CASES AND STRATEGIES
FOR PREVENTIVE ACTION

The Center for Preventive Action's Preventive Action Reports

A series sponsored by
the Council on Foreign Relations and
the Twentieth Century Fund

Toward Comprehensive Peace in Southeast Europe: Conflict Prevention in the South Balkans (Report of the South Balkans Working Group)

Cases and Strategies for Preventive Action (Papers from the Center for Preventive Action's Third Annual Conference)

To order any of the Preventive Action Reports, please call
1 (800) 552–5450

PREVENTIVE ACTION REPORTS
VOLUME 2

CASES AND STRATEGIES FOR PREVENTIVE ACTION

Edited by Barnett R. Rubin

SPONSORED BY THE COUNCIL ON FOREIGN RELATIONS
AND THE TWENTIETH CENTURY FUND

1998 • The Century Foundation Press • New York

Twentieth Century Fund/The Century Foundation

The Twentieth Century Fund/Century Foundation sponsors and supervises timely analyses of economic policy, foreign affairs, and domestic political issues. Not-for-profit and nonpartisan, the Fund was founded in 1919 and endowed by Edward A. Filene.

Library of Congress Cataloging-in-Publication Data

Center for Preventive Action. Conference (3rd : 1996 : New York, N.Y.)
   Cases and strategies for preventive action / edited by Barnett R. Rubin.
     p. cm. -- (Preventive action reports : v. 2)
   Includes bibliographical references and index.
   ISBN 0-87078-412-9 (alk. paper)
     1. Political violence--Prevention--Congresses. 2. Conflict management--Congresses.
3. Political violence--Cases studies--Congresses. 4. Ethnic groups--Political activity--
Case studies--Congresses. 5. Ethnic relations--Case studies--Congresses. 6. Burundi--
Politics and government--Congresses. 7. Africa, Sub-Saharan--Politics and
government--1960--Congresses. 8. Yugoslavia--Politics and government--1992--
Congresses.
I. Rubin, Barnett R.   II. Title.   III. Series.
JC328.6.C45   1997
303.6'9--dc21
                                                               97-41268
                                                                  CIP

COUNCIL ON FOREIGN RELATIONS

The Council on Foreign Relations, Inc., is a nonprofit, nonpartisan national membership organization dedicated to promoting improved understanding of international affairs through the free and civil exchange of ideas. The Council is a forum where leaders from academia, government, business, nonprofit organizations, and the media come together to discuss the most important international issues. The goals of the Council are to find and nurture the next generation of foreign policy leaders; to contribute ideas to U.S. foreign policy and the understanding of international politics; and to reach beyond our walls with literature and broadcast programs to Americans with interest in these issues.

The Council takes no institutional position on policy issues and has no affiliation with the U.S. government. All statements of fact and expressions of opinion contained in all its publications are the sole responsibility of the author or authors.

For further information about the Council on Foreign Relations, please contact the Public Affairs Office, Council on Foreign Relations, 58 East 68th Street, New York, NY 10021, (212) 434-9400.

— ACKNOWLEDGMENTS —

This is the second volume in the Center for Preventive Action's *Preventive Action Reports*, a series that is cosponsored by the Twentieth Century Fund/Century Foundation and the Council on Foreign Relations. This volume was made possible by the generous support of the Carnegie Corporation of New York and the Twentieth Century Fund/Century Foundation. The chapters were first presented as papers at the Center for Preventive Action's Third Annual Conference, held in New York City on December 12, 1996. Comments by an anonymous reviewer helped strengthen the volume. The book could not have been produced without the meticulous and creative editorial work of CPA Research Associate Susanna P. Campbell, for which we thank her.

— Contents —

— PREFACE —

THE CENTER FOR PREVENTIVE ACTION

The Center for Preventive Action (CPA) was established by the
Council on Foreign Relations in 1994 to study and test conflict
prevention—to learn how preventive action can work by employing
it. CPA is chaired by General John W. Vessey, USA (Ret.), former
chairman of the Joint Chiefs of Staff, and directed by Barnett R.
Rubin. CPA operates under the guidance of a distinguished advisory
board representing a wide range of disciplines and expertise (see
Appendix E for a list of members). CPA is funded by the Carnegie
Corporation of New York, the Twentieth Century Fund/Century
Foundation, and the Winston Foundation.

Many of today's most serious international problems—ethnic conflicts, failing states, humanitarian disasters—could potentially be averted or ameliorated given effective early attention. CPA defines
preventive action as those steps that can be taken in a volatile situation
to prevent a crisis. CPA uses the unique resources of the Council on
Foreign Relations to accomplish its three objectives of action, analysis,
and coordination.

ACTION

CPA selected four case studies through which to test the viability
of conflict prevention: the Great Lakes region of Central Africa; the
Ferghana Valley region of Central Asia; Nigeria; and the South Balkans.
(See below for a description of each project.) CPA assembled diverse
and experienced practitioners and experts in working groups for each
case study. A delegation of each working group was sent on a study

mission to the region to map out strategies for settling or managing the conflict.

ANALYSIS

CPA draws on the knowledge gained from all four case studies, the experience of others, and previous studies to determine what strategies are most effective in the field of preventive action. In order to disseminate its recommendations with respect to its case studies and its other findings, CPA has established, in collaboration with the Twentieth Century Fund/Century Foundation, a series of *Preventive Action Reports*. *Cases and Strategies for Preventive Action* is the second volume in this series.

COORDINATION

CPA is convinced that partnerships among governments, international organizations, and nongovernmental organizations are essential for the prevention of ethnic and other conflicts in the post–cold war world. CPA coordinates with these actors on all of its initiatives.

One of the ways that CPA fulfills this goal of coordination is through convening an annual conference on preventive action. In collaboration with the Carnegie Commission on Preventing Deadly Conflict and the Twentieth Century Fund/Century Foundation, the conference aims to survey what has been learned about conflict prevention in the previous year, to promote discussion and coordination among those involved, and to introduce the idea of preventive action to key U.S. constituencies, represented in part by the Council membership. This edited volume is a product of CPA's third annual conference, held on December 12, 1996.

PROJECT ON THE FERGHANA VALLEY REGION OF CENTRAL ASIA

The Ferghana Valley region of Central Asia cuts across the three newly independent states of Uzbekistan, Tajikistan, and Kyrgyzstan and is one of the most densely populated and volatile areas of the former Soviet Union. Tensions are exacerbated by ethnic, religious, environmental, and economic problems. CPA's Ferghana Valley working group was formed to assess the potential for future conflict in the region and to suggest ways to move the region in the direction of economic and political reform and stability.

PROJECT ON THE GREAT LAKES REGION OF CENTRAL AFRICA

In 1994, Rwanda witnessed a devastating genocide that ended with the military defeat of the regime that carried it out. After the genocide, tension spread further throughout the region, especially to neighboring Burundi and Zaire. Initially, the Center for Preventive Action focused on Burundi, but as the crisis engulfed the region, CPA widened the project to encompass the entire Great Lakes region of Africa, including Burundi, Rwanda, Zaire, Tanzania, and Uganda.

One of CPA's primary activities for this project has been the cosponsorship of the Great Lakes Policy Forum with Search for Common Ground, Refugees International, and the African American Institute. This monthly forum was established to enable all international actors working to prevent further violence in the region to exchange information, coordinate strategies, evaluate their activities, and advocate policies to the U.S. and other governments.

PROJECT ON NIGERIA

Immediate tensions in Nigeria arise from the aborted democratic transition of June 1993 and the subsequent authoritarian course of General Sani Abacha's regime. Ethnic, religious, and regional tensions, as well as economic malaise, contribute to the potential for conflict. Because of Nigeria's dominant position in West Africa and its vast oil reserves, an eruption of conflict would have substantial regional and international repercussions. CPA's Nigeria project concentrates on the role of Nigerian civil society in preventing conflict and assisting sustainable democratic reform.

PROJECT ON THE SOUTH BALKANS

CPA turned its attention to the South Balkans as the wars in Bosnia-Herzegovina and Croatia neared their end. The Dayton Accords moved this troubled corner of southeastern Europe toward peace but left many problems unresolved—including the issue of ethnic Albanians in Kosovo and Macedonia, which threatens to disrupt the entire region. The South Balkans working group was formed to recommend ways to prevent the spread of the ex-Yugoslav conflict into the South Balkans and to create a more enduring framework for peace and security in the region. The project on the South Balkans has been transferred to the International Conflict Resolution Program (ICRP) at Columbia University.

STAFF OF THE CENTER FOR PREVENTIVE ACTION

BARNETT R. RUBIN, Director

ANYA SCHMEMANN, Assistant Director

FABIENNE HARA, Research Associate

SUSANNA P. CAMPBELL, Research Associate

C. NANA-OYE ADDO-YOBO, Research Associate

— 1 —

INTRODUCTION
EXPERIENCES IN PREVENTION

Barnett R. Rubin with Susanna P. Campbell

The Council on Foreign Relations established the Center for Preventive Action (CPA) in 1994 to build up and disseminate knowledge about the relatively new field of conflict prevention. In an initial phase of operations, CPA would, it was envisioned, itself engage in part of the process of preventing conflict by undertaking missions and other activities relating to a number of regions in which conflict was in danger of breaking out or escalating. The four areas chosen were Burundi, then expanded to the whole Great Lakes region of Central Africa (which also includes Rwanda, Eastern Congo-Zaire, Uganda, and Tanzania), the South Balkans (Kosovo, Macedonia, and Albania), Nigeria, and the Ferghana Valley (a densely populated region of Central Asia including portions of Tajikistan, Uzbekistan, and Kyrgyzstan). These four cases constitute a sample of different problems of conflict prevention, providing us with a diverse set of comparisons from which to learn about preventive action.[1]

In order to reinforce networks of cooperation and promote regular evaluation of what we have learned about conflict prevention, CPA has held an annual conference each December since 1994. At these conferences, to which we have invited colleagues from NGOs, international organizations, government, business, and academia, we have attempted to establish a baseline of knowledge and analyze further successes, failures, and ambiguous outcomes.

CPA's third annual conference, held in December 1996, included six workshops.[2] Three discussed papers on CPA projects (in the South Balkans, Burundi, and Nigeria), while three others considered themes that have emerged from our work on several cases: the utility of economic sanctions and incentives, the proliferation of small arms and light weapons, and the role of religion and religious actors in conflict prevention. This volume presents the papers that framed those discussions, revised to take into account comments made by participants and subsequent discussion.

Responding to New Conflicts
The Challenge of Prevention

Among the most disturbing challenges to security in this era has been the proliferation of civil wars, or intrastate conflicts, often engulfing whole regions in chain reactions of violence. The cold war structured international relations around a large-scale conflict, but the discipline it provided created a management structure for that system by integrating numerous states, including many that were nominally nonaligned, into networks of hegemonic control. The disappearance of this structure left regional states and nonstate actors freer to pursue local agendas.[3]

In Southeast Europe, the Horn of Africa, Central Africa, West Africa, Central Asia, the Caucasus, and elsewhere states have failed, well-armed militias have proliferated, and various forms of collective identity have provided the symbols that have motivated so many to kill. As has been the case increasingly in this century's wars, civilians have often been the main targets and always been the principal victims. Refugees and displaced people have crowded the routes of flight, whether mountain paths, decrepit ferries, or overtaxed international airports.

For major powers, and particularly the United States, these conflicts have posed new problems. Without the simplifications of the cold war to fall back on, they have seemed difficult to understand and to relate to a national interest or purpose. The new simplification—that the end of the cold war had unleashed "ancient hatreds"—has served as a rationale for inaction or despair. The intermittently and selectively televised spectacle of context-free death, mutilation, hunger, and disease has made the moral challenge clear but has not elucidated what acts would meet that challenge or whose responsibility—or in whose interest—it was to undertake them.

In the absence of major states willing to take political and military risks to end conflicts decisively, responses have taken the form of humanitarian aid and limited peacekeeping operations, often intended mainly to protect the humanitarian effort. Although most of these efforts have been carried out under the aegis of the United Nations, regional organizations, interested states, and nongovernmental organizations of many types, with diverse agendas and capacities, have also played important roles. Nonetheless, the rising costs of humanitarian efforts and frustration with the inadequacy and impermanence of their results have led many organizations to focus on means of preventing such conflicts.[4]

Prevention of war between states through peaceful settlement of disputes has always been the first task of diplomacy, but international initiatives to prevent wars within states or among nonstate actors is relatively new. Prevention of intrastate conflict has posed peculiar difficulties for the UN, as well as for other official bodies, because of the doctrine of state sovereignty. As civil wars became more violent, produced refugees, and threatened to expand, the worldwide body and other state-based organizations could justify intervention on the grounds that such wars posed threats to international peace and security. It has been harder to justify preventive intervention in conflicts that have not yet reached such a level of violence and might appear to be simply domestic disputes within states. Furthermore, action by governments or intergovernmental organizations will ultimately depend on whether government leaders will be able or willing to mobilize the resources and support necessary to take effective action to prevent conflict. Inaction and flawed, counterproductive action can be equally harmful.

This volume seeks to present many of the challenges of conflict prevention through exploration of specific cases and tools. Each case presents different facets of the overall problem of prevention. All of the tools and general problems discussed in the thematic chapters are relevant to each of the cases. Combining these often ambiguous general lessons with a unique approach suited to each case in a way that produces the political support needed to sustain action is the core of the art of preventive action.

DESCRIPTIONS OF CHAPTERS

CASE STUDIES/REGIONS

The three case studies presented in this volume were chosen as projects by CPA because they reflect different issues in conflict prevention. Two were drawn from very different regions of Africa and one from the post-Communist world—two broad areas where much of the conflict prevention effort has been concentrated. The three cases illustrate different stages in the development of conflict. At one extreme, Burundi has not only seen repeated massacres bordering on genocide since the 1970s but had also just emerged from another such round when CPA became involved at the beginning of 1995. Burundi was further endangered by the regional environment, including war and genocide in Rwanda and the subsequent refugee crisis in Zaire. Efforts concentrated on managing an existing violent crisis and preventing further mass killings.

The South Balkans and Nigeria are cases wherein the potential for violent conflict has not been realized to the same extent, at least recently. Neither has recently been the site of mass violence (though both have been in decades past), but tensions are high in both areas, aggravated in different ways by their respective regional environments—for the South Balkans, the breakup of Yugoslavia and subsequent wars; for Nigeria, the civil wars and state disintegration in Liberia and Sierra Leone. In two cases, Burundi and Macedonia (one of the foci of the South Balkans project), states and international institutions have been actively involved in prevention efforts, while in Nigeria, the appearance of calm, combined with disagreements among major international actors, has produced a certain paralysis or inattention. Nigeria has also provided us with a case in which significant U.S. domestic constituencies were engaged, including oil companies, human rights and environmental groups, and a divided African-American community. Hence, these three cases present sufficiently contrasting contexts of preventive action to illuminate the decisions, choices, and issues involved.

The South Balkans. In the South Balkans (Serbia/Kosovo, Macedonia, and Albania), both conflict over national and ethnic rights and the weakness of states threaten to erupt into violence. In the new state of Macedonia and the contested region of Kosovo the issues of state, nationality, and ethnicity are as tense as those that gave rise to the wars in Bosnia and Croatia, even if a variety of factors have so far prevented a similar bloody conflagration. The status of Albanian populations defined as minorities by both Macedonia and Serbia remains unsettled. The explosion in Albania as a result of the collapse of corrupt financial institutions spread more weapons throughout the region. It also effectively split that tortured country along long-standing subethnic lines, pitting the Northern Geg rebels (drawn from the clan that had dominated that country's Stalinist regime) against a government controlled by Southern Tosks.

In his chapter entitled "Nationalism and Civic Identity: Ethnic Models for Macedonia and Kosovo," Steven L. Burg takes a step back from the immediate disputes in the region to examine different institutional models for multiethnic states. The "consociational" model of Arend Lijphart, which advocates explicit recognition of ethnic differences and a polity based on interethnic elite accommodation, has dominated the political science literature. This model, however, derives from a primordial understanding of ethnicity and in practice has not proved to be a sturdy means to prevent interethnic conflict. Furthermore, recent experiences have convinced most analysts that ethnic identity is highly contextual and malleable. Where possible, therefore, Burg advocates institutional reform designed to promote crosscutting identities and a nonethnic civic society. Nonetheless, there are cases, especially involving racial identity, but also when differences and antagonisms are well established, where some form of official recognition of autonomy or other such measures is the only means of meeting ethnic aspirations. Burg concludes that Kosovo is one of those cases where autonomy or an even stronger separate status is necessary. In Macedonia, however, Burg finds that opportunities remain for integrating Albanians into political and social life through pluralistic institutions and a civic rather than purely ethno-national identity. He analyzes examples of projects designed to work toward that end and outlines a set of reforms consistent with it.

Burundi. In Burundi, relations between the main contending identity groups are far more violent than in the South Balkans, or even arguably than in Bosnia. Dominance by the Tutsi minority through control of the army, educational system, and state service has pushed the Hutu majority into revolt several times, while the harsh rhetoric of some Hutu leaders and the actual genocide of Tutsis by a Hutu-power regime in neighboring Rwanda stiffen resistance to any concessions. Like the states of the South Balkans, Burundi is part of a region of conflicts linked to the formation of states and national communities through violence and population movement, often motivated by intense fear and mistrust.

In their chapter entitled "Learning from Burundi's Failed Democratic Transition, 1993–96," Michael S. Lund, Barnett R. Rubin, and Fabienne Hara document the extent to which Burundi, like Macedonia, has become a focal point of efforts at conflict prevention and resolution on the part of a range of public and private international organizations. These efforts began after the assassination by Tutsi military officers of

Melchior Ndadaye, the country's first freely elected president and a Hutu, in October 1993. The assassination was followed by massacres on both sides that killed tens of thousands of people.

Despite all the efforts, conflict in Burundi continued to escalate, though international action may have prevented at least one major crisis.[5] Given the intensity of the conflict, any peace effort had a high risk of failure. Using indicators derived from comparative research, the authors show that Burundi is one of the countries most at risk of violent conflict, a potential that has been repeatedly realized for decades. Only comparison with Rwanda, where one of history's few incontestable genocides occurred—on television—in 1994, made it possible to characterize international action in Burundi as preventive. Indeed, Lund prefers to view the effort in Burundi as crisis management rather than prevention.

Effective stabilization of Burundi requires effective means to counter that country's pervasive violence, protected by what has come to be known as a "culture of impunity." International action, however, concentrated on supporting political agreements for democratization and power sharing. While there have been many Burundian political actors who would have preferred a peaceful society based on compromise, the degree of insecurity and the risk of assassination prevented the political institutions that were supposed to embody such values from becoming a reality. Despite repeated calls for action on the issue of security, expressed for instance in the Security Working Group of the Burundi Policy Forum, no effective action was ever taken either within Burundi or in the broader region.[6] The authors argue that effective action in crises such as Burundi will require a more forthright analysis of the role of violence and either a greater international capacity for internal policing in such regions or greater willingness to use what force is available.

Nigeria. Nigeria poses a different but no less daunting set of challenges. Sub-Saharan Africa's most populous state, the home of vast deposits of high-quality petroleum and natural gas, Nigeria has a history of ethnic civil war, military rule, and pervasive corruption. Its past intervals of elected civilian rule led to group conflict and money-driven politics that helped to legitimize military coups that in turn aggravated the same basic problems of the Nigerian state: ethnic and regional diversity that requires federalism and decentralization, combined with a lopsided dependence on oil revenues that concentrates power in the small, central elite that controls the wealth. The result, as Peter M. Lewis shows in his chapter entitled "Nigeria: The Challenge of

Preventive Action," has been the decay of institutions and the gradual slippage of this huge country toward conflict.

International debate about Nigeria intensified after the annulment of the June 1993 presidential election and the execution of nine leaders of the Ogoni ethnic group, including writer Ken Saro-Wiwa, in 1995. This group was found guilty of murder in rushed, grossly unfair military trials.[7] The activists had led a struggle against both the government and the Royal Dutch-Shell oil company, seeking greater benefits for the Ogoni from the oil wealth in their Niger Delta land. Since then debate has been polarized between those who favor stronger sanctions against both Nigeria and the corporations who operate there and those who favor more engagement with the government to press it to honor pledges of a return to civilian rule and economic reform.

Rather than judge between these two options, some combination of which is clearly necessary, Lewis argues for greater emphasis on a third component of international policy toward Nigeria—support for civil society. While dislodging the military from power and supporting a representative government are not only inherently right but also necessary to quell Nigeria's growing conflicts, they would not be sufficient to stabilize that country's future. As Lewis has argued elsewhere, coalitions of civil society groups often act as important catalysts of transition from military rule and as guardians of the process.[8] Even more important, however, civil society coalitions could help overcome the fragmentation of the Nigerian political class, resulting from years of military politics and corruption, as well as act as watchdogs on any new regime. The latter function is particularly important if the Nigerian state is to become accountable to its people and to the rule of law. Hence a more long-term program of conflict prevention for Nigeria would support efforts by Nigerian religious, human rights, business, academic, journalistic, and other groups to form coalitions both within the country and with their counterparts in West Africa and elsewhere. These ties could also help make Nigeria a genuinely stabilizing force in its region, where its activity has so far been largely military.

ISSUES IN CONFLICT PREVENTION

Through its case studies, CPA has identified tools of conflict prevention. In order to further analyze the effectiveness of particular tools, CPA commissioned papers from experts on three areas that have been relevant to each of its case studies—economic sanctions and incentives, small weapons disarmament, and religion.

Economic Sanctions and Incentives. CPA asked George A. Lopez and David Cortright, noted scholars of sanctions, to evaluate the usefulness of both sanctions and economic incentives in preventive action. In their chapter entitled "Carrots, Sticks, and Cooperation: Economic Tools of Statecraft," they argue that neither sanctions nor economic incentives are likely to be effective in changing the behavior of elites pursuing essential goals in their own domestic politics. To the extent that either is successful, their effectiveness depends strongly upon the context and the overall mix of policies. Incentives work better in the context of an overall positive relationship; both sanctions and incentives work better when the sanctioning state also has a credible (even if unspoken) alternative of using coercion. Sanctions and incentives can also be mixed so as to provide a stronger set of alternatives to the receiving state. Overall, Cortright and Lopez prefer incentives to sanctions as both more effective and more conducive to a peaceful outcome, but they recognize the possible moral hazard of offering rewards for ending aggression or violations of human rights that should not have occurred in the first place.

In the South Balkans, Burundi, and Nigeria, international actors have identified certain political leaders as responsible for conflict and imposed sanctions against them or the states they lead:

- The United States stated at Dayton that the "outer wall" of sanctions against the Federal Republic of Yugoslavia (Serbia and Montenegro), including suspension of membership in international organizations and financial institutions and of full diplomatic relations, would remain in place until certain conditions were complied with, including significant progress toward the protection of human rights in Kosovo;[9]

- The United States and some European states, assisted by the UN, banned from international travel a list of Burundian political leaders suspected of involvement in the massacres there, by supplying their names to Interpol; the Rwanda Support Group (an interstate aid consortium) adopted a Canadian-sponsored aid package for Burundi that would be released only after certain political conditions were met; and East African states, with international support, imposed a trade and transport embargo on the country after the August 1, 1996, military coup.

◆ The United States, the EU, and the Commonwealth have all imposed various sanctions on Nigeria, pending fair and free elections as well as full cooperation against narcotics smuggling. These measures have included restrictions on issuance of visas to top authorities, suspension of membership in the Commonwealth, termination of arms transfers and military training, and limits on direct air links.

In light of Cortright and Lopez's analysis, it seems that while sanctions may reduce the likelihood of new Serbian aggression in Kosovo, they are unlikely to bring about a settlement or major changes; for these, other initiatives will be needed. In Burundi, travel restrictions will probably not affect political actors who think they are fighting for their lives, though difficult-to-enforce financial sanctions against some individuals may cripple their ability to mobilize their followers for violence and to arm them. Finally, the implication for Nigeria is that sanctions must be supplemented with a more comprehensive policy including intensive communication with the regime, an offer of incentives in the event of a regime change (perhaps in the form of debt relief, infrastructure development, and even amnesty for past rulers), and positive support for civil society.

Small Weapons Disarmament. Edward J. Laurance has been involved in the development and analysis of several small weapons disarmament efforts. His chapter in this volume, entitled "Small Arms, Light Weapons, and Conflict Prevention: The New Post–Cold War Logic of Disarmament," explores how the end of the cold war both released a vast supply of arms originally intended for various cold-war conflicts and left the developed countries and others with production capacities in excess of their needs. The resulting glut on the market created a drop in prices as these devastating small arms and light weapons were circulated wherever parties to conflicts wanted them. The arms do not cause the conflicts, he reminds us, nor can their production or sale be banned, as they are still considered legitimate means of defense. Furthermore, international law recognizes that even unofficial groups have the right to take up arms in certain circumstances, though what these are remains controversial. Nonetheless, the presence in unprecedentedly large numbers of a new generation of powerful, light automatic weapons has imparted new levels of destruction to what might have been containable conflicts and made them more difficult to resolve.

Laurance outlines approaches to disarmament at different stages of conflict: preconflict, during the conflict, and postconflict. Not surprisingly, the greatest successes are in the postconflict period, but even there the obstacles to gaining control over and destroying or disabling such a valuable resource are serious. (An automatic weapon may be worth more than a year's average salary in some countries.) The unclear borderline between warfare and crime in many of these conflicts complicates the task, as citizens who arm themselves for the apolitical task of protecting their personal security may also form an ethnic or political militia. Efforts have been under way for only a few years now, but there are initiatives both to create a more effective arms control regime for small arms and light weapons (including better reporting, monitoring, and access to information, generally known as "transparency") and to develop techniques to interdict supplies to key areas. A great range of policies has been tried, especially as part of peace settlements, and Laurance presents the evidence of their relative success. Even in preconflict situations, however, Laurance argues for greater transparency with respect to arms flows, more security for legitimate weapons stocks, controls over the production and marketing of ammunition, and greater attention to fighting crime and promoting personal security. All of these measures have the potential to decrease the accumulation of capacities for lethal harm among groups potentially in conflict.

In the South Balkans, Burundi, and Nigeria, the spread and trafficking of small arms and light weapons has contributed to making conflicts more lethal. Weapons flowing into the Great Lakes region of Africa, especially to the militias and armed forces responsible for the Rwandan genocide, attracted attention in 1995 when reports from Human Rights Watch and Amnesty International led to a Security Council resolution. Reports that arms were flowing into Nigeria after the annulment of the 1993 elections were one reason CPA decided as early as 1994 to investigate Nigeria as a possible case study. And in the spring of 1997 the uprising in Albania led to the looting of arms stocks throughout the country. Reports have spread of the diffusion of these supplies to Albanian militants in both Macedonia and Kosovo, seriously raising the stakes in the region.

Religion. We asked Donald W. Shriver, Jr., a member of CPA's advisory board and former president of Union Theological Seminary, to contribute an essay on the role of religion in violence prevention. While noting religion's sometime role as a fomenter or legitimator of violence, in his chapter entitled "Religion and Violence Prevention"

Shriver finds several ways in which religious beliefs, institutions, and leaders have prevented violence and promoted peace. Some basic religious concepts, such as the common humanity of all under God, provide basic values undergirding peacemaking. Religious institutions, because of the special status they sometimes enjoy, provide protected space for civic action. And religious leaders, to the extent that they are genuine and sincere and are perceived to be so, can inspire greater trust in antagonists, if only by listening to them more deeply than others.

Depending on the religious composition of a society, religion may reinforce efforts at pluralism or veer dangerously off into identity politics. Political accords based on religious values may implicitly or explicitly exclude those who do not share them—contradicting the goal, espoused by Steven L. Burg in his essay, of a civic society. In the discussion at the conference, Andrea Bartoli of the community of Sant' Egidio emphasized that religion needed secularism in order to provide the public context in which it could do the most in defense of human rights and basic values.

In the South Balkans, Burundi, and Nigeria we have encountered the full force of religion, for good and ill. The role of the hierarchy of the Serbian Orthodox Church in supporting nationalism is well known, and attachment to some important religious sites in Kosovo is one reason cited by Serbs for their insistence on maintaining control. At the same time, the Community of Sant' Egidio, the Rome-based Catholic lay community that mediated the peace settlement in Mozambique, had built up enough trust on both sides, as a result of years of humanitarian and religious work, that it was able to do what no one else could—persuade Serbian president Slobodan Milosevic and Ibrahim Rugova, president of the unofficial "Republic of Kosova," to sign an agreement on reopening the Albanian schools.

The Community of Sant' Egidio was also able to bring together the representatives of the Tutsi military government of Burundi with those of the principal Hutu-led guerrilla force for cease-fire talks. The Mennonites were among the few international NGOs who kept people on the ground in Burundi at even the most dangerous times. And some local religious leaders in Burundi participated on one side or another of the conflict (a phenomenon even more pronounced in neighboring Rwanda, where the local Catholic hierarchy seemed largely complicitous with the genocidal regime), while others were outspoken enough in favor of peace to be assassinated.

In Nigeria we found that as overtly political opposition was repressed, religious organizations and movements increasingly became the voice of excluded segments of the society, whether through statements by major church leaders, the rise of new syncretic churches in the South, or uprisings by Islamic militants in the North. Some efforts at interreligious dialogue and conflict resolution have also indicated that religious actors could play a key role in bringing together Nigeria's fragmented civil society.

LESSONS LEARNED

Experience with CPA's cases and its various techniques has also led us to several more general conclusions about what it takes to make preventive action effective.

CONFLICT PREVENTION MUST BE INTEGRATED INTO INTERNATIONAL POLICY

An essential lesson is that the prevention of violent conflict should not become a separate agenda in international affairs, competing for attention with strategic goals, human rights, development, trade, democratization, or any other agenda. The prevention of violent conflict should be a component of an overall strategy aimed at enhancing human security and welfare through peaceful relations among accountable states that respect basic principles of human rights and humanitarian law.

As critics of the field often remind us, in the struggle for these goals conflict is inevitable and sometimes healthy; even military conflict at times seems tragically necessary to resolve problems.[10] Most violence, of course, is not a tragic necessity in the pursuit of noble goals, but a result of misfortune or even crime. In seeking to prevent such acts, however, we must bear in mind that the goal is not stability at any cost, but a legitimate order in which people have opportunities to seek their many goals and pursue their inevitable conflicts without violence. Many authoritarian rulers claim, some sincerely, that only repression or other forms of state violence can prevent chaos or mass violence. While it is naive to insist on the immediate imposition of the entire package of Western democratic institutions and rights in poor countries torn by violence and with weak or fragmented institutions, experience shows that repression does not provide a sustainable solution. It can only insulate predatory rulers and postpone the day when society will demand accountability, the sole lasting alternative to violent protest.

The Great Lakes region illustrates that prevention of conflict per se cannot always be the main goal of policy. The predatory regime of Mobutu, a relic of cold war clientelism for which the Western powers that had supported him failed to take responsibility, was a principal source of endemic conflict across the region. Attempts to broker peace with that regime in order to prevent civil war would have preserved a major long-term destabilizing force in the name of peace. Nonetheless, rebuilding—or building—the political, economic, and security structures of the region so as to prevent further conflict is a preeminent preventive task.

The intertwining of prevention with a broader agenda requires its integration into policy at all stages of conflict. The model of prevention as intervention in a growing conflict before the outbreak of mass violence treats conflict as a particular event with a finite life cycle.[11] This model may be particularly applicable to conflicts set off by unique historical events, such as the breakup of the Soviet Union. Most conflicts, however, are chronic rather than acute; they are conditions of life that flare up, die down, and flare up in new forms over time. While we should continue to look for early warning signs of new conflicts and attempt to prevent outbreaks of violence before they occur, we should also integrate concern over the potential for violent conflict into a broad range of policies. As we develop better tools of conflict prevention and better understanding of the causes of violent conflict, we should integrate those tools and that knowledge into the pursuit of all other policy goals. Economic development strategies that provide for equitable means of dispute resolution with respect to the stresses caused by large-scale social change will be more sustainable than policies that ignore the potential for conflict. Democracy promotion policies that recognize partisan competition's potential for igniting fears and insecurities and incorporate means to overcome them will make for more sustainable and peaceful democracies (as Lund, Rubin, and Hara show in the chapter on Burundi).

A REGIONAL APPROACH IS NEEDED

Today's pervasive conflicts generally occur in and spread through entire regions of weak states.[12] The nature of the conflicts that we now confront fits poorly with existing juridical categories and with the diplomatic modalities that exist for dealing with them. International law distinguishes interstate conflicts from others, which are usually described as domestic or intrastate. Recent conflicts, however, require severe conceptual stretching to fit models of either domestic or interstate conflict. In many respects, intrastate conflict is the continuation of interstate conflict by other means. More precisely, these conflicts often constitute a new form of transnational warfare, including armed groups with cross-border ties to states, social movements, markets, criminal cartels, and corporations. In the Great Lakes conflicts, while Rwanda, Burundi, and Zaire each exhibited a unique history and particular configurations of actors, coalitions also formed across borders in a conflict that can only be described as transnational and regional.[13]

The regional dimension means that sustainable prevention of conflict will require a comprehensive regional approach. Yet within a common region, some areas or countries may not yet have experienced armed conflict, others may be in the midst of it, and others may be emerging into a peace settlement or moving from one condition to another. Preventing violence in the areas that have not experienced it may require stable conflict resolution and postconflict settlements in other parts of the region, and these settlements must be based on principles that tend to promote conflict resolution elsewhere. Recognition of the Bosnian Serb Republic at Dayton led to greater militancy among Albanians in Kosovo; failure to address the chronic problems of Zaire (including the presence of Rwandan Hutu militias) rendered peacemaking in Rwanda and Burundi (not to mention Angola and Uganda) far more difficult. And the effect of the Nigerian military regime's apparent success in leading a peacekeeping operation that presided over elections in Liberia may be to strengthen its legitimacy or to strengthen the emerging African norm against military governments.

The need for a regional approach (especially when the regions that are politically relevant may not coincide with specific international organizations) finds many inherited forms of international action wanting. Diplomats are generally accredited to individual states or agencies; most agencies, official or not, have national programs that interact with their diplomatic counterparts. The regional nature of conflict, however, requires institutional innovations such as the appointment of special envoys to entire regions, the convening of regional meetings, and attention in mediation activities to cross-border alliances, rather than assuming that each country's conflict can be negotiated separately. The need for a regional approach also means that conflict prevention cannot be neatly segregated from other stages of conflict management. Prevention of armed conflict in one country may require resolution of an ongoing conflict or successful postconflict reconstruction in a neighboring one.

THE IMPORTANCE OF UNOFFICIAL ACTORS
AND CIVIL SOCIETY MUST BE RECOGNIZED

In response to the rising importance of many actors other than international organizations and governments, CPA has focused much of its attention and analysis on the growing and potential role of unofficial actors. The number of nongovernmental organizations (NGOs) working in conflict resolution and prevention (as well as the allied field of early warning) has grown more quickly than one can easily keep track of.[14] Some of these organizations work on policy analysis, some in the field; some work in only one conflict or region, while others attempt to be more global; but taken together they have all augmented the capacity of the international system to deal with conflict, at the same time presenting it with new dilemmas.

In focusing on unofficial actors, however, CPA does not have in mind only those NGOs whose missions explicitly deal with conflict. An analysis of each of the three cases in this volume of incipient or developed crisis has shown that the weakness of civic organizations in processing and absorbing conflict and in holding state leaders and institutions accountable is a chronic condition that leaves societies vulnerable. Governments can create a framework within which civil society can work, but by its nature civil society can develop and flourish only through nongovernmental initiative. Although much more evaluation of this experience is needed to determine how and to what extent these networks strengthen the capacity of various societies to prevent violent conflict, all of our work leads us to suspect that international networks of mutual support can play an important role in sustaining institutions that enhance civic peace.

Implicit in our approach has been the recognition that changes in communications technology, migration patterns, the cost of travel, financial markets, and other institutions have blurred the boundaries between domestic and international politics. While international affairs has never been monopolized by states, the range of actors with international links has expanded. Religious groups, corporations, labor organizations, scholars, professionals, and other sectors of society have expanded direct contacts with their counterparts to the extent that we may speak of an incipient transnational civil society, a network of ties through which resources, information, and advocacy flow according to a logic partly independent of states.

Nonetheless, the goals and impact of nongovernmental organizations, the private sector, and many other unofficial actors may or may not be consistent with that of conflict prevention. Some religious organizations, such as the Community of Sant' Egidio, the Mennonite Central Committee, the Society of Friends, or the Fellowship of Reconciliation, are among the most effective mediators.[15] On the other hand, other religious groups may promote conflict through aggressive proselytism or unbalanced support lent to one or another group in a divided society or region. Business may seek stability, security, predictability, and the rule of law, all of which are consistent with the goals of conflict prevention; it may also have an interest in the goodwill of host governments, in avoiding sanctions, in quiescent labor, and in extracting valuable resources from territories controlled by illegitimate authorities—all factors that may aggravate conflict. Business and others are also engaged in a debate as to whether management's sole responsibility is to shareholders or whether it also, to one extent or another, has obligations to a broader set of "stakeholders" in the enterprise and in the communities where it operates. Human rights organizations support institutions of accountability and transparency that are essential to managing conflict peacefully and deterring future acts of violence; in their pursuit of these goals, however, they may oppose compromises such as amnesties for past abuses that may seem necessary to convince antagonists to lay down their arms. Similar analyses apply to other sectors. These examples also illustrate that conflict prevention is not a self-evident, all-encompassing goal. Like other interests, values, or goals, it may come into conflict with others—the free dissemination of religious faith, the pursuit of wealth, or the punishment of crimes against humanity.

Despite the contradictions, the potential power of such unofficial actors is too important to neglect. They are both active themselves on the ground and form important constituencies for (or against) action by governments. Finally, only well-organized societies can hold their governments accountable and create the institutionalized channels of collective problem solving and dispute resolution that can make violence obsolete.

THE EFFORTS OF A MULTIPLICITY OF PARTNERS NEED COORDINATION

The multiplicity and variety of actors involved in generating conflicts requires a similar multiplicity of international partners to resolve them. The UN, regional organizations, states with global reach, important regional states, humanitarian organizations, NGOs working with civil society, conflict resolution organizations both religious and secular, potential and actual investors, international financial institutions, aid donors, and many others bring specific, needed capacities to bear. At the same time, the multiplicity of partners can pose difficulties. Their efforts can undermine each other, communicating different messages; and relevant actors may either play different would-be interveners off against each other or seek to incorporate some of them into their own political coalitions.

Hence, one of the major needs in dealing with conflicts and the situations that give rise to them is for new forms of coordination among international and local actors. While the UN in one or another guise is often the logical home for this coordination effort, much more creativity is needed. The UN finds it difficult to coordinate the sometimes disparate efforts of powerful member states, which need to find their own means of policy coordination. As an organization of states staffed largely by diplomats conscious of the limits sovereignty places on their mandate, the UN may find it difficult to work directly with many NGOs, or with civil society organizations or religious groups. Aid donors and international financial institutions must make their activities consistent with whatever political efforts are under way.[16] Various attempts are in progress to institutionalize interaction among all of these groups in order to promote at least transparency and regular discussion.[17]

Action by this multiplicity of partners requires more than coordination, of course; it requires genuine complementarity in pursuit of common goals. Complementarity is the key: NGOs, official international organizations, and governments can each bring different capacities to bear, but they cannot substitute for each other. The rise of NGOs does not mean that foreign policy (and political responsibility) can be conveniently privatized. The three case studies in this volume provide examples. In Kosovo a combination of firm official pressure and discussion with the government of Serbia is necessary to create the conditions for NGO-organized dialogue on the ground that might lead to an interim settlement. (Such dialogue, in turn, must not raise expectations of external assistance that cannot be met, leading to disappointment and, perhaps, further radicalism.) Humanitarian and conflict-resolution work by NGOs and international organizations in the Great Lakes region came to naught when governments failed to suppress the remaining genocidal organizations. Aid to civil society in Nigeria will fail without pressure on the government to permit political space for it to flourish, and pressure on the government will not lead to democratic accountability without civil society partnerships that can sustain that accountability.

ALL PREVENTION IS POLITICAL

Acknowledging the need for complementarity is, in a sense, a mild way of expressing a much greater problem: Not all would-be interveners aim solely or primarily to prevent violent conflict or to promote human rights and accountability. Conflict prevention does not consist of actors (in some Third World country) who cause problems and interveners (in developed countries or international organizations) who try to solve problems. All the actors have political interests, and all are involved in a common problem. Both official and unofficial organizations that intervene have multiple goals, and both may be part of the problem as well as (or instead of) part of the solution. Those who see themselves as external interveners aiming to prevent or resolve conflict are themselves part of the political process that generates and reproduces the conflict. Not only is intervention itself a political act that the protagonists will try to exploit, but also those actors intervening to prevent or resolve conflict may be acting in other arenas in ways that generate or aggravate the conflict.

Attempts at intervention may also have unintended consequences. Mediators, as we have seen, may convey different messages, undermining each other's work. An even more serious problem has been the gap in time between the announcement of a planned intervention and its implementation—or, even worse, cases when an intervention is announced and then not implemented. As Lund, Rubin, and Hara discuss, Secretary-General Boutros-Ghali's call for an international preventive force in Burundi, followed by months of inconclusive debate, may have encouraged fighters on both sides to escalate military activity in order to prevent any such intervention or to assure themselves of an advantageous position when it arrived. In the event, it never arrived, leaving the victims of violence defenseless. The vaguely defined "security assistance" to which the Burundian negotiators agreed at Mwanza, Tanzania, in the summer of 1996 set off a similar reaction, including the military coup against President Sylvestre Ntibantunganya, assuring that the "assistance" could not be delivered. Announcement of the September 1996 agreement on reopening the schools in Kosovo before the details of implementation had been worked out was followed by an escalation of threats by Serbian nationalists and violence by the Kosova Liberation Army, creating a political environment in which the agreement could not be implemented.

More fundamentally, conflict prevention can at times seem like a weak palliative applied to problems generated by the "normal" functioning

of the relationships—economic and other — that define the international system. In no sector is this more evident than in the manufacture and
trade in small arms and light weapons. Few of the societies subject to devastating conflict (the former Yugoslavia being a notable exception) have the
capacity to produce the weapons and ammunition needed to continue
waging war. As Edward Laurance shows, the legitimacy of the production
and sale of arms and ammunition in general and the particularly weak reg-
ulatory regime for small arms and light weapons provides the environment
that makes illegitimate and destabilizing arms transfers and secondary markets possible. The international financial system that hides and circulates
ill-gotten wealth makes destabilizing predatory rule much easier and more
rewarding, as the history of both President Mobutu and the various corrupt
rulers of Nigeria shows, as well as the less well known underworld of drug
traders and car thieves that supports South Balkans violence.

Nigeria provides an arresting example of how the normal operation
of the international economic system creates conditions that facilitate
conflict. The coincidence of immense ethnic diversity (a result of colonial bureaucratic statemaking) and centralized oil revenues derived
from one small region of the country have defined that dysfunctional
state. The social structure requires decentralization, while the economic
structure (dependence on oil revenues) dictates extreme centralization.
Control over the revenues from the international oil market provides
rulers with the means to undermine federal or other institutions that
they fear may weaken their control or threaten their power. Hence
financial corruption undermines many Nigerian institutions. International efforts to pressure the predatory military regime toward reform
have foundered in part on the complicity of oil-consuming societies
with the processes that support that regime. Nor is it so simple as blam-
ing the oil companies, who are responding to our developed societies'
vast and still growing demand for energy. As Peter Lewis shows in the
chapter on Nigeria, a more stable Nigeria will require changes in the
way the rest of the world does business with Nigeria, not just a change
in Nigeria itself.

Hence, while reacting to events and palliative tactics remain necessary, long-term prevention of violence may require institutional
changes, not just in the societies at direct risk but also in how they
interact with the rest of the world. Such changes will, of course, affect
important interests, and it is not surprising, therefore, that policies
depicted by their proponents as needed to prevent violent conflict may
be resisted by others. Since conflict in one form or another is inherent
in all collective human activities, no single policy alternative is likely

to present itself as a unique way of avoiding conflict. Different political forces will have different interests in and beliefs in the rightness of different policies, some of which may prevent at least some kinds of conflict. The issue cannot be segregated in an apolitical, humanitarian discourse. The political reality of prevention efforts is the reason, as argued above, that they must be integrated into a broader set of strategic policies, rather than treated as a separate "humanitarian" concern.

THE PRIMACY OF RELATIONSHIPS

The most complex, difficult, and yet in many ways strongest lesson of our experience thus far has been that both conflicts and conflict prevention or resolution result from relationships among people. Both social scientists and strategists normally analyze these relationships in terms of power and wealth. And few indeed would be naive enough to claim that violent conflicts involving vast resources and claiming the lives of thousands, even millions, of people result only from psychological causes. Real issues are at stake. But at the same time, people imbue these struggles with meaning and feeling. Competition over resources or power leads to mistrust, images of enmity, dehumanization, hatred. Outsiders are sometimes able to design solutions that would seemingly ameliorate many of these conflicts, provide for sharing of resources, and build institutions of coexistence. Even when the plans for a solution are valid (as they are not always, of course), the process through which a mediator can gain a hearing for such proposals—or through which the parties to the conflict can trust and communicate with each other well enough to devise, consider, or adopt such proposals—itself encounters many psychological and interpersonal barriers. Both the material and the psychosocial relationships among the parties to the conflict must change, and neither can change without the other's participation.

Starting and sustaining such a process often requires a leap of faith: trust in some person, institution, or ideal; belief in something that transcends the overwhelming reality of conflict. While religion can motivate parties to a conflict with a transcendent reason for combat, a transcendent belief system can also provide the faith needed to test the possibility of peace, as Donald Shriver argues in his chapter. Diplomats, NGOs, and others working in conflict resolution, while never neglecting the practicalities of power and resources, must also attend to the spiritual resources that may ultimately be necessary to escape from conflict. We cannot neglect the difficult practical work of devising the right mix of sanctions and incentives (as analyzed by Cortright and Lopez), building institutions of ethnic separation or power sharing (as analyzed by Steven Burg), curbing the flow of small weapons and disarming former or potential combatants (as analyzed by Ed Laurance), providing security to potential negotiators (as Lund, Rubin, and Hara argue the international community failed to do in Burundi), or working with partners to strengthen civil society until it is strong enough to hold a predatory state accountable (as Peter Lewis argues is necessary in Nigeria). But without cultivating long-term relationships—based on solid values—with our fellow humans caught in the trap of violence, we cannot even begin.

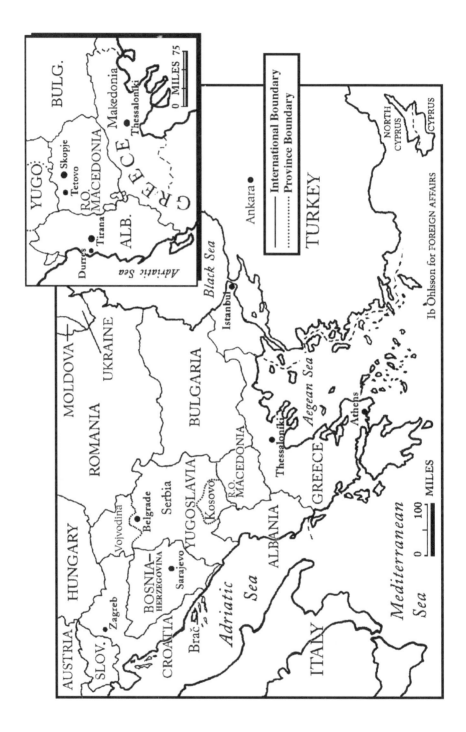

Ib Öhlsson for FOREIGN AFFAIRS

— 2 —

NATIONALISM AND CIVIC IDENTITY
ETHNIC MODELS FOR MACEDONIA AND KOSOVO[1]

Steven L. Burg

The art of preventing the outbreak of violent ethnic conflict requires efforts to address both the immediate causes of tension and the underlying sources of conflict in intergroup relations. At present, two primary approaches to the resolution of intergroup conflict are presented in academic literature. The dominant approach accepts intergroup conflict at the mass level as a given and focuses instead on structuring the process of elite interactions to manage the conflict. This "consociational" approach emphasizes state restructuring according to power-sharing formulas that reflect the salience of existing ethnic cleavages and hence institutionalize the ethnic dimensions of conflict. The alternative, "integrationist" approach focuses on action to ameliorate intergroup tensions and conflict by emphasizing or creating incentives to cooperate across ethnic cleavages. This approach is applicable at both the mass and the elite level.

Each of these approaches has important implications for the work of those attempting to prevent or resolve interethnic conflict. Neither is universally applicable. The integrationist approach, however, represents a relatively underutilized option at present. This paper makes the case for this approach in Macedonia and cautions against neglecting this option in other cases. While the report of the Center for Preventive Action's Working Group on the South Balkans makes clear that it will be difficult to pursue contradictory approaches to conflict resolution and prevention in Macedonia and Kosovo, differences between these cases suggest that while some form of power sharing may be required to de-escalate the conflict in Kosovo, efforts to increase intergroup contact and cooperation may be the best strategy for preventing intergroup conflict in Macedonia.[2]

This paper reviews conditions in Macedonia and Kosovo in analytical terms and categories intended to facilitate comparative discussion of conflict resolution.

Because conditions in Macedonia and Kosovo are significantly different and offer quite different challenges and opportunities for preventive action, they are treated separately here. The activities of nongovernmental organizations and multilateral governmental actors in Macedonia to stabilize the political environment of the country and prevent intergroup conflict suggest that a pluralist or integrationist strategy might succeed there. In contrast, a brief review of the situation in Kosovo and of nongovernmental and multilateral attempts to resolve the conflict there suggest that its peaceful resolution is likely to require the adoption of extensive power-sharing arrangements between the Kosovar leadership and the Serbian or Yugoslav leadership. The differences between these two cases underscore the need to adapt conflict prevention techniques to the specific characteristics of each case; no one formula, approach, or set of practices can be expected to be universally appropriate. Hence, the present emphasis on power-sharing formulas in the emerging literature on conflict prevention and resolution should not be allowed to obscure the potential applicability of the integrationist or pluralist alternative in some cases.

In adopting any strategy of conflict prevention in Macedonia, it is important to bear in mind one of the central messages of the Report of CPA's Working Group on the South Balkans: that the dynamics of interethnic relations in Macedonia and Kosovo are closely linked. Thus, the ability of both international and domestic actors to adopt any particular strategy in one case may be constrained by its anticipated impact on, or the effect of developments in, the other. Adoption of a strategy of conflict prevention in Kosovo based on extensive power sharing, for example, may make a strategy based on integration far more difficult to implement in Macedonia. Thus, the prevention of interethnic conflict must be conceived as a multidimensional task, involving not only the internal dynamics of the conflict, but the relationships between the conflict and its external environment as well.

COMPETING APPROACHES TO CONFLICT MANAGEMENT

As noted above, the academic literature on preventing or managing ethnic conflict is dominated by two competing approaches: the pluralist or integrationist approach; and the consociational or power-sharing approach.[3] The latter is most closely associated with the scholar Arend Lijphart.[4] It is the most widespread basis for solutions proposed by scholars studying current ethnic conflicts and is often cited as an explanation for alleged successes in cases that might have been expected to be failures.

Scholars differ with respect to both the definition of the consociational approach and the conditions for its success. Lijphart himself has varied his definition.[5] But it is fair to say that this approach can be boiled down to a few simple ideas. First, ethnic conflict is understood as originating in contact between groups holding incompatible, culturally rooted values. Accordingly, the isolation of groups from one another at the mass level through entirely separate networks of social and political organizations—segmentation—is a central component of this approach. Second, in recognition of the differing values of such groups, and in the apparent conviction that they cannot reach compromise, each of the cultural segments or communities is to be granted a high degree of autonomy over its own affairs. Third, with respect to decisionmaking on issues of common interest to all groups, the consociational paradigm calls for proportional systems of representation in common institutions that ensure the participation of representatives of all such groups in decisions. Fourth, each of the groups represented in authoritative decisionmaking processes should be granted veto power over the resulting decisions when its "vital interests" are at stake. Because intergroup contact at the mass level generates conflict, such contact is to be restricted to elites. Hence, decisionmaking on issues of common interest and the exercise of group vetoes on issues concerning "vital interests" are to be exercised by elite representatives of each of the groups. Indeed, elites exercise a monopoly even over the definition of what constitutes the common interests of all and the "vital interests" of each. The obvious vulnerability of such a system to intransigent elite behavior can be avoided, according to Lijphart and others, through the exercise of goodwill among elite representatives of the ethnic segments—a condition essential for the model's success.

Elite domination of these systems is reinforced by structural ethnic segmentation. Each ethnic group forms its own distinct religious, cultural, and political organizations. Organizationally segmented or isolated communities provide the constituencies for ethnically defined political parties and their leaders, who claim to represent these populations—rather than specific interest or functional groups—in state decisionmaking processes. Where ethnic populations are distributed in more or less territorially compact patterns, territorialized autonomy—whether limited devolution, federalization, or confederalization—becomes the logical expression of such an approach to conflict management. Belgium, the case most often cited by Lijphart and others as an example of successful management of ethnic conflict through consociationalism, has passed through precisely these stages of increasingly complete dismantling of the common state and the creation of distinct, ethnically defined territorial entities with increasingly comprehensive, independent decisionmaking authority. At present, it may be argued there is little left of the Belgian state over which the territorial entities can argue, other than the existence of the state itself.[6]

What appears to have held Belgium together throughout the dismantling process was the continued presence of a shared Belgian identity that overrides the ethno-regional identities and the existence of common interests and class identities that cut across the ethno-regions and provide the basis for joint political action in central decisionmaking institutions. The most important of these has been class identity. The presence of common, crosscutting interests and identities, then, contributed to the peacefulness of the dismantling process.

Perhaps the most important factor contributing to peace in Belgium, however, has been the strongly democratic character of the state and the resultant high level of legitimacy of institutionalized decisionmaking processes. Democratic legitimacy created the certainty that no single actor could or would attempt unilaterally to override a decision arrived at through established decisionmaking processes. Each of these factors—a strong national identity, class interests, and democracy—contributed to moderating the expanding mutual veto power enjoyed by each of the ethno-regional groups, making compromise on the dismantling of common state institutions and the devolution of state powers possible.

Several factors now hold Belgium together: the apparent absence of any further economic or material gains if the regional leaderships were to eliminate the common state entirely; the difficulty of resolving the status of certain ethno-linguistic border regions (including Brussels); and the unpredictability of the consequences of full dissolution for the components' membership in the European Union. In the absence of such factors, the consociational features of the Belgian system might very well have provided the institutional and organizational foundations for secession.

Indeed, it can be argued that recent experiences in Czechoslovakia, the former Yugoslavia, and Bosnia-Herzegovina underscore the inherent vulnerabilities of such arrangements to secession.[7] In Czechoslovakia and the former Yugoslavia, federal institutions and decisionmaking practices created de facto ethno-regional vetoes over federal decision-making. In Czechoslovakia, this instrument was used by Slovak nationalists both to block elite-brokered solutions to the conflict over the relationship between the two federal units and to prevent resolution of the issue through popular referendum. The deadlock produced through intransigent use of the veto led directly to dissolution of the state. Whether this was the intended outcome or not is subject to differing interpretation but is irrelevant for our purposes.

While dissolution remained a peaceful process in Czechoslovakia, a similar deadlock in federal-level decisionmaking led to violence in the former Yugoslavia. In both instances, power-sharing arrangements between elite-dominated ethno-territorial entities that enjoyed substantial autonomy created structural conditions that intensified conflict, rather than moderating or resolving it as the consociationalists have argued. In these cases, intransigent use of the veto nullified the already weak crosscutting or common interests in these states and paralyzed common institutions. The Belgian situation did not prevail: Only a small proportion of the Yugoslav population shared a relatively weak overarching identity,[8] and there was none in Czechoslovakia. Structural conditions helped transform the electoral competition that accompanied democratization into an ethnic competition and provided a ready framework for dominant groups to ethnicize the definition of successor states.

In Yugoslavia the predominantly ethnic definition of regional structures (republics and provinces) contradicted the multiethnic character of the populations in Croatia, Bosnia, Serbia, and Macedonia. This contradiction further intensified the negative consequences of power sharing among ethno-regional elites by facilitating the exclusion of regional minorities by ethno-nationalist successor leaderships. A similar dynamic unfolded in Slovakia in the course of the Czechoslovak dissolution. In Yugoslavia, however, the territorial dimension of power sharing was, at least in formal constitutional and abstract theoretical terms, to be balanced by power sharing among ethnic communities. The federal and republic constitutions of Yugoslavia recognized and empowered nonterritorial ethnic communities in much the same way that the contemporary Belgian constitution recognizes both regional (territorial) and ethno-linguistic communities.[9]

In Bosnia-Herzegovina, the ethnicization of politics in a disintegrating Yugoslavia ensured that the empowerment of three major ethnic groups and the establishment of a mutual veto among them would produce political deadlock. The complex patterns of ethnic settlement in Bosnia meant that any effort to resolve conflict by dismantling the state and devolving authority to territorial entities along Belgian lines, or even along nonterritorialized principles akin to those cited by Lijphart in his study of the Netherlands, would have required exceedingly complex negotiations among elites committed to a peaceful settlement.[10] Tragically, while power-sharing arrangements delivered powerful weapons of intransigence into the hands of Bosnian elites, few incentives to cooperation were present, and there was little likelihood that they could be developed in the short term. Democratic institutions and norms were too weak to constrain the behavior of nationalistic elites and to overcome the centrifugal forces produced by socioeconomic and political factors inside Bosnia and in the surrounding environment.

It seems certain that consociational power sharing will encourage rather than prevent conflict, deadlock, and secession in the absence of either cultural-historical norms or socioeconomic and political incentives to cooperation, such as exist in the Netherlands, Switzerland, and Belgium. Yet, proposals for such arrangements are often among the very first actions of international actors attempting to resolve or prevent intergroup conflict.

Elsewhere in this volume, Michael S. Lund identifies three broad categories of sources of conflict: the socioeconomic structure of group relations, the institutional and procedural framework of participation and decisionmaking, and elite behavior. Of these, he argues, the socioeconomic structure is beyond the immediate control of those seeking to prevent conflict, while institutions "are somewhat more malleable" and elite behavior is "relatively more amenable to change in the short run." Based on this distinction, Lund suggests that preventive action should focus most immediately on elite behavior, in the medium term on transforming institutions, and only in the long term on the underlying socioeconomic structure of group relations.

But while the short-term behavior of elites may be amenable to change through the application of pressure, sanctions, or even coercion, such changes in behavior will last only as long as those measures continue to be applied. Once such external forces are removed, internal socioeconomic forces can be expected once again to determine the behavior of elites. Similarly, while institutional reforms that introduce elements of consociationalism or power sharing can empower group elites to defend their self-defined vital interests, such reforms by themselves will not induce cooperative behavior. Lund himself points out the vulnerability of relying on such an institutional approach in his discussion of Burundi. He notes that "new institutions [could] simply become new bases of operation through which party leaders separately pursued their partisan aims, by . . . passing discriminatory legislation, doling out patronage, and repressing other groups, thus inviting government disintegration, deadlock or rebellion."[11] Indeed, this is precisely what happened in Yugoslavia over the course of the 1980s and, in a much more intensified process, in Bosnia-Herzegovina following the 1990 election.[12]

The Yugoslav and Bosnian cases suggest that durable solutions to conflict require changes in the underlying socioeconomic structure of group relations, encouraging cooperation across ethnic barriers as a means of either repairing social relations in the wake of conflict or averting conflict by fostering shared interests and identities. In the absence of such changes, institutional solutions are unlikely to succeed. Incentives to cooperation can be found in the society itself, in the form of identities and interests that intersect with, and moderate the appeal of, ethnicity. This is the essence of the "crosscutting cleavages" hypothesis widely cited in political science as the source of political moderation and cited by Lijphart himself as a condition that contributes to the success of power sharing. But crosscutting cleavages contribute to the moderation of conflict only when they become the basis for political identity, electoral competition, and participation in representative institutions and decisionmaking processes. Their ability to moderate ethnic conflict can be thought of as roughly proportional to the extent that the interests and behavior associated with identities that cut across ethnic group boundaries gain strength relative to those associated with ethnicity or ethno-regional identity.

Hence, in situations of politicized ethnic identities and potential intergroup conflict, the identification and encouragement of crosscutting cleavages in political decisionmaking processes can be an effective strategy for moderating conflict. This was a central argument in Professor Leatherman's background paper on Macedonia for CPA's Working Group on the South Balkans.[13] In the absence of such crosscutting cleavages, incentives to cooperation between political parties and their leaders can be built into electoral systems and representative institutions. But the adoption of mutual vetoes of the kind prescribed by advocates of power sharing should be approached with extreme caution; as the experience of Yugoslavia suggests, such a veto is likely to promote intransigence rather than cooperation.

The pluralist approach to ethnic conflict management is based on a radically different understanding of the effects of intergroup contact.

Stated most concisely, pluralists argue that, under critically important conditions of open communications and equality, contact between groups generates mutual understanding and cooperation, not conflict. While consociationalists view institutions as primarily reflective of ethnic segmentation, pluralists hold that institutions can not only reflect, but also *transform*, ethnic relations. Contact in shared institutions is not necessarily an agent of cultural assimilation; but sustained contact under conditions of open communications and equality may contribute to the emergence of a shared culture of interaction and cooperation, known as "civic culture."

The openness of intergroup contact and communication is essential to the pluralist paradigm. Consociational systems tend to perpetuate existing deficiencies in intergroup understanding, because structural ethnic segmentation blocks intergroup communications. The pluralist paradigm, in contrast, suggests the importance of efforts to overcome such segmentation of communications. Efforts to ensure the openness of mass media to intergroup communication are a potentially powerful means by which to begin to construct the social foundations for identities and behavior that transcend ethnic communities. Similarly, while the consociationalist approach might argue for the segmentation of education, the pluralist approach suggests that common educational institutions that value group identities and cultures equally—especially at the university level—are a potentially powerful means by which to foster intergroup contact, communication, and understanding and encourage the discovery of shared values and interests. Hence, the pluralist or integrationist approach directs attention to the social and economic factors that define group orientations; that is, it directs attention to that source of conflict which consociationalists view as a given.

The consociational approach is based on the disputable assumption of goodwill among elites for whom competition is the source of personal power. The pluralist approach is based on the assumption that individuals at the grass roots are able to recognize opportunities to secure social and economic benefits through intergroup cooperation, and that the success of such cooperation in securing benefits for all those who participate will foster goodwill. Whereas the consociational approach accepts and reinforces the politics of identity, the pluralist approach seeks to foster the politics of interest at both the grassroots and institutional levels.

Where the consociationalist approach institutionalizes ethnic segmentation in the state itself, the pluralist approach calls for avoiding definition of the state, or of state institutions, in ethnic terms. From a pluralist perspective, behavior based on ethnic identities should be required to compete with behavior based on nonethnic identities and interests on an equal, rather than a privileged, basis. The dilemma inherent in the pluralist approach, of course, involves the protection of ethnic minority populations from unfair treatment at the hands of an ethnic majority, especially under conditions of democratic electoral competition and representation.

In cases where the social differentiation associated with modernization precedes the politicization of ethnicity, nonethnic identities and interests are likely to cut across ethnicities and to have acquired enough political salience at least to moderate ethnic conflict, as in the case of Belgium. In the former Yugoslavia and much of Eastern Europe, in contrast, the development of national consciousness and its politicization preceded the modernization and social differentiation processes. The establishment of Communist regimes and the elimination of private ownership in states that were still only partially modernized appears to have prevented (or cut short) the emergence of genuine class- or church-based politics of the type central to the historical development of cross-cutting cleavages in West European pluralist systems. In the multinational Communist states, ethno-national identity remained the only officially sanctioned political cleavage. With the collapse of communism, therefore, and the onset of electoral competition, no other cleavage could provide as powerful a basis for mobilization.

Where the politicization of ethnicity dominates other bases of political behavior, as in Kosovo and Macedonia, the challenge in pursuing a pluralist approach to ethnic conflict management consists in establishing a balance between the ethnic and the nonethnic mode in participation, representation, and decisionmaking. In some cases—Kosovo may be one such—the challenge lies in facilitating the emergence of any nonethnic dimension at all. To pursue a power-sharing strategy aimed at institutions alone, however, would mean institutionalizing ethnic cleavages and creating the structural foundations for intransigent vetoes and, ultimately, secession. It may be possible to lay the foundations for the emergence of social and political forces that might counterbalance this tendency toward secession by also pursuing a pluralist strategy at the grass roots. In the wake of the breakup of the multinational states of Eastern Europe, no political leadership is likely to embark on a strategy of power sharing in the absence of such counterbalancing tendencies, lest it create the institutional foundations for secession.

Electoral rules represent a potentially important instrument at the institutional level through which to pursue a pluralist strategy of moderating intergroup tensions and preventing ethnic conflict. Electoral rules affect the scope and character of both participation and representation in a given system. Proportionality systems recommended by the consociationalists ensure the representation of all groups but also encourage ethnic bloc voting. Where ethnicity has been politicized, the result of such electoral rules is the conversion of electoral competition into an ethnic census. Donald Horowitz has directed attention to the need under such conditions for strong structural incentives to elite cooperation.[14] He has argued that adopting particular vote-counting schemes, demarcating ethnically diverse constituencies, and requiring an elected majority in each constituency may both foster positive interaction among groups in the electoral process and produce representatives more inclined to intergroup cooperation. Where the incentives for cooperative behavior are strong, they are likely to result in heightened emphasis by leaders on practical material issues of common concern to all individuals in a given constituency, rather than on divisive ethno-cultural issues. Even in strongly institutionalized democracies such as the United States, electoral rules have been altered with such goals in mind. But as the history of efforts to secure minority voting rights and representation in the United States demonstrates, devising electoral solutions is not easy and can be highly controversial.[15]

If ethnic domination and/or deadlock in decisionmaking institutions are to be avoided, the pluralist approach suggests that much of what are considered the "vital interests" of ethnic communities should be depoliticized. Such interests should, whenever possible, be placed outside the realm of partisan competition and state decisionmaking rather than merely devolved to autonomous entities, where they would remain political, or subject to a "mutual veto." With respect to "vital" issues, whether members of an ethnic group act as individuals, in groups, or as a collective community should be a matter of private choice, not public policy. Decisionmaking in state institutions should focus on issues more easily subject to compromise, such as material issues. Even material issues, however, may be perceived as "vital" by members of an ethnic community, including those elected under rules that maximize incentives to cooperation. Thus, even a pluralist strategy requires formulas by which members of an ethnic community can protect themselves from being outvoted on issues they perceive as "vital."

Weighted parliamentary voting systems, rather than simple vetoes, offer potentially important instruments by which groups might be empowered to defend their interests. As James Coleman has argued, weighted voting systems—by endowing members of parliament with multiple votes that they may apportion among issues as they wish—

can simultaneously empower members of parliaments to defend their special, or vital, interests and create opportunities and incentives for them to build cross-cleavage alliances through vote exchanges. A minority's ability to use multiple votes to veto any action may moderate the behavior of a majority, as consociationalists have argued. At the same time, however, the weighted voting scheme Coleman has developed creates a strong structural incentive not to indulge in intransigent behavior; it creates a limited rather than unlimited ability to block legislation. The successful use of multiple votes by any one group to veto any item reduces its ability to veto future legislation. This not only makes intransigent behavior potentially costly; it places a premium on coalition-building strategies as a substitute for the veto.[16]

Both consociationalists and pluralists would agree that the ethnic definition of state institutions is to be avoided. In economically less developed contexts, control of the state itself is the major economic resource. Therefore, employment in state institutions must be open equally to individuals from all groups. In multilingual settings, openness will require multiplication of the languages used in everyday administration and hence will increase the cost of state institutions. Cost considerations may act as a brake on the growth of state administration and create a further incentive to reduce its functions. Nonetheless, participation by all groups on an equal basis contributes to legitimization of the state and its "civic" rather than "ethnic" definition. From the pluralist perspective, it also creates opportunities for cooperative activities across ethno-linguistic cleavages.

However limited the functions and institutions of the state, local governments will continue to provide such basic services as the protection of public safety and the maintenance of public infrastructure. Local governmental institutions must operate according to the same principles of openness, including operation in multiple languages where appropriate. The same principle should be applied to private entities that perform public services, such as utility companies. In this way, local populations can pursue their interests in better roads, clean water, and reliable power supplies—activities the pluralist paradigm sees as inherently conflict-moderating—directly and cooperatively across ethno-linguistic cleavages. The creation of opportunities for such grassroots cooperation is essential to the success of a pluralist, integrationist strategy. It is such cooperation, over the long run, that can be expected to give rise to domestic social forces and electoral pressures that alter the power calculations of elites and compel them to cooperate.

The pluralist approach is thus oriented toward openness and participation. Consociational or power-sharing approaches are at best elitist and at worst antidemocratic. In the present, post-Communist period of European political development, the popular attractiveness of democratic ideology and demands for empowerment should act as deterrents to the adoption of such an approach as a long-term strategy for resolving intergroup tensions and conflicts. Some practices associated with the power-sharing paradigm, such as the establishment of governments based on "grand coalitions" among groups, may be useful as short-term preventive techniques. But in the longer term, the greatest promise for moderating intergroup tensions and preventing conflict comes from the identification (or creation) of crosscutting cleavages, their representation in political decisionmaking processes in the state, and the creation of conditions that encourage cooperative action across ethnic cleavages on the social level.

CONDITIONS IN MACEDONIA AND KOSOVO

International concern for conditions in Kosovo and Macedonia arises out of the strategic importance of these neighboring territories for stability in the South Balkans as a whole. Kosovo is an overwhelmingly ethnic-Albanian province of Serbia, in which a well-organized nationalist independence movement has mounted sustained, nonviolent resistance to Serb control. That movement has been suppressed by a combination of military and police repression. There is some evidence of rising tensions, punctuated by isolated incidents of violence in the region. The potential for massive violence in the region increased in April 1997 with the apparent influx of significant numbers of weapons into the region from neighboring Albania.[17] An outbreak of fighting in Kosovo would further destabilize Albania, as well as neighboring Macedonia. At the same time, however, there is some evidence of movement among both Kosovar Albanian and Serbian leaders toward a willingness to negotiate a solution to their conflict. Thus, the opportunity to pursue a peaceful resolution of this conflict still exists.

The situation in Macedonia is, on its own, less volatile but no less serious. According to the results of a special, internationally supervised census conducted in 1994, Macedonia's population of just under two million is 66.6 percent ethnically Macedonian, 22.7 percent Albanian, and 4.0 percent Turkish.[18] It is the relationship between ethnic Albanians and Macedonians that is at the heart of the political insecurity of Macedonia. The ethnic Albanian population is concentrated in the western counties of Macedonia, adjacent to the borders with Kosovo to the north and Albania to the west. The Turkish population constitutes a smaller but significant minority in several counties in both the west and the east. (See Table 2.1 for the ethnic composition of counties in western Macedonia.) Thus, in the west, Macedonia is a multiethnic state; in the east, however, it is largely Macedonian, with the proportion of Macedonians ranging from 82.9 percent in Titov Veles to 98.6 percent in Probistip.[19] The exceptions are to be found in the southeast: in Radovis, where Turks constitute 14.0 percent of the population and Macedonians 85.3 percent, and in Valandovo, where Turks constitute 12.1 percent and Macedonians 81.9 percent. Whereas the Turkish population poses serious questions of minority rights for the Macedonian state, Albanian discontent—especially in the context of a nationalist independence movement in neighboring Kosovo and political chaos in neighboring Albania—poses the threat of an incipient secessionist movement across a large portion of the country, and the destabilization, if not dismemberment, of the Macedonian state with unpredictable consequences for all its neighbors. Macedonia is a post-Communist state characterized by weak political institutions and a very weak civil society. Political parties in Macedonia include both Albanian and Macedonian nationalist parties, along with parties committed to a civic or nonethnic vision of the state. Politics is characterized by open competition for electoral support among these parties, including

TABLE 2.1
ETHNIC COMPOSITION OF TEN WESTERN COUNTIES IN MACEDONIA, 1994
(IN PERCENTAGES)

County	Major Ethnic Groups				
	Macedonian	Albanian	Turk	Other	Total
Tetovo	20.8	74.4	2.3	2.5	100.0
Gostivar	18.6	63.7	12.7	5.0	100.0
Kicevo	39.7	49.2	7.2	3.9	100.0
Debar	21.1	44.4	26.3	8.2	100.0
Struga	44.4	45.2	5.3	5.1	100.0
Kumanovo	50.5	36.9	0.3	12.3	100.0
Krusevo	55.8	22.9	5.5	15.8	100.0
Skopje (region)	65.4	20.8	2.4	11.4	100.0
Resen	76.1	9.8	10.6	3.5	100.0
Brod	68.6	0.2	30.8	0.4	100.0

Source: Statistical Office of the Republic of Madcedonia, "Population According to Declared Ethnic Affiliation, Religious Affiliation, Mother Tongue, and Citizenship," The 1994 Census of the Population, Households, Dwellings, and Agricultural Holdings in the Republic of Macedonia I (Skopje: November 1996), Table 1.1a, p. 23.

competition between nationalist and nonnationalist parties within both the Albanian and Macedonian communities. The civic-oriented, but largely Macedonian, Social Democratic Alliance and Liberal parties have been able to forge governing coalitions that included moderate nationalist and nonnationalist Albanians. Basic features of the post-Communist political system, such as electoral rules, are still in formation. There is a relatively low level of agreement on procedural rules in state decisionmaking institutions. In some cases—including parliamentary rules of procedure—these are carryovers from the Communist period, and there is a correspondingly low level of adherence to them. Their legitimacy is still challenged by those dissatisfied with the outcomes they produce. Even those who themselves participate in decisionmaking processes, such as members of parliament—including, in some instances, members of parties that are part of the governing coalition—have challenged the legitimacy of outcomes.

While weak institutions do not contribute to moderating intergroup conflict, the fact that Macedonia is still in the process of transition from Communist to non-Communist principles of organization and operation, and the relatively low levels of attachment to existing institutions, means that almost all political actors in Macedonia seem to agree that the current system must be changed. This may make it easier to modify existing organizations and institutions or to create entirely new ones. All of the areas identified earlier—electoral rules, decisionmaking rules (informal and formal, governmental and parliamentary), state employment practices, language use policies, and the organization of higher education—are areas in which CPA's Working Group on the South Balkans identified changes that might be implemented in Macedonia in order to reduce intergroup tensions. In some of these areas, international nongovernmental organizations are already active and have achieved notable successes.

In Macedonia, as in other post-Communist East European states, the separation between the public and private spheres is not well defined. There are few well-institutionalized barriers to the penetration of public policymaking and state influence into aspects of life that might be considered private in more well developed liberal democratic states. Control over the state in Macedonia continues to be viewed by many political activists as a means of securing the survival of one's own group, and its control by others is viewed as a potential threat to group survival. These conditions suggest a clear opportunity to engage local actors in efforts to reform existing institutions in ways that can contribute to moderating intergroup tensions and preventing conflict in

Macedonia. Institutional reform will have only a limited impact, however, if social interests and political forces that cut across ethnic cleavages are not strengthened.

The weakness of civil society in Macedonia is a product of the economic underdevelopment of the country and a legacy of the past efforts of the Communist regime to suppress the emergence of politically significant autonomous social activity. Reform of the economy is not far advanced: The autonomy of major enterprises is limited, and private, market-oriented economic activity is not well developed. The mass media are still dominated by the state, although the independent sector—including television—is growing. These weaknesses magnify the significance of ethnic solidarities for political behavior and reinforce the ability of ethnic entrepreneurs to mobilize voters, as there are few if any cross-cutting cleavages that affect political behavior. These conditions suggest the necessity of efforts to foster the growth of civil society. Peter Lewis has proposed a similar approach for Nigeria: what he calls "a strategic focus on Nigerian civil society," or "capacity-building initiatives to strengthen the role of civic organizations." He argues that "pressures from organized societal groups can be a catalyst for democratic transition, and the process of negotiation and accommodation within civil society offers an important arena for conflict resolution in divided societies."[20]

The pluralist paradigm would suggest that those intent on reducing tensions among ethnic groups in Macedonia should identify opportunities for procedural or institutional reform, or for the establishment of new institutions that foster conflict-ameliorating contact and communication between groups and encourage the emergence of crosscutting cleavages. Given the advanced level of politicization of ethnic identities in Macedonia, mechanisms must also be established that will allow ethnic representatives to defend interests they perceive as "vital." But as our earlier discussion of power-sharing formulas might suggest, any such mechanism must avoid deadlock and state paralysis. Weighted parliamentary voting systems represent a potential institutional response to this danger. As Lund's three-part categorization of conflict-prevention activities suggests, another response might be directed at the behavior of elites. One leader of an organization engaged directly in efforts to build understanding among ethnic groups in divided societies reported that his organization has found that self-interest and incentives are "absolutely critical" in motivating cooperation, and that "outsiders can help local actors identify their interests" in an effort to encourage cross-cleavage cooperation. Such efforts at building cross-group communication at the elite level seem necessary if the adoption of power-sharing schemes is not to lead to intransigent behavior; but they are unlikely to be sufficient to prevent such behavior.

Conditions in Kosovo are radically different. Here, one ethnic group (the Kosovar Albanians) has been subjected to the repressive and often violent rule of another ethnic group (the Serbs) that controls the military and police of a still-authoritarian post-Communist state. Each group attaches legitimacy to its own institutions: the Serbs insist on the legitimacy of the formal institutions from which the Albanians have largely withdrawn or been expelled, while the Albanians consider the parallel social and political institutions they have constructed since 1989 as their legitimate institutions. There are no institutions that enjoy legitimacy in the eyes of both groups. The formal demands of each side are mutually exclusive: The Serbs demand that the Albanians recognize Serbian and Yugoslav institutions, while the Albanians demand full independence. The demands of one are backed up by force as well as the strength of formal international recognition of existing borders. The demands of the other are backed only by the moral force of claims to human rights and self-determination and the threat that continued failure to address them will lead to violent rebellion.

While in Macedonia it is appropriate to speak of intergroup tensions and the potential for conflict, in Kosovo one must speak of existing conflict, a sometimes violent conflict between two fully mobilized, deeply divided, and completely segmented ethnic communities, with a potential for far higher—and more tragic—levels of violence. Yet in Kosovo, the task of those trying to resolve this conflict is not different in kind from the tasks in Macedonia or other less advanced conflicts: it is to identify areas of mutual interest and to foster agreements between the two groups that permit them to pursue those interests. As CPA's Working Group on the South Balkans has suggested, these areas of mutual interest might provide the basis for a mutually acceptable interim solution while further negotiations over a more permanent resolution of the conflict continue. Under such conditions, discussions of a permanent solution would almost certainly incline toward extensive power sharing, if not outright separation.

In the Macedonian case, it is possible to argue that individuals and groups on both sides of the ethnic cleavage may still share the same interests and goals. Joint, cooperative effort among Albanians, Macedonians, and others in Macedonia can be expected to produce, within a reasonable amount of time, a sense of shared "civic" identity. Hence, not only are there still opportunities to pursue a pluralist strategy of reconciliation, but there is also a reasonable hope that such a strategy might succeed. In Kosovo, on the other hand, the impact of mutual interests is tempered by the accumulated animosities associated with violence and repression and the incompatibility of the ultimate goals on the two sides of the conflict. There is little likelihood that a pluralist strategy of reconciliation will succeed in any reasonable period of time in Kosovo; and in light of the extreme demographic imbalance in the region, it might never succeed. A permanent solution to the conflict in Kosovo, therefore, will likely require implementation of extensive power-sharing arrangements, perhaps amounting to de facto separation, between Kosovo and Serbia.

CONFLICT PREVENTION IN MACEDONIA

Macedonia has received the attention of numerous international actors. The presence of the United Nations Preventive Deployment force (UNPREDEP) played a key role in averting external conflict and has contributed to moderating internal tensions. Several nongovernmental organizations have been conducting projects, explicitly intended to prevent interethnic conflict, that fall squarely within the pluralist paradigm. Their successes are consistent with the view that this strategy can work in Macedonia.

Search for Common Ground in Macedonia (SCGM), for example, has been engaged in a number of efforts to encourage both intergroup contact and communication and active cooperation in the pursuit of shared interests, in the hope of fostering greater intergroup empathy and understanding.[21] The "How We Survive" journalism project sponsored by SCGM resulted in the simultaneous publication, in the major Albanian-, Macedonian-, and Turkish-language newspapers, of a series of feature reports on how people of all ethnicities were coping with problems of daily life. It also generated greater cross-group empathy among the journalists who participated. The journalism project exploited the existence of common professional interests across the ethnic divide, mobilized institutional support for interethnic contacts, increased the flow of sympathetic information across the cleavage in the form of newspaper articles, and helped to create empathy among journalists, who play an important role in helping to shape mass perceptions and opinions. SCGM is following this up with a current project encouraging the publication of contrasting opinions on important issues as a means of acculturating readers to the idea that one characteristic of democracy is "conflict of opinion without conflict." SCGM-sponsored monthly roundtables at Skopje University encourage direct interethnic discussions on issues of common concern, and its projects on environmental protection support interethnic cooperation in direct efforts by local populations to clean up their communities. The ongoing successes of SCGM projects provide powerful evidence of the utility of the pluralist paradigm in Macedonia.

Because education, and especially higher education, has been such a contentious issue in Macedonia, CPA's Working Group on the South Balkans devoted considerable attention to this issue during its visit to Macedonia and in its deliberations afterward. Its recommendations for depoliticizing the issue included allowing the establishment of private universities, opening the state-funded university to greater enrollment of ethnic Albanians by expanding the domain of Albanian-language instruction at the university (and taking steps to ensure that more Albanian students receive adequate preparation for higher education), and increasing the role of international educational professionals in goal setting, policy development and implementation, and evaluation. Although these recommendations were developed by the members of CPA's Working Group without reference to the pluralist paradigm, they conform to it. Allowing the establishment of a private university would encourage the development of civil society in Macedonia and underscore its legitimacy. Making the state-funded university more open to all ethnic groups would underscore the civic definition of state institutions. Professionalizing educational policy would allow educators of all ethnicities to participate as equals in cooperative activities on matters of common interest. The Macedonian government has continued its efforts to open the University of Skopje to ethnic Albanian enrollment and has prepared legislation to permit the establishment of private universities. But draft national legislation continues to require Macedonian as the language of instruction and limits the use of minority languages to teacher training courses and subjects not promoting cultural and national identity (e.g., theater).[22]

These proposed reforms in education represent another important affirmation of the attractiveness of the pluralist strategy for Macedonian leaders committed to reducing intergroup tensions and establish an important precedent for further cooperative efforts in other areas identified by CPA's Working Group. But large demonstrations by Macedonian students against government efforts to expand Albanian-language instruction at the University of Skopje provided ample evidence of the difficulties involved in implementing such a strategy. Efforts to increase opportunities for communication and contact across ethnic barriers will meet with resistance from those on both sides of the divide whose power and privilege depend on mobilizing nationalist sentiments and who fear the consequences of greater equality. Others may resist integration out of genuine belief in the superiority of cultural separation and autonomy.

The National Democratic Institute for International Affairs (NDI) has also demonstrated that the strategy of professionalizing issues that might otherwise engender additional intergroup tensions can be successful in Macedonia. NDI reported in 1996 that, at the request of the Macedonian government, it had arranged for expert review of the government's draft law on local elections; 80 percent of NDI's recommendations were accepted. NDI then organized an all-party public roundtable on the draft law, which precipitated a wider public debate including newspaper, television, and radio coverage of the event and the issue.[23] By these actions, NDI helped Macedonian party leaders depoliticize the issue and resolve their differences amicably. This process established an important precedent for meaningful public consideration and debate of proposed government policies.

A major explanation for the successes of organizations such as SCGM and NDI, and for the more modest success of the CPA Working Group on the South Balkans, lies in their sustained attention to the issue. The fact that both SCGM and NDI have maintained a continuous presence on the ground in Macedonia has allowed these organizations to accumulate experience and professional contacts with local actors bearing on the dynamics of issues. This is an invaluable resource in any effort to resolve or prevent conflict.

The more modest success of CPA's Working Group can be attributed to the fact that it has sustained its attention largely from afar. The members of CPA's Working Group and the members of the mission to the region brought a broad range of skills and experiences to bear on the issues before them: These included substantial area expertise (including relevant language capabilities) and hands-on experience in dealing with the politics of conflictual issues, assets that were multiplied many times over among the full membership of the Group. Because most members of the mission had not been deeply involved in the details of the issues up to the formation of CPA's Working Group, they were able to approach the issues in Macedonia from a fresh perspective. And because most of them would not remain directly engaged in the issues over a long period, they were intensely interested in identifying opportunities for the conflicting parties themselves to act in constructive ways. Area expertise combined with an openness that allowed fresh approaches to the issues, experience in the politics of conflict resolution, and an orientation toward identifying what the parties themselves, rather than outsiders, could do to improve the situation on the ground all contributed to the ability of CPA's Working Group to draft useful recommendations.

RESOLVING THE KOSOVO CONFLICT

The conflict in Kosovo is unlikely to be manageable through a pluralist strategy of reconciliation. At the same time, power-sharing arrangements that encourage intransigent use of a veto or, especially, secession will not be accepted by the more powerful party to the conflict. Yet no effort to achieve peace in Kosovo will succeed unless it addresses and satisfies real interests on both sides. Hence, peacemaking efforts in Kosovo must focus on identifying measures that address outstanding issues in ways that benefit both sides. CPA's Working Group concluded that there were some areas in which both sides might agree to actions that benefited each side in a different way, and that successful actions of this type might contribute to de-escalating the conflict and building mutual confidence between the parties. This, in turn, might permit them to address larger, more contentious issues at some point in the future.

CPA's Working Group singled out the return of schools, including Prishtina University, to normal operation "at the earliest possible moment" as an important opportunity to begin a process of normalization in Kosovo. The schools were singled out because of the enormous human cost to the Albanian population of continuing to rely on the alternative school system to educate its youth, and because of the enormous symbolic significance for the Serbs of restoring the operation of state institutions in Kosovo. The success of the Community of Sant' Egidio in mediating an agreement in September 1996 between Ibrahim Rugova, the Kosovar leader, and Slobodan Milosevic to normalize operation of the educational system of Kosovo appears to confirm the general approach outlined by CPA's Working Group and suggests that similar agreements concerning public health and other institutions might also be concluded.[24] A meeting between David Phillips, director of CPA's project, and Ibrahim Rugova, almost a year after the mission to the region and more than six months after the recommendations became public, that secured Rugova's agreement to implement an important part of the accord by naming representatives to a joint implementation commission underscores the importance of sustaining follow-up on the recommendations of CPA's Working Group for a period long enough for them to affect political calculations in the region. It should be noted that little progress has been achieved in implementation discussion up to now. The successful implementation of this accord will require the continued involvement of Sant' Egidio in identifying areas of common interest between the two sides.

A similar process of facilitating agreement between Kosovar Albanians and Serbs on the principles that might guide discussions leading to negotiation of a solution to their conflict has been unfolding under the sponsorship of the Project on Ethnic Relations (PER). PER-sponsored discussions between Albanian and Serbian political leaders in New York in April 1997 led to the identification of some basic principles on which both sides could agree. The Helsinki Commissions of Serbia and Kosovo subsequently asked the Center for Preventive Action to cosponsor a dialogue they planned among leading representatives of the two parties. These efforts may lead to further, more detailed discussions that would include representatives of the ruling party. Thus, nongovernmental organizations may be able to play a role in identifying opportunities for cooperation in Kosovo similar to the role they have played in Macedonia.

However, the success of efforts to exploit these opportunities in Kosovo may not be due entirely to internal factors or to the activities of the nongovernmental organizations themselves. External actors—particularly the United States government—are pressing both sides very hard to pursue such agreements. Both sides are eager to please the United States in the wake of the Dayton agreement and the assumption by the United States of a leadership role in bringing peace to the Balkans. Thus it appears that nongovernmental organizations can also play an important role in resolving the Kosovo conflict by keeping governments— and especially the U.S. government—apprised of apparent opportunities for agreement and progress, when doing so does not jeopardize the opportunity. Even aside from U.S. pressure, leaders on both sides of the conflict in Kosovo have strong incentives to achieve at least some progress so as to strengthen their position among their own peoples. Hence, continued efforts to facilitate contact and communication between the two sides are an important part of the effort to resolve this conflict.

POSSIBLE ROLES FOR OUTSIDE ACTORS

This brief review of academic paradigms and practical experience in conflict prevention and resolution in the South Balkans suggests some important conclusions about the role of outside actors in resolving the conflicts in Kosovo and Macedonia. While this paper argues in favor of pluralist strategies of furthering contact, communication, and cooperative engagement across ethnic cleavages, it seems clear that this strategy is more appropriate for Macedonia than for Kosovo. Conditions in Kosovo simply do not appear to favor such grassroots efforts by outside actors. It is very important to point out, however, that some independent internal actors are themselves quietly pursuing this strategy. For example, the Forum for Ethnic Relations in Belgrade has sponsored direct discussions between Kosovar Albanians and Serbs and is conducting a joint Serb-Albanian project examining the Kosovo crisis and the prospects for Serbian-Albanian relations. It has produced a series of volumes examining the various dimensions of the conflict.[25] A less formal organization, The Group of Women Psychologists, has been sponsoring discussions between Kosovar Albanian and Serbian women to explore how the current situation might be changed for the better. The continuation of such activities may require financial support from external actors, but they are best left in the hands of local actors so as to avoid their politicization. They in fact represent very modest evidence of a revival of civil society.

In both Kosovo and Macedonia, conflict prevention activities have succeeded where they have focused on identifying areas of mutual interest between the parties in conflict and facilitated discussion, organization, and action around them. They have not succeeded where external actors have attempted to intervene in disputes or around issues where there is little or no mutual interest or basis of agreement between the parties. The Project on Ethnic Relations has achieved modest success with respect to the Kosovo conflict by fostering contact and communication between leading political figures from Kosovo and Serbia without intervening in the emerging dialogue to impose solutions on the actors. Discussions in New York in April 1997 allowed both sides to explore principles on which a solution might be approached. The continuation of discussion between Kosovar Albanian and Serbian political leaders, and especially their expansion to include representation of the ruling Socialist Party of Serbia led by Slobodan Milosevic, seems to offer some hope for movement toward an interim agreement that would improve conditions in Kosovo while opening the door to negotiation of a more permanent solution.

Close attention to what might be called the basic hopes and wishes of participants in the conflict, and not just on their articulated views and demands, can help identify opportunities for constructive action. Among other things, it requires openness to contact with as complete an array of actors on each side as possible. It is inherently difficult, however, to move beyond views and demands to hopes and wishes. Another asset can be individuals with personal relationships with the actors that antedate the prevention effort and members of a team who can establish personal rapport with local actors. In the case of CPA's Working Group some members of the mission were able to achieve this, and their insights helped shape the final recommendations.[26]

The successes of SCGM and NDI and the more modest success of the CPA Working Group in Macedonia all point to the importance of combining expertise in the area of conflict with experience in conflict resolution and prevention. This is a lesson well worth emphasizing for every nongovernmental actor, multilateral governmental actor, and national government wishing to become involved in efforts to resolve or prevent conflicts. Misapplication of abstract approaches to conflict resolution owing to ignorance of their meaning or implications for local actors can, in fact, aggravate conflicts. Advocacy of power-sharing arrangements by outside actors, for example, can easily be seen by local actors as signaling support for secession if such advocacy is not accompanied at the same time by efforts to build bridges across ethnic cleavages. Similarly, scholarly knowledge of a region is less useful in the absence of sensitivity to the special demands of conflict prevention. These observations suggest that an important role for the Center for Preventive Action and its working groups may be to encourage contact, communication, and mutual learning between practical and diplomatic practitioners of conflict prevention and resolution, on the one hand, and academic experts, on the other, in an effort to enhance the capabilities of both to deal with conflict. An organization such as the Council on Foreign Relations may make a practical contribution to conflict prevention without violating its nonpartisan, nonoperational character by sponsoring expanded contacts between its working groups and those involved directly in conflict prevention and resolution efforts.

The most important conclusion about the role of outside actors, however, may be to remind ourselves, as scholars and practitioners of conflict resolution, that we cannot solve conflicts. Only the parties themselves hold the power to agree to and implement peaceful solutions to conflicts. Thus, the most effective action we can take may be to adopt what Peter Lewis has called "a strategic focus . . . on civil society" that will facilitate the emergence of social organizations and forces that will deny popular support to political entrepreneurs intent on exploiting conflict to gain power.

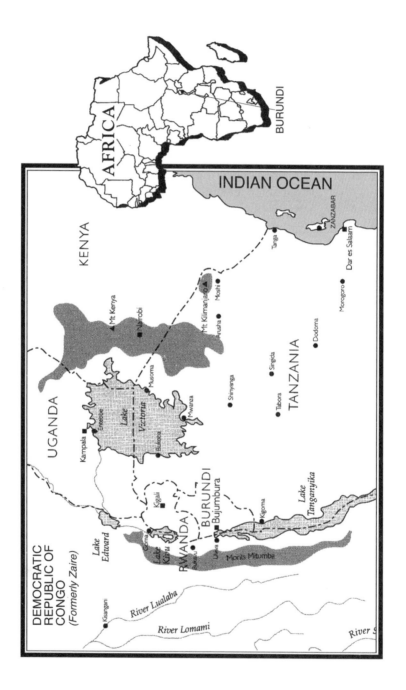

AFRICA

BURUNDI

INDIAN OCEAN

ZANZABAR

KENYA

Tanga

Dar es Salaam

Mt Kenya

Nairobi

Mt Kilimanjaro

Moshi

Arusha

Morogoro

Musoma

Dodoma

Mwanza

Shinyanga

Singida

TANZANIA

Lake Victoria

Tabora

Entebbe

UGANDA

Kampala

Bukoba

Lake Tanganyika

Kigali

BURUNDI

Bujumbura

Kigoma

RWANDA

Lake Edward

Lake Kivu

Goma

Bukavu

Uvira

Monts Mitumba

DEMOCRATIC REPUBLIC OF CONGO
(Formerly Zaire)

Kisangani

River Lualaba

River Lomami

River S

— 3 —

LEARNING FROM BURUNDI'S FAILED DEMOCRATIC TRANSITION, 1993–96

DID INTERNATIONAL INITIATIVES MATCH THE PROBLEM?

Michael S. Lund, Barnett R. Rubin, and Fabienne Hara

INTRODUCTION

In October 1993, when Tutsi army officers assassinated Burundi's first Hutu president, the international community mounted one of its most extensive efforts in preventive action. Though some crises may have been averted, violence escalated to a full civil war, and a Tutsi military regime finally took power on July 25, 1996. Why, despite the vast array of efforts, did this unprecedented international effort fail? Was the situation simply too intractable, or can we draw lessons for more effective interventions?[1]

SIGNIFICANCE OF THIS CASE

In comparative terms, Burundi presents a "middle" case of international engagement in post–cold war national conflicts: not aptly described as "too little, too late," yet not as timely or extensive as other recent efforts. UN secretary-general Boutros Boutros-Ghali described the international effort with regard to Burundi as "preventive diplomacy," but the label is misleading if one reserves that notion for proactive involvement before significant violence has arisen. The international efforts toward Burundi are better described as low-intensity conflict management. (See Table 3.1, pages 73–75, for a list of conflict management programs in Burundi.)

In contrast to the international responses to Somalia, Yugoslavia, and Rwanda, third parties deliberately initiated toward Burundi several explicitly conflict-oriented activities, bilateral and multilateral, in addition to development and humanitarian programs, and these were introduced relatively early in the course of what has since become a low-level but deadly civil war. But in terms of its timing, compared to the international preemption of potential violence in Macedonia beginning in late 1992, for example, or the quick international response to Congo-Brazzaville's postelection violence in summer 1993, the attention to Burundi came only after a major violent cataclysm: the massacre of 50,000 to 100,000 people in the countryside following an attempted coup and the murder of Burundi's new Hutu president, Melchior Ndadaye, in October 1993. Considering that this partial coup effectively erased the results of the earlier elections and that so many were killed, international action in Burundi has had an after-the-fact quality. It thus is analogous to the efforts currently directed at Nigeria's leaders and the belated response to the genocide in Rwanda in May 1994.

The international community has been responsive out of all proportion to the significance in traditional strategic or economic terms of this Maryland-sized country of about six million people. The response has included a UN and several other special envoys, a UN commission of inquiry, an OAU military observer mission, regional summits and negotiations, several high-level fact-finding and jawboning delegations, a number of NGO initiatives, an ongoing Washington policy forum, and, ultimately, regional economic sanctions. U.S. and European media frequently have reported on the country, and op-ed pieces have been published. However, these actions still do not match the spectrum of military, diplomatic, and other measures deployed in and around Macedonia, for example, or the multifaceted international effort directed against South Africa's apartheid.

Burundi did receive an unusual degree of international attention; yet Burundi's violence had nevertheless escalated by July 1996 into virtual civil war punctuated by another military coup, followed by continued stalemate with few signs of a settlement. The questions analysts and policymakers need to ask are: Why did the international efforts fail to advance Burundi toward a functioning, popularly elected government and to contain the growing violence? Were the actions too late, or not enough? Did international actors do the wrong things? Did they help a little by preventing even worse escalation, while ultimately failing because the basic challenge was too great? Did they worsen the situation?

This chapter applies a method for evaluating the impacts of early-stage outsider interventions into national political crises. The method first identifies the major background and more immediate sources of these conflicts and examines their dynamic interactions over time. The next section identifies three levels of causation behind Burundi's political conflict, from the June 1993 elections to the coup by Major Pierre Buyoya in July 1996; these involve historical and other systemic sources, institutional and process factors, and precipitating events. After a historical overview of the conflict and the international response to it, we describe the conflict strategies embedded in the various third-party efforts that were made and seek to determine the extent to which these strategies addressed those causes and dynamics. The varied international initiatives that may be deployed toward a country in distress—mediation, sanctions, peacekeeping, humanitarian assistance, economic aid, track-two diplomacy, democracy projects—each have an implicit "peace theory" or conflict management strategy behind them that incorporates assumptions about what causal factors are most important and how they can be influenced. By first identifying the various layers of causation and then inventorying and profiling the kinds of policy intervention techniques applied, this method of assessment seeks to uncover gaps that can lead to developing more cost-effective strategies in this and other conflicts.

Following the description and evaluation of the effects of major third-party responses to the conflict, we draw conclusions and suggest policy lessons.

THE CONFLICT IN BRIEF—AND THE RESPONSE TO IT

Before and since 1993, Burundi exhibited an unusual number of inherited and institutional factors that other studies of ethnic conflicts have identified as creating a high potential for violent conflicts. These included, for example, a violent recent history, deeply polarized and distrustful communities, ethnicized political parties, and weak and fragmented state institutions. But while these factors laid the groundwork for the continued violent pursuit of politics, they did not make violence inevitable. What made the country repeat its past cycles of violence was the deliberate use of various forms of deadly force by members of a small, largely self-appointed and self-advancing elite, acting in the name of the two main ethnic communities in their ongoing struggle for political power and material privilege. Armed actions by both sides soon brought an escalating spiral of violence over which the protagonists increasingly lost control.

As to the effectiveness of the international efforts, some initiatives did encourage certain institutional changes and prevented escalation at tense moments, as illustrated by a brief review of the major events. In September 1987, Major Pierre Buyoya took power from his cousin, Gen. Jean-Baptiste Bagaza, apparently with the aim of instituting reforms. Following the August 1988 massacres, first of Tutsis by Hutu guerrillas and then of Hutus by the army, international pressures mounted to inaugurate market and democratic reforms. International assistance helped fund and guide both a structural adjustment program and the June 1993 legislative and presidential elections. Following an October 1993 attempted coup d'état, the international outcry caused its leaders to back down, although this came too late either to prevent the president's assassination or to limit the subsequent massacres. In addition, timely diplomatic pressures, particularly in 1994, had an observable influence in containing violence at potentially explosive moments and in keeping alive the hope of effective reconciliation through various political agreements.

But international efforts ignored several causal factors that were crucial to perpetuating the cycle of violence. Initially, too much faith was placed in institutional engineering and popular elections, as if they could transfer effective power, as against simply providing broad legitimacy, in this highly ethnically divided, Tutsi-dominated but numerically mainly Hutu nation. Thus, no provisions were made for protecting the security of the newly elected leaders and the subsequent government against the prospects of threats by discontented losers and other elements on both sides. Despite efforts to forge a legitimate government, the violence grew and took on more forms. Continual negotiations with top leaders at the same time as they initiated or sanctioned violent acts may have increased their incentive to continue this behavior. By 1996, when the violence had become too pervasive to ignore, the international community publicly proposed several forms of military intervention, none of which could be implemented. The open discussion of these proposals, however, precipitated violent reactions by those who opposed them in Burundi.

The international response ultimately failed to reverse the upward trend in violence and repolarization because it continually misdiagnosed the conflict's most critical perpetuating forces and the effects of its own actions. Following the 1993 coup, the international community viewed the conflict largely as a legitimacy problem of nondemocratic government and a constitutional and diplomatic problem of lack of agreement among the contending party and governmental leaders. In fact, however, it was literally a life-and-death struggle among competing individuals and factions within Burundi's small governing elite who could and did use several forms of coercion and armed force against each other to obtain or retain wealth and power. The international actors could not control the resulting escalation of the conflict and arrest Burundi's political disintegration because they did not interdict the political violence and governmental coercion that were being actively and continually engineered by these elites. As a result, any gains made by negotiations and the regular governmental process were subverted or exploited.

The misdiagnosis and the resulting mismatched response were due in some part to conceptual and organizational features of the principal external multilateral organizations, governments, and nongovernmental organizations involved in Burundi. Most external attention to the conflict tended to focus on the killing and its humanitarian effects, but not on its basic political and military causes. And because the conflict had many sources and facets, many long-term and short-term problem definitions circulated among these entities and resulted in policy confusion. Though each notion of the problem captured a piece of reality, no focal point or process existed that could carry out a sustained and authoritative analysis of the evolving conflict pattern and generate a conflict management or preventive strategy that methodically addressed, in some prioritized way, the conflict's interconnected leading causal forces.

DISSECTING BURUNDI'S CONFLICT
LAYERS OF CAUSATION

Before we can judge the effectiveness of the international effort in managing Burundi's conflict, we need to look at the various factors that have produced the conflict and analyze how they interacted over time. But when first observing a particular, already advanced national conflict like Burundi's, we find multiple and complex sources that seem inextricably and confusingly intertwined. Portrayals of such conflicts thus typically catalogue myriad causes: resource scarcity, cultural attitudes, arms flows, group hatreds, individual personalities, chance events, and so on. The "situation report" approach, on the other hand, simply takes repeated snapshots of the issues in contention and of the main observable parties and what they do, rather than looking into abiding patterns. Alternatively, analyses may stress one cause, such as the army's crackdowns, to the exclusion of others.

But these approaches are not helpful to policymakers or practitioners in the field, who must make the best possible use of limited financial and political resources. They need a multidimensional yet integrated account of the main forces at work, their relative weight, and their interactions, so that they can identify strategic points at which interventions can have real results. The conflict analyst is challenged to disentangle a conflict's distinguishable threads, even if this seems artificially "academic," and construct from them a coherent account.

Fortunately, whether and how national conflicts over political differences get settled through a largely peaceful political process or, alternatively, are expressed through violent or coercive means is not an utterly mysterious question. Although each situation is unique in its details, a number of the factors that are frequently present in peaceful or violent situations can be identified by looking at multiple examples of similar kinds of conflict situations.

Consulting individual case studies and comparative assessments of similar conflicts can help identify key "swing factors," or variables, that in many settings apparently influence whether political disputes result in violence or are settled peacefully.[2] Sources of conflicts can be distinguished, moreover, in terms of certain categories that entail different policy implications. At any particular moment in the course of a conflict, some causal factors are predisposing but latent, rather than decisive and active. They operate broadly through the social life and economies of the countries affected: their degree of social and cultural integration, for example, or of inequality. They are more or less built into the structures and culture of a society, at least for certain periods of time. Rather different factors arise out of the processes, institutions, and leaders at the center of a conflict and reflect particular behaviors and attitudes on the part of the immediate parties. The former causes produce acts of violence *remotely and indirectly*, whereas the latter are more *direct and immediate*. To elaborate, we can delineate three kinds of causes:

+ **Received legacies and socioeconomic conditions** that arise out of the environment of the main protagonists in the conflict. Generally speaking, these factors are relatively constant and largely inherited by particular players. They lie outside the immediate control of specific protagonists or even of governments and are the most difficult to change, at least in their entirety and in the short run.

- **Institutions and political processes**, such as constitutions, representative bodies, and group associations that shape whether background forces find political voice and how the most affected organized interests pursue their competition. These mediating channels are somewhat more malleable, although not immediately changeable.

- **Actions of protagonists**, which show how particular leaders and leadership groups perceive the situation and react to it. These factors are more subject to individual and group will, so they may be relatively more amenable to change in the short run, though not necessarily easily.

The level of hostilities characterizing a particular country's political conflict is like the net result of an algebraic formula having several components or functions, each with particular positive or negative values. By applying such a formula to Burundi, we can extract from the complexities of its conflict the most important background, institutional, and behavioral sources of conflict and gain a sense of their relative weight. But when one looks to see which of these factors are present in Burundi, it is striking that the country exhibits almost all of these features to a significant extent.

RECEIVED LEGACIES AND SOCIOECONOMIC CONDITIONS

The potential for violent conflict is increased to the extent that the following factors are significant.

Past Discrimination. Certain groups have been relegated by colonial regimes or subsequent governments to an inferior status and have suffered unequal treatment in relation to other groups. In Africa and other regions, colonial powers often imputed superior status to and bestowed material privileges on some tribal or ethnic groups relative to others. In Burundi, Belgian authorities applied European pseudoscientific race theory to the distinction between

Hutus and Tutsis and bestowed greater advantages on Tutsis, the supposed natural leaders. Since independence in 1962, increasingly Tutsi-dominated regimes continued to discriminate against Hutus in educational opportunities and with respect to positions in the civil service and army.

Weight of Violent History. Currently active political groups have engaged in violent conflicts in the recent past.[3] The greater the number of violent conflicts that have recently occurred, the more mistrust and fear there is among the groups. This provides fertile ground for political leaders to revive memories of past killings perpetrated by another group and thus to incite a community to further violence. A culture of violence can take hold, in which the only way to handle conflicts of interest is violence or domination. Burundi's postindependence history is strewn with recurrent coups or attempted coups and intercommunal violence, as in 1965, 1966, 1972, 1976, 1987, 1988, 1989, and 1991. High tensions and violence have been more or less continuous.

Group Sharing of Common Territory. Politically mobilized groups live interspersed in the same territory, rather than separately, and thus compete for the same resources. Hutus and Tutsis have been relatively evenly spread across the country's many hills, at least until the escalated conflict from 1994 to 1996. At that point, the pattern of conflict increasingly resulted in Tutsis concentrating in Bujumbura, the towns, and displaced persons camps, relegating Hutus to the rural areas or to refugee camps outside the country.

Ethnic Duopoly. Duopolistic societies are composed of a majority and a minority mobilized group, as compared to more heterogeneous, oligopolistic societies comprising three or more sizable groups. When a pair of groups compete with each other for the same political space, intense mutual hostilities can build up because of the zero-sum nature of the conflict, and the politically dominant group, whether numerical majority or minority, will feel insecure. In a more heterogeneous society there are more incentives to create coalitions among several groups, thus requiring compromise.

In Burundi, the politically dominant Tutsis constitute about 14 percent of the population, while the politically and socially suppressed Hutus constitute 85 percent. The former feel deep insecurity about the supposed plans of the latter to annihilate them, while the latter nurse deep grievances at their exclusion from power in a country where they are a vast majority.

Low Modernization and State Monopoly of Social Goods. The population is preponderantly rural and engaged in subsistence agriculture. Where the population is almost completely dependent on its own farming or grazing for subsistence, a number of related conditions make it easier for small modernizing elites to mobilize and manipulate the masses to engage in violent conflicts. These conditions are all present in Burundi: industry is poorly developed, urbanization and educational levels are low, and the identities of individual members of society tend to be influenced more by traditional distinctions such as ethnic and status differences. Economic advancement and the allocation of modern material goods, such as job opportunities, education, social position, and political offices, are decided almost exclusively by state policies, which groups therefore compete to control. But state control also limits the ability of the economy to stimulate entrepreneurialism that might increase the country's competitiveness in world markets and generate new wealth—thus keeping the country generally impoverished. The national economy thus has few industries or outside trade and commercial links that might create an urban proletariat, middle-class entrepreneurs, or other groups with higher stakes in national political stability because of their involvement in modern business or professional livelihoods that crosscut traditional distinctions.

Ninety-four percent of Burundi's population resides in rural areas and is primarily engaged in subsistence agriculture. Burundi ranks low in access to education. Its small industrial sector is confined largely to local products or uncompetitive exports such as coffee and tea, produced until recently by state industries. Little civil society exists independently of political parties and the state.

Reinforced Social Cleavages. Where social groups differ consistently along many dimensions—ethnicity, economic conditions, religion, language, region—it is easier to attribute one's grievances or fears to the other group, and harder to establish communications and mutual understanding, than where crosscutting cleavages are found.[4]

The two main ethnic group identities in Burundi correspond to wide differences in economic circumstance, social and political position, and (urban versus rural) residence. As a result of ethnic cleansing and encampment policies, the two groups are increasingly separated physically.

They largely share a common language, religion, and culture but attach opposing meanings to various common symbols and historical events.

Regional Aggravation. States or groups in neighboring countries have cultural ties to and actively support one or the other party to a domestic conflict financially or militarily, and group conflicts in neighboring countries provide threatening precedents.[5]

During the period under study in Burundi the conflict became increasingly regionalized, especially under the impact of the Rwandan genocide. That attempt to wipe out all Rwandan Tutsis (and political dissidents) intensified the fears of Burundi's Tutsis. The refugee and military camps of Rwandan Hutus in Zaire (now Democratic Republic of Congo, DRC) and, to a lesser extent, Tanzania provided bases and supplies for Burundian Hutu guerrillas.[6] In response there has been limited military cooperation along border regions between the predominantly Tutsi armies of Rwanda and Burundi, reinforcing the Hutu belief in a regional Tutsi conspiracy. Rwanda actively organized and supported the anti-Mobutu revolts in eastern Congo that led to the destruction of the Hutu camps, which in turn forced the Burundian Hutus to move their bases either to Tanzania or back inside Burundi.

INSTITUTIONS AND POLITICAL PROCESSES

Although these historical legacies and systemic conditions generate tremendous pressures on Burundian politicians and governments to embrace violent means of advancing their conflicting interests, many other poor, small countries also exhibit these factors without experiencing violent conflict. How a country reacts to circumstances is shaped as well by its institutional and political infrastructure.

Ethnically Based Political Parties. Where the most important national-level political parties are organized around ethnic groups or other dominant social cleavages, rather than according to different shared interests or political ideologies, then when elections are held, winning parties reflect the size of different groups in the society, so elections become political censuses. In the absence of countervailing bases of organization, political instability is increased because these groups are otherwise also polarized. But parties that crosscut such dominant cleavages can create a counterbalance to ethnic influence.

In Burundi, the two main political parties, UPRONA (Union pour le Progrès National) and FRODEBU (Front Démocratique du Burundi), are officially nonethnic and include at least some individuals of both groups. UPRONA originated as an interethnic nationalist movement. But both parties have become predominantly ethnic political movements that articulate respectively Tutsi and Hutu grievances and fears.

Uncertain Distribution of Power. A centralized regime that has monopolized power but feels it is losing its grip will tend to suppress opposition, thus provoking more rebellion. Where no clear balance of power exists, and the relative power possessed by contending national or regional groups is shifting, violence is also more likely to flare up as groups test their capacities and act out of fear of being overwhelmed.

Despite the longstanding domination of Burundi's government and social institutions by Tutsis, the numerical preponderance of Hutus has made possible periodic rebellions. The 1993 multiparty elections that installed the first Hutu president and a Hutu-dominated parliament weakened Tutsi domination without affecting the strength of the principal institution through which it is exercised, the army. The resulting uncertainty provided incentives for seeking increased power through violent revolt, on the one side, and repression, on the other.

A Weak State and Noninstitutionalized Politics. Where one or more groups use the authority and resources of government to serve their own group's parochial interests and dominate others, or several groups exploit the separate offices and agencies of the state they have captured, such as particular ministries or portions of the security forces, and in the absence of state institutions that can enact and enforce laws, the political power struggle is arbitrated, conflicts of interests between major social groups are negotiated, and national policies are enacted and implemented outside the formal processes of government.[7] When the state is not the venue for political conflict resolution and disputes are conducted largely outside regular channels, they are subject to volatile power moves or the whims of individuals, and coercion is more likely to be used to gain sway.

Alternatively, through power sharing, elite compacts, and other negotiated agreements, especially to the extent that they are institutionalized in a body of laws, governmental institutions can mute or blunt differences by incorporating and constraining major groups' interests, thus acting as an effective third party that pursues transcending interests.[8] The underlying feature of states where political disputes are managed without violence or coercion is that the rules of political struggle are regularized and predictable.

For much of its postindependence history, Burundi was dominated by a Tutsi party and leaders largely to the exclusion of Hutu interests. After politics was opened up to Hutu participation, much of the activity within government has either favored one or another group's political agenda or it has been deadlocked, eroding and discrediting formal institutions.

A related variable deserves special attention.

Lack of a Legitimate Monopoly on the Use of Force. Violence or coercion is more likely when the military and police apparatus serves the partisan aims of political factions vying for control of the state and public policies; violence is less likely where military and security forces are controlled by public officials in accordance with constitutional order, and these forces have the effective upper hand over factional militias or political terrorism. But in many recent violent conflicts, leaders of the political factions on the disputing sides have assumed early effective control over their own distinct armies and militias. In Burundi, the army has been used to serve mainly Tutsi group or subgroup interests; it has progressively lost control over major parts of the country to insurgent groups; and the army itself is fragmented and difficult to control. The leadership of the Hutu opposition has increasingly shifted toward guerrilla commanders.

ACTIONS OF PROTAGONISTS

Like the systemic factors, institutional factors do not completely dictate a course of action to particular players and thus cannot fully explain why conflicts escalate. Despite the history of Tutsi predominance in education, the economy, and government; army repression; recurrent Hutu rebellion; Hutu versus Tutsi communal violence; and Tutsi fears of Hutu retaliation, a violent path was not foreordained. We must also look to the deliberate human actions that themselves can either trigger or suppress hostile behavior.

Divisive Leaders. Especially at particularly tense or politically critical moments, the main leaders of government and organized groups in Burundi have engaged in demagogic rhetoric, unilateral provocative acts, uncompromising policies, or coercion and force to seek their objectives, rather than moderating their words, actions, programs, and policies; making conciliatory and reciprocal gestures; or seeking bilateral or multilateral negotiations and give-and-take bargaining.

According to Gérard Prunier, a keen observer of the Great Lakes region and one not known for euphemism, "The Burundian political 'elite' is criminally blind and monstrously selfish."[9] Among many cases, one might mention that after two opposition cabinet ministers were dismissed in January 1995 the UPRONA leader, Charles Mukasi, called on the Burundian people to overthrow the government within forty-eight hours. FRODEBU leaders, too, have taken unilateral and often covert steps to shape the outcome of national issues, the most dramatic of which were actions by local FRODEBU activists who fomented the killing of Tutsis in October 1993, following the killing of President Ndadaye.

To sum up, the extent to which any particular country tends toward violent or coercive modes of handling national political disputes can be explained largely by the prevalence of certain definable systemic, institutional, and behavioral variables. Burundi ranks high on most of these factors, thus appearing to be a worst-case illustration of a propensity toward national ethnic conflicts.

THE EVOLUTION OF THE CONFLICT IN BURUNDI

Listing the sources of conflict derived from comparative study of conflicts can broaden and focus the policymaker's conception of a conflict's several interacting causes. The standard, often one-dimensional, explanations of such conflicts invoking less nuanced variables, such as poverty, ethnic divisions, population density, and lack of democracy, appear nonspecific and simplistic. Yet simply making a list of key factors is too mechanical, for in reality these variables interact with one another. A more dynamic, composite picture is needed. A useful way to identify the essential dynamics of a conflict is to describe how the identified factors interacted with each other over time and what energized those interactions.

THE ESSENTIAL TRANSITION CHALLENGE:
INSTITUTIONALIZING POWER STRUGGLES

The basic context in which all these factors came into play in Burundi was a regional and national transition away from authoritarian rule to a more open system. In poor, postcolonial societies, competition over who will wield power and gain material advantages occurs mainly among factions led by educated political elites. In the first decades of independence, many such countries sought to avoid violent competition through various forms of authoritarian rule, enforced by single national parties, all-embracing ideologies, and strong armies.

The transition toward more democratic, participatory, and peaceful forms of government and politics requires that the exercise of power be governed by impersonal rules, rather than by particular leaders and their followers. The challenge is to create confidence and trust in the unpredictable workings of autonomous impersonal and legitimate processes, rather than in particular groups, leaders or ideologies. Stable democracy is "institutionalized uncertainty," as one analyst has put it.[10] Highly uncertain but regulated channels of conflict, such as constant haggling, compromise, pressure group politics, political campaigns, policy half-measures, and tedious legal proceedings must become the norm for achieving group and individual interests, rather than the seemingly more conclusive alternatives of the use of arms or other forms of coercion. It is not the lack of development per se that directly causes such conflicts—many developing countries exist in peace—but rather the inability of a new political system to regulate the inevitable competition over scarce resources in a nonviolent way.

Where many of the variables we described are strongly present, the transition challenge is even more difficult. Hostile communities that have pursued differing interests at each others' expense now need to begin to communicate and bargain in accordance with common procedures and institutions. The country's government and territories can no longer be owned by one side or another or continually fought over among warring factions and their warlords.

How the sources of Burundi's conflict thwarted its ability to make a transition to a new political order can be seen by reviewing three dovetailing but distinguishable phases in the evolution of the Burundi conflict from 1988 through July 1996. Each phase began with moves to create a more encompassing political order on a new legitimate basis, but each was followed by the erosion of this framework. Effective power oscillated between the formal level of government and politics—which was peaceful, at least on the surface—and the extrainstitutional arenas, which were violent. But the extrainstitutional violence has increasingly dominated the formal, public level of normal politics.

FROM REFORM TO BACKLASH AND ITS AFTERMATH, 1988–93

Although he seized power from his cousin, President Jean-Baptiste Bagaza, through a coup in September 1987, Major Pierre Buyoya responded to a new round of Hutu guerrilla killings and anti-Hutu army reprisals in 1988, and to the democratic sentiment rising in Africa, by inaugurating from 1988 to 1991 an unprecedented series of political and economic reforms. The economic reforms included a World Bank-designed structural adjustment program, including privatization of state enterprises, strengthening the currency, and diversification of exports beyond the traditional tea and coffee.[11] The political reforms sought to regularize direct popular influence on government and strengthen respect for human rights by ending military rule, abolishing the state security court, and setting up inclusive commissions on national unity, constitutional democracy, and elections. A plan for the first popular, multiparty elections for the presidency and parliament was adopted by popular referendum in 1992. Buyoya's reforms also sought to redress the social and political inequities between Hutus and Tutsis by putting more Hutus in high government positions and opening up more opportunities in education, employment, and the armed forces for Hutus.

The popular election of June 1993, however, precipitated Burundi's increasingly violent and ultimately self-destructive political conflict. The country's first multiparty elections brought the decisive victory of Melchior Ndadaye as its first Hutu president, backed by a FRODEBU-dominated parliament. Buyoya's reform era had behind it the stabilizing influence of the Tutsi-led army. But once national governing power was subject to the dictates of a mass electorate, Burundi faced a crossroads. The fundamental question was not simply whether it would have "democracy" in the sense of majority rule, but whether its newly legitimized offices and institutions—the parliament, presidency, bureaucracy and subnational governments—could actually carry out public business through regularized, collaborative, and thus peaceful procedures. Would these become effective channels through which politicians would wage a peaceful political struggle to influence national policy? Or would the new institutions simply become new bases of operation through which party leaders separately pursued their partisan aims by wielding their respective political weapons against each other—passing discriminatory legislation, doling out patronage, and repressing other groups, thus inviting government disintegration, deadlock, or rebellion? Would the institutions consequently become mere shells, circumscribed and undermined by extraparliamentary and extragovernmental methods of wielding influence and power, such as ethnic demagoguery and the covert or overt use of violence and coercion, including further coups?

The stakes were raised by an economic coincidence. The world price of coffee, the main source of the country's foreign exchange and the source of livelihood for much of the Hutu peasantry, fell in 1993.[12] The only alternative for many Hutus was the hope of placing a relative somewhere in the state structure as the result of a successful election outcome.[13]

Although the election campaign had been deeply imbued with ethnic overtones, for a time the country was generally calm. The new government appeared to be assuming effective control and to be finding acceptance from the army and Tutsi leadership. It began to introduce reforms in administration, state employment, and land tenure. But the potential for disruption through violence or military takeover was reflected in the actions from June through September of several discontented elements, including protesting Tutsi youth demanding cancellation of the legislative elections, Tutsi farmers evicted by returning Hutu refugees, renegade army officers who attempted a coup in July, Hutus carrying out rural reprisals against Hutus who had supported UPRONA and sabotaging rural communal projects.

The initial success of a second revolt by army officers seeking a return to the past led to the defining events of recent Burundi history. On October 21, an army unit attacked the presidential palace and captured and killed President Ndadaye and four other top Hutu officials. Though senior army officers claimed that they faced pressure from junior officers, they most likely acquiesced in or supported their actions.

Within hours of the news, widespread killings mainly of Tutsis were carried out in the name of revenge for "killing our president." In some places the massacre was organized by FRODEBU activists and newly appointed Hutu local government officials, who mobilized the populace to block roads and bridges against the army, distributed machetes and gasoline bottles to youth, divided up students ethnically in the schools, and rounded up and executed UPRONA members. For their part, army paratroopers began first to rescue threatened groups but then carried out massive reprisals against Hutu peasants and local officials, attacking civilians indiscriminately, including some Tutsis, with machine guns and incendiary grenades.

Although the army leadership soon halted the coup and declared support for the remnant of the elected government, the political order newly founded on the legitimacy and authority of popular elections had been destroyed. A violent national convulsion had occurred, in which 50,000 to 100,000 are estimated to have been killed, large numbers were implicated in some way, and the apparatus of government was used by both sides against the other.

In sum, an electoral process and functional parliament had broadened and invigorated competition among the individual leaders within Burundi's small, ethnically mixed political elite, but without increasing the scarce resources available from the state, the economy, and society. The economy was in fact shrinking, and the new state was vulnerable to brute force. The responsibility for maintaining public order and individual security for most Burundians shifted from the hands of a Tutsi-dominated military state to officials with an abstract, diffuse, and uncertain public electoral mandate, bound by constitutional rules within a framework of office sharing but lacking more than nominal control over the army and other security forces. The elections rapidly and officially weakened the established means for regulating the ways by which Burundi politics, as well as economic and social opportunities, could be pursued. Prunier captures the uncertainties and rising tensions that formed the context for the violence:

> Life had functioned in Burundi for the last 25 years, well or badly, but according to a certain pattern. The election of Melchior Ndadaye and the restructuring of the administration first, then of patterns of land tenure, of job opportunities and finally of army structure, represented a tremendous leap into the unknown. Everybody had lost their bearings, positive or negative.[14]

FAILED POWER SHARING, 1994–96

A "collegial" government took charge of necessary business in late 1993 until a new president could be elected by the parliament three months after the assassination, as called for by the constitution. Mass killings in the countryside subsided, but street violence and ethnic cleansing of Hutu neighborhoods began in Bujumbura during the next two months of political uncertainty and constitutional disputes. On January 6, 1994, for example, the extraparliamentary Tutsi extremist party RADDES (Rallye pour la Démocratie et le Développement Economique et Social) called for a general strike that shut the city down, the first of a series of "journées ville morte" (dead city days) when armed gangs of Tutsi youth enforced total stoppage of work and commerce.

Urban violence did not abate even after the constitution was revised to allow the parliamentary election of a president, a power-sharing agreement was concluded, and a new coalition government, blessed by the army, was formed in January and February. Fighting in various Hutu-dominated districts of the capital became more common, as FRODEBU youth were reportedly receiving arms from Rwanda, which was still controlled by the Hutu-power regime. In response, the army's inauguration in March of operations to disarm the insurgents ended up in major clashes with urban guerrillas in the Kamenge district of Bujumbura and the province of Cibitoke. Hundreds died in these battles.

Newly elected President Cyprien Ntaryamira was then killed on April 6 in the Kigali plane crash that also killed Rwandan president Juvénal Habyarimana, setting off the Rwandan genocide. The Burundian presidency passed to the speaker of the National Assembly, Sylvestre Ntibantunganya, and a process of negotiation involving twelve parties and focusing on the presidential succession proceeded.

The resulting Convention of Government, finally signed in September 1994, put the government on a provisional footing leading to elections in 1998. The agreement gave 45 percent of the cabinet positions to Tutsi opposition parties. A prime minister elected by opposition parties had to countersign all presidential decisions. The convention also established a National Security Council (NSC) to approve all government decisions. While the political leaders on the NSC were ostensibly split evenly between FRODEBU and the opposition, the military representatives who were also included gave the Tutsi opposition an effective two-thirds majority and a veto over any action by the elected government. This power-sharing agreement appeased Tutsi fears by granting UPRONA and other opposition parties important government positions; but these same concessions made many Hutus feel that the coup's results had effectively deprived the majority of its election victory, even while retaining a Hutu from FRODEBU as nominal president.[15]

But even while negotiations were going on, officers had attempted another coup. Soon after the installation of the new government and president, Tutsi opposition-inspired work stoppages and grenade attacks again erupted in the city in response to the Tutsi prime minister's actions (which displeased Tutsi extremists) and the election as speaker of a prominent FRODEBU leader accused of calling for massacres in 1993 from exile in Rwanda. This intimidation eventually forced the prime minister to resign. Strikes spread to the provinces.

After the conclusion of the Convention of Government in September 1994 the number of rural insurgency attacks, army reprisal campaigns, and local ethnic clashes increased, as the conflict spread around the country. Hutu interior minister Léonard Nyangoma broke with his party and set up a new political movement whose armed wing trained Hutu guerrilla forces in eastern Congo. The increased rural violence was also being fueled by other Hutu groups arming in the countryside. On the one hand, the decades-old guerrilla group PAL-IPEHUTU (Parti de la Libération du Peuple Hutu) and its dissident offshoot FROLINA (Front de Libération Nationale) were training Hutu refugees in Rwanda and Tanzania. Increasingly, Hutu insurgents attacked military bases and government installations. On the other side, Tutsi gangs motivated by vengeance were forming in displaced persons camps, which were put under the guard of the army. In response to insurgent attacks, the army conducted more and more indiscriminate reprisal attacks, killing many civilians, sometimes in joint operations with Tutsi militias. Military skirmishes rose, and assassinations, including the killing of foreign aid workers, increased.

Efforts were still made to restore central political unity. In spring 1995, the president joined with opposition members in the government to expand security forces and measures to control the violence. Government members banded together to denounce the violence on both sides. Optimism rose that the government was regaining some unity, as parliament supported a new security program, involving new army efforts to dismantle terrorist gangs. FRODEBU denounced Hutu extremists, and UPRONA condemned Tutsi extremists. The university reopened, and a national reconciliation campaign began. The national debate called for by the Convention of Government was about to be inaugurated. But the campaigns against the Hutu districts in the capital continued, while insurgent attacks became bolder and more widespread around the country. As a result, the conflict became driven more and more by the dynamics of escalation and the spiraling of violence, over which the governing political elite increasingly lost control. As insurgent attacks and army actions continued to increase throughout the country, from mid-1995 the conflict took on the character of an ongoing civil war involving deliberate military strategies by organized insurgent forces and frustrated army campaigns ending in large numbers of civilians massacred.

The violence increasingly discredited the political institutions that the international community was trying to save. The uncontrolled methods of the army suggested to more and more Hutus that their president was no longer able to protect them. In the political vacuum that developed after various calls for foreign intervention went unheeded, increasing violence led President Ntibantunganya to seek refuge for his own safety. The army took power and installed Pierre Buyoya as president again on July 25, 1996.

How can we characterize and explain this steady deterioration? At first, it happened mainly because the leading participants undermined the political process from within the government. During the election and subsequent period they continued the high-stakes struggle among elites for control over the state and the assets and perks of officialdom it offered decisionmaking authority, position and remuneration, status and prestige, and patronage. But the struggle was now being conducted on a more uncertain plane. A more legitimate but less predictable politics created an "ethnic security dilemma." To reduce the uncertainty of their individual and group positions, all the chief players in this struggle, including high government officials such as the president and prime minister, the army chief of staff and other high officers, along with the UPRONA, FRODEBU, and other party leaders, and later, the leaders of the Hutu and Tutsi insurgent groups, began to use forms of armed force and violence to pursue their objectives. This process started with the assassination and massacres of late 1993 and continued afterwards, though initially hidden from most foreign observers.

On the Tutsi-UPRONA side, the tools of coercion and death became the fomenting of street violence, plotting assassinations of officials, arming and leading youth militias, government (army)-authorized ethnic cleansing, attempted and actual coups, army reprisal campaigns, and renegade army actions. On the Hutu-FRODEBU side, the politics of violence entailed mainly the strengthening of increasingly organized armed urban militias and insurgent movements in the countryside. Thus, members of UPRONA and other Tutsi opposition parties supported urban armed gangs that disrupted public life and intimidated the population; individual officials plotted assassinations against each other; some Hutu members of the government authorized training and support of Hutu insurgents; army officials looked the other way or actively assisted unauthorized coup attempts and military campaigns; and so on.[16]

A new basis for governance had created an electoral and parliamentary politics that was more legitimate in principle but could not provide effective protection against deliberate sabotage or political exploitation through ethnic demagoguery and covert use of force. With new incentives for political competition yet no effective restraints on the divisive and violent pursuit of power, ambitious leaders and politicians lost any assurance of their political or even physical survival. In view of the distrust engendered by their past experience with each other, for the sake of their own defense, as well as to achieve particular political objectives by preempting their political opponents, both sides hedged their bets in the uncertain new order by resorting to unilateral, coercive, covert, and eventually overt forms of force, in addition to using more legitimate procedures, such as electoral campaigning, parliamentary debate, and constitutional negotiations.

These struggles were highly fragmented and did not obey any single overriding logic. Major political parties fought over the control of government; but leaders also competed within any given party. At times personal rivalries outweighed ethnic loyalties. Hence the UPRONA leader is a Hutu, and some individual Tutsis have joined both FRODE-BU and its offshoot insurgency movement, the Centre National pour la Défense de la Démocratie (CNDD), led by Léonard Nyangoma. There are also concealed factional struggles within groups, such as between southern and northern Tutsis or among different clans of the dominant southern (Bururi) Tutsis in the army. These personality-based rivalries among leaders lead to demagogic outbidding for followers.

From 1993 through early 1995, the conflict was largely pursued by individual party leaders and small factions undermining each other in Bujumbura, even as they maintained some semblance of cooperation and common control over basic government functions. Increasingly, however, public order was undermined by influential populist leaders who had defected from the Bujumbura elite to create their own political-military movements. The movement from one phase of conflict to the next thus also saw the escalation of violent behavior and the expansion of its loci, targets, and perpetrators.

In this light, the more common ways of characterizing the Burundi conflict—as an "ethnic conflict"; as the struggle between "moderates" from both sides against ethnic "extremists," or between "centrists" and "spoilers"; or as a "creeping coup" by Tutsi opposition parties and the army—all fail to capture the pervasively fragmented and volatile nature of Burundian politics. A better description is that of a deadly two-level "double game" composed of an outwardly civil politics subverted by a volatile underworld of contending factions in which murder and other violence are perpetrated from within the trappings and conventions of public institutions. Hiding behind the veneer of party politics and parliamentary-executive debates, and the decisionmaking of the formal governmental institutions of parliament, the presidency, the prime minister's office, the cabinet, the ministries, the university, and parastatals (state corporations), the players threaten and manipulate various forms of violence and organized force against one another, as all constantly struggle to ensure their own political as well as physical survival within a land and society of meager and declining resources.

That for most of this period the Tutsi-led parties and Tutsi-dominated army held the most power, and that the fight was thus on the whole unequal until perhaps 1996, does not detract from the fact that it followed the classic logic of escalation of a two-sided conflict. Each attack by one or the other side provoked a counterreaction, thus ratcheting up the conflict to higher thresholds of intensity. Violence and coercion continually increased, took more different forms, spread geographically, widened their targets, became more organized and offensive and less reactive, and implicated more members of the general population.

THE INTERNATIONAL RESPONSE

In addition to the indigenous accelerators and brakes acting on an emerging political conflict, another set of variables determining any conflict's course is the response by significant actors outside the immediate arena. Some observers have noted that international actors became part of Burundi's domestic politics; the Burundian protagonists also became unwitting actors in international political struggles, especially those over the future role and leadership of the United Nations. These struggles sometimes undermined the ability of international actors to apply an effective strategy in Burundi, as so many of their actions were dictated by political needs unrelated to the specific dynamics within that unfortunate country. For example Secretary-General Boutros-Ghali seemed to make Burundi a test case of his leadership. In a letter to the Security Council of February 15, 1996, he wrote:

> Much has been said about the need for preventive diplomacy in the post–cold-war era. . . . Burundi is a test case for the United Nations' ability to take such action. Indeed it could even contribute to the continuing search for a workable system of collective security at a time when civil wars and ethnic conflicts are becoming increasingly frequent. . . . The warning signs in Burundi have been with us for some time. If another tragedy befalls the Burundian people and the international community again proves to be unprepared, despite all the warnings, it will cause untold human suffering and gravely damage the credibility of the United Nations.[17]

But the same language could be used with respect to the long list of states, NGOs, and other international organizations that attempted to halt Burundi's slide into violence. While the worst has still not happened, the effort has failed to achieve its major goals, and massacres continue.

The international initiatives toward Burundi changed with the phases of the conflict. A few development and humanitarian organizations, such as Catholic Relief Services, Action Aid, and others had worked in Burundi for years, some in the rural areas. More policy-oriented organizations became active with the introduction of President Buyoya's reforms. From, then until the assassination of President Ndadaye, efforts concentrated on supporting those reforms, including both the structural adjustment policy for the economy and a democratization policy for the polity. During this period the dominant view was that these institutional reforms would prevent the recurrence of the violence that had repeatedly swept the country. The lead agencies seemed to be the World Bank, various European development agencies, USAID, and the National Democratic Institute for International Affairs (NDI), which provided technical assistance in the 1993 elections. Humanitarian organizations were present, to deal with old-case refugees from Rwanda, internally displaced people from various rounds of past violence, and Burundian refugees in Tanzania or Zaire. But most of the NGOs work in the country concentrated on development assistance or poverty amelioration not directly tied to conflict.

The second phase started after the killings in the fall of 1993. The 1994 Rwandan genocide and the regional crisis it set off further intensified both the Burundian crisis itself and the concern expressed by international actors. A mixture of guilt, determination to learn from experience, and desire to avoid blame for any repetition of such events colored much of the international activity in Burundi. The UN secretary-general himself spoke of the desire to "avoid a repetition of the tragic events in Rwanda."[18] Especially after the publication of a major evaluation of the failure to prevent genocide in Rwanda, many actors seemed to position themselves so that they could not be blamed for similar events in Burundi. The first significant outside action in direct response to the assassination of President Ndadaye and the subsequent violence in October–November 1993 was the assignment to Burundi of a special representative of the UN secretary-general in November. The special representative was Ambassador Ahmedou Ould Abdallah, former minister of foreign affairs of Mauritania, who had served the UN in several posts. He remained in Bujumbura for two years.

Until approximately the end of 1995, the principal goal of Ould Abdallah's efforts was strengthening Burundi's official political system.

At times assisted by a delegation from Parliamentarians for Global Action (PGA) and others, Ould Abdallah worked to assure the success of negotiations leading to the September 1994 Convention of Government. Afterwards several organizations worked for its implementation and on many nonofficial conflict resolution, training, and problem-solving workshop programs, many of them at least loosely coordinated with Ould Abdallah's office. Ould Abdallah left Bujumbura in October 1995, however, and his post remained vacant until the appointment of his successor, Canadian Marc Faguy, in January 1996. Abdallah's freelance style of operation, close work with NGOs, and perceived personal ambitions (he was later mentioned as a candidate to succeed Boutros-Ghali when the United States blocked the latter's reappointment as secretary-general) were reported to be factors in his departure. Faguy never played the same assertive role.

At the request of the Burundi government, the Organization of African Unity also deployed about sixty military observers there in April 1994. The mandate of the OAU Mission in Burundi (OMIB) was to monitor the behavior of the army. It also aimed at working toward the promotion of dialogue among the government, the army, and political and civil groups and at promoting the reestablishment of constitutional rule in the country.

By the end of 1995, the increase in violence was attracting greater international attention. Throughout the post-1993 period the various representatives of the "international community" had become an essential element of the Burundian political arena, but they now became even more central. In a December 29 letter to the UN Security Council, Boutros Boutros-Ghali spoke of "an increasingly marked genocidal trend" and suggested preventive deployment of a military force to Zaire in order to intervene in the event of a "sudden deterioration" of the situation in Burundi. Debates about this and similar proposals increasingly dominated discussion about Burundi both internationally and domestically. Several different plans for an international military intervention were discussed, but the fierce reaction against such proposals by the army and most Tutsis, the collapse of the government after a severe round of violence, and the assumption of power by the military on July 25, 1996, put an end to such discussions. Indeed, the coup and the violence that precipitated it were in part reactions to these proposals for international military intervention.

Humanitarian organizations subsequently increased their presence to deal with the challenge of the displaced. In the aftermath of the massacres, Tutsi survivors moved into urban centers or government institutions, where, guarded by the army or militias, they were known as *déplacés*. There they received World Food Program rations principally distributed by humanitarian NGOs. Internally displaced Hutus generally took to the hills or forests, where they were known as *dispersés* and received no aid. Burundian Hutu refugees in Rwanda, Tanzania, and Zaire became wards of the UN High Commissioner for Refugees (UNHCR). After the Rwandan genocide and the victory of the Rwandan Patriotic Front in July 1994, however, Rwandan Hutu refugees fled to northern Burundi, where they became the main focus of humanitarian work in the country. This effort, led by UNHCR, increased tensions, especially among Tutsi *déplacés*, who felt that they, survivors of a genocide (as they characterized the 1993 massacres), were being slighted in favor of perpetrators of the Rwandan genocide. These tensions may have been responsible for the killing of some aid workers.

Concern about Burundi itself also grew after the events in Rwanda. After the April 6, 1994, airplane crash in Kigali, Ould Abdallah's quick action in mobilizing the paralyzed government to quash rumors, arrange for succession to the dead president, and mobilize forces to keep the peace was instrumental in preventing another round of violence.[19] As more organizations set up operations in Burundi in order to prevent "another Rwanda," Ould Abdallah asserted his role as coordinator and leader of the effort. He not only pursued the UN's own programs but also tried to gain leverage over the activities of many NGOs and of various states in order to mobilize forces in support of his conflict prevention efforts. He catalyzed the formation of forums that acted largely as support groups for his work in both London (convened by International Alert) and Washington (convened by the Center for Preventive Action, Search for Common Ground, Refugees International, and the African American Institute).

The basic strategy of the international effort during this time was to support political "moderates" in both FRODEBU and UPRONA in their efforts to form a working government, then to implement the Convention of Government and lay the basis for democracy. Some, however, argued that marginalizing the "extremists" made them more dangerous. According to this view, efforts should be made to bring all parties into the negotiation process. By 1996, as the center was weakened, and especially as CNDD replaced FRODE-BU as the leading voice of the Hutu majority, the latter approach gained ground. Until then the two approaches were in conflict, and the multiplicity of initiatives—some aiming to marginalize the extremes, as Ould Abdallah wished, and others seeking to include them—meant that neither strategy could be pursued consistently.

An amazing number of organizations undertook efforts of different sorts (see Table 3.1). Ould Abdallah closely monitored these efforts and at times recruited NGOs to perform functions that he thought were needed. These projects aimed to train politicians in the skills and values required by democratic institutions, promote human rights and humanitarian law, train Hutus and Tutsis in conflict resolution, teach the "culture of peace," promote reconciliation through working togeth-er on common problems, broadcast radio programs teaching conflict resolution and interethnic peace, fund indigenous NGOs of various sorts (women's, peace movement, dialogue groups), sponsor dialogues, take selected leaders on trips to study conflict resolution and intereth-nic or interracial projects in South Africa and the United States, pro-duce educational materials on democracy, coordinate efforts and strategic thinking among the various organizations involved, work with elders to reintegrate displaced and dispersed people into their *collines* (hills—the units of rural settlement in Burundi and Rwanda), and more. Many other tasks, however, remained undone. No resources were made available to curb "hate radio" that preached violence and even geno-cide. The aid needed to integrate Hutus into the state structure and train police and judiciary did not materialize. Funding for human rights monitors proposed by the UN High Commissioner for Human Rights was far less than needed—it supported only five monitors. These were tasks that exceeded the capacities of the NGOs, and no states made available the resources to carry them out.

Most significantly, no robust measures were taken to curb the vio-lence. The international community only faintly recognized that con-tinuing violence posed the greatest threat, in that it continually renewed and strengthened the mutual fear and distrust that under-mined efforts at peace building. The violence was seen as a result rather than as a cause. It was mostly blamed on "extremists," and the problem conceptualized as "impunity": no one had been arrested or punished for the killing of President Ndadaye or for the continuing assassina-tions. The Convention of Government recognized the impunity prob-lem and the inability of Burundian society to deal with it alone; it therefore requested that the United Nations establish an International Commission of Inquiry (ICI) to investigate the assassination of the president of Burundi on October 21, 1993, the massacres that followed, and other serious acts of violence and political crimes committed since 1993. Prior to its establishment, an investigator sent to Burundi by the

TABLE 3.1
CONFLICT MANAGEMENT PROJECTS IN BURUNDI, 1993–96

Organization	Type of Organization	Project (s)
Accord	South African NGO	Exchange with South Africans
African Development Foundation	Independent agency funded by U.S. Congress	Assistance to NGOs
African Dialogue Center for Prevention, Management and Resolution of Conflicts	Arusha-based NGO	Support for mediation by former Tanzanian president Julius Nyerere
African American Institute	New York-based NGO	Conference on role of military in democracy in Bujumbura; co-convener of Burundi Policy Forum
Africare	Washington-based NGO	NGO training
Amnesty International	London-based NGO with global membership	Monitoring and reporting on human rights practices and arms flows in the region
Carter Center	Atlanta-based NGO	Convening regional heads of state in Cairo and Tunis
Catholic Relief Services	Humanitarian agency of U.S. Catholic Bishops Conference	Humanitarian assistance; project on reconciliation with Burundian Catholic bishops; support for research on conflict prevention
Center for Preventive Action, Council on Foreign Relations	New York-based NGO with national membership	Coconvener of Burundi Policy Forum
Centre Canadien d'Etudes et de Coopération Internationale	Montreal-based NGO	Democracy assistance
Community of Sant' Egidio	Rome-based Catholic lay religious community	Mediation
Human Rights Watch	New York-based NGO	Monitoring and reporting on human rights practices and arms flows in the region
International Alert	London-based NGO	Conflict resolution training; mediation; NGO capacity building; exchanges with South African peace activists; SRSG support group in London; support of Burundian peace group, Comité des Apôtres de la Paix (CAP)

TABLE 3.1 cont.

Organization	Type of Organization	Project (s)
International Center for Conflict Resolution	Capetown-based NGO	Mediation
International Commission of Inquiry	UN-appointed commission	Reporting on the assassination of Pres. Ndadaye and subsequent killings
International Committee of the Red Cross	Geneva-based NGO	Humanitarian assistance; education on international humanitarian law through art exhibitions and mobile theater troupes
International Crisis Group	London (now Brussels)-based NGO	Advocacy of humanitarian intervention
Mennonite Central Committee	Pennsylvania-based Protestant denomination	Reconciliation work in villages
National Democratic Institute for International Affairs	Washington-based, congressionally funded political party institute	Technical assistance and training for elections; parliamentarianism; national debate; election observation; democracy education
NGO Commission of Inquiry	International coalition of human rights NGOs	Investigation of human rights violations following the killing of the president in 1993
Nordic Africa Institute	Government-funded, Scandinavian research institute on international affairs	Dialogue facilitation and research
Office of the Special Representative of the UN Secretary-General	International organization	Preventive diplomacy on behalf of UN; coordination of overall effort
Organization of African Unity	Regional international organization	Posting military observers; high-level missions
Parliamentarians for Global Action	New York-based NGO with global membership	Collaboration with Burundi parliamentarians and democracy building
Radio Agatashya/ Fondation Hirondelle	Lausanne-based NGO	Pro-reconciliation radio broadcasts from Eastern Congo
Radio Umwizero- European Union	Regional international organization	Pro-reconciliation radio broadcasts
Refugees International	Washington-based NGO	Reintegration of displaced and dispersed people (pilot project); advocacy of regional UN super-envoy; elimination of hate radio

TABLE 3.1 cont.

Organization	Type of Organization	Project (s)
Reporters Sans Frontières	Paris-based NGO	Support and advocacy for freedom of the press
Search for Common Ground	Washington-based NGO	Coconvener of Burundi Policy Forum; pro-reconciliation radio broadcasting; women's peace movement and center; mediation
Swedish Agency for International Development Cooperation	Swedish government agency	Mediation; training; democracy assistance
Synergies Africa	Geneva-based NGO	Regional consultations with NGOs and heads of state; sponsoring of civil society projects; dialogue facilitation
United Methodist Church	Nairobi-based church	Dialogue facilitation
UNESCO	Paris-based UN agency	Education in the "culture of peace," mediation
UN High Commissioner for Human Rights	Geneva-based UN agency	Technical training; dissemination of standards; human rights education; stationing of human rights observers
U.S. Catholic Conference	Washington-based association of U.S. bishops	Support for the Burundian Episcopal Conference
World Vision	Washington-based evangelical humanitarian organization	Humanitarian assistance; collection of data on ethnic fears and needs; reconciliation project with Burundian Episcopal Church

Note: The above list is partly based on self-reporting by organizations to the Burundi Policy Forum (now the Great Lakes Policy Forum). It omits many organizations engaging in humanitarian assistance with no reported conflict management component, including the UN High Commissioner for Refugees, UNDHA, WFP, the International Rescue Committee, CARE, Médecins sans Frontieres, Médecins du Monde, ACF, OXFAM, Christian Aid, Concern, Action Aid, IHA, Danchurchaid, Terre des Hommes, FOCSIV, Aide et Action, Handicap International, Pharmaciens Sans Frontières, GTZ (Deutsche Gesellschaft für Technische Zusammenarbeit), Equilibre, Belgian Red Cross, IMC, and UNICEF. It omits funding organizations such as USAID and ECHO, which paid for many of the above activities. It omits development organizations, such as UNDP, EUDG VIII, and the World Bank. It does not include most of the advocacy and lobbying organizations that sponsored conferences on Burundi, produced newsletters or commissioned policy reports, such as Eurostep (Brussels), CCAC (Brussels), Survie (Paris), NCDO (Amsterdam), Minority Rights Group (London), Pax Christi (Brussels), etc. It also omits government diplomacy such as the many special envoys and high-level visitors, as well as several Security Council delegations and one-time missions on behalf of the UN secretary-general. In January 1995 the UN special representative of the secretary-general estimated that about seventy delegations had visited Burundi since his appointment in November 1993.

secretary-general argued that an ICI would be viable and useful only if its mandate guaranteed the enforcement of its recommendations in order to prosecute and punish those responsible for the violence. Nonetheless, the ICI that was eventually established for Burundi had no power to indict anyone or to recommend anyone for indictment by any national or international court. The ICI's report was presented to the secretary-general only on July 23, 1996, two days before the coup that finally did remove Burundi's Hutu president, though without killing him this time.[20] The UN High Commissioner for Human Rights also established a UN Human Rights Observer (UNHRO) Mission to monitor violations of human rights and sponsor human rights education projects in schools. Other proposals for the attack on impunity during this period were not implemented. These included the deployment of human rights observers throughout the country, inclusion of Burundi in the mandate of the International Tribunal on Rwanda, and massive efforts to train police and judicial personnel.

These efforts were reinforced by considerable jawboning and high-level pressure, which proved a poor substitute for actual programs that would have cost money and perhaps involved risk. An activist U.S. ambassador traveled throughout the country at some risk to himself (his convoy was attacked in June 1995) and issued strong statements about army atrocities. (As a result of the latter activity, the French minister of cooperation called him a "warmonger.") Boutros-Ghali visited Burundi in July 1995 supposedly to reinforce the message of Ould Abdallah, who left his position a few months later. The United States at various times sent National Security Adviser Anthony Lake, then UN representative Madeleine Albright, USAID administrator Brian Atwood, Assistant Secretaries of State John Shattuck (Human Rights) and George Moose (Africa), and special envoys Howard Wolpe (Burundi) and Richard Bogosian (Rwanda and Burundi). The OAU sent several high-level delegations in the spring and summer of 1995. The EU troika (past, present, and future presidents) sent their ministers of cooperation.

In 1995, as the Rwandan Hutu former army and Interahamwe militia reorganized and rearmed themselves in Eastern Zaire and started their attacks on Rwanda, while assisting the Burundian Hutu forces of the CNDD/FDD, the international community began to pay more attention to the regional dimension of the problem. In messages to his NGO partners, Ould Abdallah emphasized that higher priority needed to be given to the regional refugee situation, which was the major destabilizing factor.[21] Refugees International and others had for several years called for a regionwide super-envoy of the secretary-general; an effort by the secretary-general's office to explore the possibility of a regional conference in 1995 collapsed, but former U.S. president Jimmy Carter took up this effort. The Carter Center convened the presidents of all states in the region in Cairo in November 1995 and in Tunis in March 1996. Their joint declarations agreed on a framework for refugee repatriation, an end to cross-border raids and arms trafficking, support for the International Tribunal on Rwanda, and many other useful things.[22]

These agreements, however, remained unimplemented. Instead, violence was escalating throughout the region. There were several well-publicized incidents of large massacres by both Hutu guerrillas and the army or Tutsi militia groups, and many more remained unpublicized, especially those against Hutus who had less access to the international media. As the violent substratum of Burundian politics became more visible, the international agenda narrowed once more. The development agenda of the pre-Buyoya years had already been lost; the structural adjustment program had largely failed, and the massive violence and continuing political conflict made further efforts in that direction impossible. The efforts to salvage democracy seemed headed for the same fate, and for the same reason. By the end of 1995, international spokesmen focused more and more on one issue: preventing escalation into mass killings or genocide in Burundi.

Open discussion of armed intervention began in mid-1995. In July, when UPRONA rejected an invitation from the OAU to come to Addis Ababa for negotiations with FRODEBU and others, OAU Secretary-General Salim Ahmed Salim warned that Burundi might face an armed intervention to stop the killing. In his letter to the Security Council of December 29, 1995, Boutros-Ghali, after noting an "increasingly marked genocidal trend of a socio-ethnic nature," suggested placing a military presence in Zaire able to intervene rapidly in the event of "a sudden deterioration of the situation in Burundi." He characterized such a deployment as "a preventive measure that could help to avoid repetition of the tragic events in Rwanda." He also suggested "white-helmet" guards for humanitarian workers and human rights observers and sent the UN High Commissioner for Refugees, Sadako Ogata, to evaluate the security of humanitarian workers.[23]

The secretary-general further elaborated on this proposal in a subsequent report drafted upon Ogata's return. In this document he stated that "the objective of the international community must be to prevent the escalation of present tensions in Burundi into full-scale civil war, ethnic violence, and genocide." In the event that preventive diplomacy failed, he proposed the formation of a multinational force for "humanitarian intervention," such as member states had prevented him from forming for Rwanda in 1994. He argued that such a force should be authorized by the Security Council under Chapter VII of the UN Charter so that it could be deployed even without the agreement of the authorities in Burundi. He noted that at least part of the reason that such a force had become necessary was that the international community had failed to respond adequately to recommendations for assistance of various types in integrating Hutus into the state and economy, silencing hate radio, supporting the political process, or isolating the extremists by freezing their assets or denying them visas.[24]

During the next several months, the UN sponsored a process of "contingency planning" for such a force. This process accentuated divisions in the international community and failed because of reasons having little to do with Burundi. France, badly burned by continuing accusations of its support for the genocidal forces in Rwanda and the negative reaction to its Turquoise operation there, refused to participate. Indeed, the contingency planning was one of several events that aroused French suspicions of Washington's intentions in Africa, as the United States dominated the effort and volunteered to assist with planning, logistics, and communication. But in accordance with the policy on peacekeeping adopted after the domestic political disaster occasioned by the deaths of Army Rangers not under UN command in Somalia, the United States refused to act as the lead state or provide ground troops. The Americans argued for UN leadership, while the UN argued that experience had shown that only a coalition led by a strong member state could carry out a successful Chapter VII operation. The U.S. Army War College carried out a planning exercise on how to establish "safe areas"; the Defense Department sent a mission to evaluate the capacity and readiness of those African militaries that might participate; but the entire effort came to naught. Everyone was able to claim, however, that the main reason for the lack of action was someone else's incapacity or hesitation.

Though no preventive force arrived, the discussion of the proposal did affect the situation in Burundi. UPRONA, the army, and all the Tutsi parties vigorously opposed it. The extremists, led by Bagaza, vowed to wage war on such a force if it came. An apparent increase in violence and massacres in the spring of 1996 may partly have been a response to the call for a contingency force; the armed groups were showing what they were capable of. By August 1996, after Buyoya's coup had largely rendered the discussion moot, the SG revealed that he had written to twenty-one countries, of which only three had offered to supply troops.[25]

In the spring of 1996, as it became clear that the broader international community was unlikely to take any decisive action, Burundi's East African neighbors began to mobilize, largely under the leadership of former Tanzanian president Julius Nyerere. Nyerere had participated as cochair of the Carter Center's Tunis conference, and he had agreed to take primary responsibility for Burundi. In March a meeting in Addis Ababa including representatives of both the UN and the OAU recognized him as lead negotiator on Burundi, though without any specific organizational mandate.

Alarmed by Nyerere's subsequent inability to bring the parties together, however, the major East African states opened a summit on Burundi in Arusha, Tanzania, on June 25, 1996. Observing the progress of the contingency planning in New York, the African leaders, whose countries were directly threatened, apparently concluded that they had to seize control of the effort themselves, in a foreshadowing of the collective effort by some of them a few months later to instigate or support the overthrow of Zairian president Mobutu Sese Seko. Burundi was represented at the summit by both its FRODEBU Hutu president, Sylvestre Ntibantunganya, and its UPRONA Tutsi prime minister, Antoine Nduwayo. The parties agreed to an all-party meeting in Arusha the next week. According to the official communiqué, the states also agreed to study a request for "security assistance" from "Burundi." Such assistance would have consisted of a joint military force, mainly drawn from the armies of Uganda (seen as pro-Tutsi) and Tanzania (seen as pro-Hutu) and the Kenyan police (seen as pro-Hutu), in order to protect politicians, government employees, and economic installations and train the army and police.

While these goals were indeed those demanded by the situation, announcement of the force led instead to the complete unraveling of whatever political consensus still remained among the "moderates" of the two parties. As one journalist put it, "The president wants foreign troops to come and protect him from the military. The prime minister wants foreign troops to come and support the . . . military."[26] As the force was aimed at curbing violence by the army, Tutsi militias, and the CNDD, all of these opposed it. Tutsis in Bujumbura, including UPRONA, mobilized against it. A massacre of Tutsis led to attacks on the president at the funeral of the victims as the army stood by. Afraid for his life, President Ntibantunganya fled to the U.S. ambassador's residence. The army took power, which it handed over once again to

Pierre Buyoya. The East African states responded to the coup by placing trade sanctions on Burundi.

International efforts have continued since that time. Nyangoma
(of CNDD) and Buyoya opened up secret bilateral talks through the
Community of Sant' Egidio in Rome. Various mediators, including
Nyerere, who was increasingly seen as pro-Hutu, continued to work.
While the sanctions against Buyoya initially tipped the scales in favor
of the CNDD, the war and the change of power in the DRC redressed
the balance by driving Nyangoma out of his bases in South Kivu.[27]
Buyoya and Nyangoma made the Sant' Egidio negotiations public in
May 1997, when they signed an agreement (largely unimplemented as
of this writing) on certain interim questions, including a cease-fire.
Although the killing has continued, with new abuses (such as the forced
settlement of Hutu peasants in "regroupment camps"), negotiations
also continue, and Burundians might eventually find a way out of their
decades-old inferno, mainly as a result of the classic effect of mutual
stalemate and exhaustion. Nonetheless, it is worth analyzing the impact
of the failed international interventions between 1993's bloody, failed
coup and 1996's bloodless, successful one.

THE IMPACT OF INTERVENTION

As Boutros-Ghali stated, Burundi was indeed a test case of
post–cold war prevention intervention in a domestic conflict. Given
the difficulty of the situation it is difficult to say that the international community failed the test, but it certainly did not pass it with any
distinction. At times Burundi did not receive enough attention, or a
series of partial measures were launched in response to particular
events. When it did receive high-level international attention, political agendas largely unrelated to circumstances in Burundi shaped the
debate.

In fact, reforms in Burundi promoted by international actors without a good understanding of their consequences were among the leading causes of the new round of violence that these same actors then
undertook to prevent. International actors unanimously supported the
rushed pseudodemocratization of the country without any attention to
the security issues that majoritarian elections under universal suffrage
would pose for a divided society like Burundi. They seemed to assume
that holding democratic elections would produce democratic politics.
As described above, however, the problem of *institutionalizing* politics is
key to a successful transition and depends on the construction of many

institutions that can wield effective authority, not simply on the existence of political parties and electoral commissions.

It is true that the danger might not have appeared to be as great in 1989–93, as Buyoya prepared for elections with the apparent support of the army. But certainly one of the lessons of Burundi (and other cases) is that superficial or pseudodemocratization—holding competitive elections without the reform of basic institutions, such as the armed forces—is as liable to provoke conflict as to prevent it, endangering the young democratic institutions themselves. Those who can wield armed force can easily provoke renewed intercommunal hostilities. Elections function as instruments of democracy only when there is an at least rudimentary rule of law in place. Reform and training of the police, the judiciary, legal personnel, and the army should have preceded elections. At the same time, one must recognize that it might be hard to generate pressure for such reforms without the mobilization that accompanies open politics. The two processes have to run together so as to be mutually reinforcing. Leaving basic institution building until after a national electoral contest for control of the state, however, seems a recipe for failure. Uganda, Rwanda, and DRC under Kabila seem determined to postpone electoral competition until after settling basic institutional issues, though there is a strong element of self-serving, power-seeking behavior in their leaders' decisions to do so. In a discussion on the Congo, the EU's special envoy to the Great Lakes, Aldo Ajello, staked out a plausible middle ground. He argued that the international community should insist on some basic principles (free and fair elections, separation of legislative, executive, and judiciary powers, and respect of human rights) but not try to impose a particular model of Western democracy (majority rule, role of the opposition as a permanent element of democratic dialectic). To the extent that the basic principles are respected, each country should be given the freedom to choose its own model in accordance with its culture, history, traditions, and ethnic composition. The international community should support such efforts at state building, especially in countries emerging from years of violent conflict.[28] This seems a valid lesson from the experience of Burundi and that of others.

The unbalanced approach that makes electoral procedures primary seems to have generated an imbalance in the capacities of the actors in the international system. There were always organizations available for providing "democracy assistance," but very few who could provide aid in training the judiciary, the army, and the police and in making them work properly. While the United States has a number of programs to promote the "rule of law," there seem to be few that can be applied to countries with a French-style system of civil law rather than common law, with its quite different relationships among police, judiciary, and the legal profession.

Once the new round of violence was under way in Burundi, international action exhibited a similar mix of strengths and weaknesses. There were some belated attempts to find an organization to train the police and the judiciary: the Security Working Group of the Burundi Policy Forum in Washington, for instance, worked to get funding for police training from the International Criminal Investigative Training and Assistance Program, but it never materialized. A group of Belgian NGOs mobilized to provide training for police and judicial personnel in Rwanda, but their efforts were a small fraction of what was needed in that country and could not be extended to another. There was no international police corps from UN member states that could be mobilized to assist with security and with the investigation and punishment of crimes (mainly murder) in Burundi.

Besides humanitarian aid, whose dispensation sometimes exacerbated conflict by providing more resources to refugees (i.e., Rwandan Hutus) than to displaced persons (i.e., Burundian Tutsis), the main international efforts before the proposals for military intervention focused on crisis management through direct pressure, democracy building, and various combinations of mediation and conflict resolution. These had some observable effects.

Containment of violence or coercion. The international and domestic response (including suspension of development aid) to the putsch and massacres in October 1993 seems to have reversed the possible inclination of the army higher command to allow the attempted coup to stand for as long as it could and moved it, instead, to declare support for the elected government. Diplomatic interventions by the UN's special representative calmed down tensions at high crisis moments, such as when the president died in the Kigali plane crash in April 1994. Similarly, the monitoring activities of the OAU military observers have helped reduce army excesses in those few areas where they have been allowed to accompany those forces. Foreign humanitarian staff provided eyes and ears that sometimes discouraged or restrained local acts of violence where they were present. The regular meetings of the Burundi Policy Forum, which received considerable attention in Bujumbura, also added to the sense that the world was watching. The ICI's report eventually forced some officials from office and made the point that coup plotters and massacre abettors need to hide their tracks even better or face some sort of exposure. Cumulatively, the awareness of the aggregate international presence of foreign missions and the monitoring role of such agencies as the UNHRO has helped to contain the violence from reaching higher levels and thus perhaps slowed down the conflict's escalation. But these efforts did not reverse the overall trend toward escalation and toward destabilization of the country.

Engaging the parties and reaching settlements. Several diplomatic initiatives also exerted timely leverage and facilitation in getting the parties to negotiate and reach certain political settlements. Examples include the January 1994 UN and OAU help in getting a new president appointed and the UN special representative's catalyzing of the Convention of Government in September 1994 with the participation of Parliamentarians for Global Action.

Changing attitudes and norms. Burundi-specific mass media programming—provided, for instance, by Search for Common Ground's radio project—broadcast information aimed at combating rumors and promoting ethnic reconciliation. UNESCO's culture of peace program and the ICRC's program of dissemination of humanitarian law through local theater groups had similar goals. The National Democratic Institute produced a booklet on Burundian concepts of democracy. Search for Common Ground and International Alert put Burundians in contact with activists of the South African peace movement, who taught them how they had combated intercommunal violence in the townships. There were other such programs, but there has been no formal evaluation of any of them. As we go to press, we have learned of a multidonor evaluation of International Alert's work, including that on Burundi. In any case, such programs aim at long-term transformation and are not likely to be successful at stopping immediate violence. Arguably, considering the political-military environment from 1993 to 1996, putting resources into such projects was an error of priorities. Given the few resources that these programs received, this does not mean they should have received fewer. But the failure to devote even more resources to ending the violence, and the impunity that protected it, reflects a lack of candid analysis and will.

In sum, while the excesses of violence were trimmed and provisional agreements arranged, the political process itself was not transformed from an essentially armed struggle into an institutionalized peaceful process of political give-and-take. Conflict escalation eventually destroyed the fragile political framework and led to an effort by an already embattled military to reimpose an unequal order.

One shortcoming of this strategy was that diplomatic mediation among elites to restore the proper workings of central governmental institutions, such as through power sharing, assumed that the top leaders held effective power over the members of their respective organizations. In fact, the new competition among members of the elite occurred at multiple levels, from the president and prime minister on down, so there have been few lasting and effective hierarchical controls and little consistently effective discipline exercised by the top officials in the army, the political parties, and the cabinet over those nominally subordinate to them. With competition in effect at several levels, loyalties have been determined by shifting calculations of individual and factional convenience.

A fragmented international reaction to some extent reinforced the fragmented nature of Burundi's political scene. The number of official and unofficial mediators and special envoys steadily grew, as did the programs of international agencies and NGOs. As all looked for participants to engage with and a particular area where they could contribute, they contacted different members of the various political parties and social groups; such contacts provided them with resources and prestige. While Ould Abdallah considered that multiple organizations and approaches were necessary (indeed, he even recruited some organizations, as he believed that NGOs were quicker to react and more flexible than the UN bureaucracy), he felt it was necessary to keep them under strict supervision and coordination. He succeeded to a limited extent, though even during his tenure he felt that his efforts were occasionally undermined by others.[29] Some resented what they regarded as Ould Abdallah's insistence on personal control over the entire effort, and some disagreed with his approach; but that control provided some crude coordination and kept activities roughly in line with a strategic vision.

After Ould Abdallah's departure, however, there was less such coordination or strategy. The concurrent increase in violence led to a change in focus, toward prevention of further escalation of violence or reaction to such an escalation. Again, none of the proposals for military intervention was ever implemented, and the threat of intervention may actually have intensified the violence. Furthermore, it is far from certain that the interventions were aimed at the right goal.

Secretary-general Boutros-Ghali's proposal for a preventive deployment force received some support from NGOs, who also expressed guilt about the failure of the international community to react in Rwanda.

The International Crisis Group, whose most prominent spokesman on this issue was former U.S. congressman Stephen Solarz, carried out an independent military assessment of the requirements of such a mission and called for the immediate deployment of 25,000 men to stop the killing. Other advocacy groups, such as Refugees International, took similar positions. Gérard Prunier, however, argued that the fear of a "Rwanda-like" genocide was misplaced: "Given the general deterioration of administration in the country nobody in Burundi today [February 1996] has the organizational capacity to perpetrate a genocide."[30] In many ways the rhetoric about preventing another Rwanda, while laudable in its motivation, betrayed a lack of understanding of the difference between the two situations. The Rwandan genocide resulted from a systematic, state-organized effort to mobilize the politically dominant majority to exterminate the minority. That genocide might have been stopped by removing the planners and organizers of the operation—though a great deal of killing, perhaps on a Burundian scale, might have continued, as it does in Rwanda today. There was no such single control center in Burundi. A military operation could have eliminated the army high command but would have been powerless to control the diffuse Hutu guerrillas in the countryside, with their bases in Zaire and Tanzania. For these among other reasons Prunier concluded:

> The proposal by Secretary-General Boutros Boutros-Ghali to deploy United Nations peacekeeping troops in Zaire in the hope that this will somehow improve the situation in Burundi is well intended but completely unrealistic. In fact, the only line of action, already recommended by Ahmedou Ould Abdallah when he was in Bujumbura is to support elements of the civil society who are ready to struggle for peace (if properly backed up) and to put very heavy international pressure on the extremists, who are after all in limited numbers, even though they now occupy the forefront of the political scene.[31]

The proposal from the East African states for security assistance seems to have been closest to providing what was really needed—security to enable negotiators to proceed with less fear. Indeed, one East African diplomat present at Arusha said that the idea emerged from sidebar discussions at which Burundians explained that they could not put their genuine compromise proposals on the table for fear of being assassinated when they returned. The proposals, however, seem to have been formulated in a hurry, without adequate appreciation of how they would be perceived in the fear- and violence-charged atmosphere of a country where everyone has lost relatives and friends to the conflict and distrust is the universal solvent of all social and political relations.

Policy Lessons: Conceptual and Organizational Impediments

What explains the lack of a more appropriate response? Lack of "will"? Lack of time and attention? Lack of knowledge? Lack of resources? Lack of process and organization? Overall it is true that the UN Security Council, the major powers, and the leading players of the international community were far from viewing Burundi as a strategically crucial crisis and thus from watching Burundi on a full-time basis. Had they been more engaged and less distracted and thus willing to devote more staff time to analyzing the conflict, assessing a range of possible options, and drawing up coherent strategies, they might have arrived more quickly at what measures were necessary to effectively address the escalatory spiral of Burundi's politics. But even if in the aggregate there was more total commitment, that alone might not have removed certain impediments that explain why the considerable actions that *were* taken did not work. These impediments have to do with the way the international community perceives the problems in the Burundis of the world and is currently organized for conflict analysis, policymaking, and action with regard to them. These impediments led to rationalization about what the needed international actions were and limited the international community's ability to maximize its efforts, even within the limited resource parameters it faced.

Fragmented Definition of the Problem

One problem has been the multiple, competing definitions of the basic problem in Burundi and the corresponding multiplicity of proposals for dealing with it. There has been a failure to distinguish between the systemic and the more proximate sources of conflict and a tendency to throw resources at all levels of the problem, willy-nilly, as if any effort helps. Is Burundi's problem economic underdevelopment, lack of democracy, gross human rights violations, refugees, or refugees and displaced persons? While all these perspectives have a place in a coherent strategy, certain short-term and long-term perspectives prevailed more than others. Because of the dramatic poignancy of the human suffering and the continuing killings, policy discourse about Burundi has been especially dominated by humanitarian and human rights definitions of its problem. Indeed, making progress in addressing causes of the crisis has been held back by the constant absorption of most political energy in mitigating these symptoms of the conflict.[32] But the human rights and humanitarian approaches focus on symptoms and are energized by moral sentiments; they do not produce an integrated analysis of causes and dynamics that might inform an effective strategy. On the other hand, development programs, when they were still operating, focused primarily on long-term economic systemic sources of conflict while largely ignoring the ways in which their resources might be targeted on specific proximate causes (e.g., targeted job-creation projects for unemployed Tutsi youth in Bujumbura).

In sum, thousands of professionals in hundreds of governments and international organizations are focusing on Burundi. Lots of money is already being spent. But these human and financial resources are not being targeted effectively on the specific antecedents of instability and violence.

Although the international community's considerable direct diplomatic involvement in the political process did focus on more proximate sources of the conflict, it largely missed the role that violence was playing. Many initiatives viewed the conflict as a lack of democracy, or its approximation, "power sharing." The latter did seem to be required, given the lack of consensus over constitutional issues among the political leaders who represented the main segments of Burundi society. While these individuals headed the ostensible political parties and occupied government positions, they were also, to a greater extent, sponsoring unofficial armed movements. They saw their problem as gaining power and staying alive, not gaining assent to negotiated agreements. The international actors' main strategy was to seek to achieve agreement over legal and constitutional questions among party leaders and government officials, when insecurity, preemptive tactics, and raw power were dictating the parties' actions.

The principal third-party diplomatic methods used—mediation and official and unofficial facilitation—did not offer significant carrots or sticks to wean the main players away from the use of covert force or interdict the perpetrators of covert violence (coups, militias, assassinations) or the more overt forms (army reprisal campaigns). The common view that mediation will not work unless the parties have the "political will" to cooperate or unless methods of coercive diplomacy are used to induce it applies here. But this conventional wisdom slaps a label on the situation without identifying the specific sources of that lack of will. Increasingly, because of the widening opportunities for elites to outbid each other for leadership positions, these leaders have been increasingly unable to deliver their respective constituencies, even if, individually, they saw some gains in a particular negotiation. By the time the high-level jawboning efforts were made in 1996, including the cutoff of aid and enactment of sanctions, the parties were too entrapped in their positions to find a way out.

It is possible that the international players' failure to explicitly recognize the violent nature of Burundi's politics, mainly because they were unwilling to use military force as a possible solution, constituted a perceptual blinder that limited their ability to accurately define the problem in the first place. There were several missed opportunities in not considering more seriously ways to provide public security—for example, a postelection preventive deployment, the early proposals to provide security for officials, expanded police training and assistance, and the idea of some form of security assistance in 1996. Working more closely with the armed forces while they still claimed to be a national institution (even though often not behaving as such) might have helped to staunch the physical threats that were governing politicians' behavior. A sizable preventive deployment or a significant military-to-military relationship might have countered the atmosphere of insecurity more concretely and provided leverage and contacts through the military presence for making the political process more secure, as has occurred in Macedonia through UNPREDEP. Complementary policy options to gain leverage against "men behaving badly" might also have tried to deter individual behavior through freezing individual assets, punishing individuals' behavior, and rewarding good individual behavior.

Unfortunately, high-level discussion of the use of military force or pressure has been limited to the option of responding to a full-scale humanitarian crisis. Rather than seeing conflict prevention as a rolling process of fine-tuning programs already on the ground (e.g., through development assistance conditionality), a top-down crisis perspective, resident in the traditions of the Security Council and the UN, has waited for a major Rwanda-style cataclysm, which has not erupted. In the meantime, the political and military situation has escalated steadily, so that it is now too risky and politically unfeasible to use military force.

LACK OF POLICY PROCESS

Outsiders already have abundant information, knowledge, and analytical ability to identify the main patterns in the workings of conflicts like that in Burundi. The problem is not simply that there is some diffuse lack of political will and thus no action. It is also that even the abundant existing information and analysis are not pulled together anywhere in authoritative analyses, so that they can be used to develop a policy or strategy. Although able diagnosticians of the conflict on the ground exist in the academic community both outside governmental bodies and inside them, those specialists seem to have little continuing contacts with the high-level diplomats and officials who make decisions about conflict responses, and there is no institutional linkage for low-priority situations. Strategy development has been hampered because those who are able to delve into the overall causal dynamics of such countries' politics and conflicts do so largely outside governments, in the universities and think tanks, while those in government with ostensibly analytical roles are in fact absorbed in crisis remediation or routine program administration. Between detailed analyses by outside specialists, on the one hand, and discrete actions taken ad hoc, on the other, coherent analysis seems to have little room to influence the actions that are taken. We have specialists, initiatives, programs, and projects on Burundi, and diplomats knowledgeable about Burundi, but no policies.

These conclusions lead to at least two recommendations for official organizations engaged in preventing or managing conflicts like that in Burundi:

♦ **Educating the policy elite.** The existing knowledge about ethnic conflicts, early warnings of conflict and crisis, and the array of policies in the "toolbox" for preventing or managing conflicts needs to be disseminated to policymakers with decisionmaking authority who operate at higher levels.[33] We know a lot more now about ethnic conflicts, their systemic and proximate antecedents, and their solutions than we did even a few years ago, when notions that these conflicts were caused by "ancient hatreds" seemed to hold sway. Some measures such as preventive deployments that might plausibly have stemmed the erosion of stability in places like Burundi were not promoted vigorously or felt to be politically feasible. But now, the cumulative experience from a series of post–cold war failures in Africa and elsewhere, as well as a number of contrasting successes, might make such measures more acceptable at early stages of international crises, were the lessons known to top policymakers. The immediate challenge is to apply what we know about early stages of such conflicts in the routine monitoring of countries vulnerable to them, and to spread this knowledge of the comparative advantages of various tools of conflict management more widely among the middle and top levels of the policy elite in major governments and multilateral organizations. These elites might then feel more emboldened to decide to devote a portion of staff and budget to outgoing on-the-ground monitoring, integrated analyses of specific conflicts, and assessment of successful preventive measures.

Were an assessment of the risks and opportunities in many African and other developing societies to be carried out, policymakers might find that, while the bad news is that there are some places like Burundi that are especially burdened with several factors predisposing to conflict, the good news may be that many other societies, even in Africa, are faring quite well. And if developing countries vary a great deal in their proneness to violent conflict, then we do not face a world of impending chaos. Policymakers might be able to relax somewhat about the imagined huge commitments entailed in getting serious about conflict prevention, and they could concentrate their most explicitly preventive actions on avoiding the worst outcomes in a small number of cases.

♦ *Organizing for conflict prevention.* The functions of tracking ongoing political developments for early warning of conflict or crisis in vulnerable societies, and of making decisions to implement various ongoing programs to address manifestations of conflict as they emerge, need to be linked better in ongoing policy planning units that are dedicated specifically to prevention. These units should operate both in the headquarters offices (e.g., the Burundi desk and the in-country missions) and in the in-country field missions (e.g., in embassies of donor countries, the UN, regional multilateral organizations, and NGOs).

While these measures might improve the performance of existing organizations, they fail to address a number of larger questions. First, analysis of what seems to have been needed in Burundi has exposed several gaps in the capacity of international institutions. In particular, as events in Bosnia have also shown, there is little capacity for preventive policing or for the training and strengthening of police and judicial officers. The lack of an international criminal court also means that entities like the International Commission of Inquiry have no means of translating their findings into actual legal proceedings. In the absence of institutions capable of apprehending and punishing those who commit political murders or assassinations, exposing their deeds may only strengthen the sense of impunity, as the perpetrators continue to operate freely despite such exposure.

More fundamentally, the difference in political commitment between those who are pursuing the conflict and those outsiders who intervene to try to halt it creates an asymmetry that seems almost insuperable. Burundi shows that even in a tiny, weak, poor country, a relatively small group of extremist elites who are willing to devote all their energy and resources to a conflict, and to take and risk life, are quite capable of resisting the efforts of a divided and distracted, even if relatively mobilized, international community—all of whose agents, in the end, have the option of leaving.

As in those cases, and others of counterinsurgency, it seems that the only durable alternative is to seek out and strengthen those in the society itself who are willing and able to devote an equal measure of commitment to ending or mitigating the conflict and to provide them with the assistance they need. The moral hazard of doing so, of course, is that such support encourages them to take actions with dangerous consequences, from which their external supporters may not be able or willing to protect them. Indeed, the fundamental lesson of the analysis is that while there are definitely potential allies and resources to work with, conflict prevention is an open-ended, long-term process with no assured exit strategy. For both practical and moral reasons, it requires a long-term commitment. That is one reason that supporting and strengthening initiatives by neighboring states and societies, who cannot remove themselves from the region, is likely to be more effective in the long term.

What is most lacking in the international community's approach to a country like Burundi, of no strategic or economic interest to rich and powerful states, is thus not necessarily action per se; we have seen that humanitarian concern, guilt, and various inter- and intraorganizational rivalries propelled numerous states and organizations into action. What is most lacking is the strategic direction and coordination that comes from the exercise of power. That, above all, is what distinguishes Macedonia, which despite its obscurity is located in Europe on NATO's frontier, from Burundi. The United States has placed troops there and issued a clear warning to Belgrade against violence in Kosovo. UNPREDEP and this warning provide a context that strengthens all other preventive activities in the country.

The experience of Burundi shows that activity by NGOs and even by international organizations cannot substitute for strategic commitment by states. This does not mean that NGOs and international organizations are unimportant; despite all the obstacles, they have accomplishments to their credit in Burundi. But they are complements to, not substitutes for, political commitment by states.

NIGER
CHAD
BENIN
NIGERIA
Kano
Zaria
Hausa
Kanuri
Yoruba
Abuja*
Nupe
Ogbomosho
Ibadan
CAME-
ROON
Tiv
Yako
Igbo
Onitsha
Lagos
Ethnic groups
Gulf of
Guinea
Ibibio
Ogoni
0 MILES 200
AFRICA
Ib Ohlsson for FOREIGN AFFAIRS
Source: Encyclopedia of World Cultures and Facts on File

— 4 —

NIGERIA

THE CHALLENGE OF PREVENTIVE ACTION

Peter M. Lewis

Nigeria is sub-Saharan Africa's most populous country and among the region's most diverse societies. Since achieving independence from Britain in 1960, Nigeria has experienced recurrent political and economic instability. A succession of democratic governments and military rulers have failed to yield a durable governing formula for the federation. A cataclysmic civil war, sparked by the failed Biafran secession in 1967, demonstrated the consequences of the country's volatile ethnic and regional fissures. After a fleeting and erratic petroleum boom in the 1970s, the nation experienced a prolonged depression that necessitated a difficult path of economic austerity. Amid these challenges, Nigeria has aspired to play a leading role in continental affairs, and it has been among the United States's foremost trading and investment partners in Africa.

Since mid-1993, Nigeria has been embroiled in a national crisis of broad dimensions. The immediate tensions arose from the abortive political transition of June 1993 and the increasingly authoritarian course of General Sani Abacha's regime.[1] The ongoing confrontation—between a fervent prodemocracy opposition movement, concentrated in the country's southern states, and an entrenched military government comprised mainly of northern Muslims—presents an essential challenge to stability. In a more basic sense, chronic political uncertainty, ethno-regional tension, and economic malaise have provoked widespread concerns over the equilibrium, and perhaps the very existence, of the Nigerian federation.[2]

At this writing the Abacha regime appears to have consolidated authority, and the government purports to be moving toward a new democratic transition in 1998. Political parties have been registered, local elections have been held, and officials have pledged their intention to carry out the transition agenda. There are significant questions as to the credibility of this promise, however, in light of past military conduct and the continuing restrictions on human rights and political participation. These circumstances have inspired domestic and foreign critics of the regime to continue their active opposition to the current leadership.

The overt political calm masks a variety of unresolved problems. The antagonism between government and opposition shows little prospect of resolution. Avenues for dialogue and negotiation have been curtailed by military repression, while domestic opposition groupings have been unable to mount a sustained challenge to military rule or to advance a viable alternative formula. The country has been shaken by recurrent protests from political, ethnic, and religious groups, punctuated by episodes of civic violence, bombings, and assassinations. These events indicate a reservoir of political discord and social frustration. In light of the inflammatory tensions surrounding the crisis, there remain legitimate concerns over incipient political breakdown and civil conflict.

The long-term stability of Nigeria is of special importance owing to the country's size, its regional significance, and its position in global energy markets. With an estimated 103 million people, Nigeria is Africa's most populous country. It is the preeminent political, military, and economic power in the West African subregion. Nigeria has played a pivotal role in the Economic Community of West African States (ECOWAS), and it has provided the leading element in the ECOWAS Monitoring Group (ECOMOG), the regional peacekeeping force in Liberia. In addition, Nigeria provides about 5 percent of global petroleum supplies, and it is the sixth largest producer in the Organization of Petroleum Exporting Countries (OPEC). From both regional and global perspectives, violent conflict in Nigeria would carry broad implications.

The current status quo in Nigeria does not form a basis for legitimate political reform, social stability, or international acceptability. Interested parties within and outside Nigeria seek new ways to expedite a settlement of the political impasse and encourage a swift restoration of genuine democratic rule. Official U.S. policies toward Nigeria, comprising diplomatic initiatives and limited sanctions, have failed to yield significant progress on human rights or political reform. A variety of alternative diplomatic approaches, including parallel efforts by two official U.S. envoys, complementary overtures from the Commonwealth and the United Nations, and track-two initiatives on the part of several unofficial actors, have also produced meager results. In addition, more stringent sanctions, perhaps including a comprehensive embargo on the purchase of Nigerian oil, have been precluded by a lack of consensus among both major G-7 countries and important constituencies in this country.

The difficulties of fashioning an effective international response to the Nigerian predicament offer lessons about the necessary conditions for preventive action. Intervention usually requires clear motivation on the part of outside actors, agreement on a strategy for change, and the coordination of policy instruments. In addition, leading protagonists in the problem area must be sensitive to external influence. Most of these conditions have been lacking in the Nigerian situation. There has been little consensus among leading foreign powers, reflecting their different assessments and disparate interests. Moreover, the Nigerian government has resisted diplomatic initiatives and remains marginally affected by most forms of economic pressure.

The shortcomings of previous approaches, as well as the palpable need to strengthen the foundations for improved governance in Nigeria, suggest a multifaceted strategy incorporating civil society as a key component of stable democratic rule. An array of interventions are available to external actors, including sanctions or inducements directed at the regime and engagement with nongovernmental groups. Initiatives toward civic organizations in Nigeria would address a neglected component of political change, while balancing bilateral pressures with other forms of external influence. A strategy that focuses on strengthening civil society provides an opportunity to mitigate conflict and encourage political reform over the longer term.

The next section provides an overview of the Nigerian crisis, set against the background of the country's postindependence development. This is followed by a consideration of existing policies toward Nigeria, the problems of preventive action in the Nigerian context, and the relative merits of alternative approaches.

THE CASE OF NIGERIA

Throughout Nigeria's turbulent postindependence history, three challenges have been paramount: diversity, governance, and development. The problem of managing diversity constitutes the first issue, as political leaders have sought means of accommodating the country's sprawling ethnic, regional, and religious cleavages. The quest for national unity has inspired a search for effective mechanisms of federalism and power sharing.[3] Through repeated constitutional revision, Nigerian elites have sought to create a viable political balance among the country's diverse segments. In addition, leaders have created new states and amended revenue distribution formulas to provide a greater sense of representation and entitlement to different communities.

Second, the quest for stable and effective governance has been an ongoing dilemma. Neither democratic nor authoritarian rule has proven stable in Nigeria. Nearly all the nation's leaders have professed a commitment to electoral government, and much of the Nigerian public harbors a belief in democratic principles. Yet, despite widespread attachment to the idea of civilian rule, the nation has been governed by the military for a total of twenty-seven years since independence and has experienced a constitutional regime for only four years in the period since 1966. Through a succession of transition programs, Nigerians have attempted to revise their laws and institutions to establish a democratic order, yet efforts to realize a stable electoral system have yet to succeed.[4] The search for durable institutions, especially with regard to the balance between civilian and military authority, is a central challenge for governance.

The challenge of economic development presents a third central issue. Since the early 1970s, Nigeria's economic and social contours have been shaped by the impact of prodigious oil wealth. This apparent bounty has produced ambiguous and often perverse effects. The main legacies of the petroleum boom have been a distorted, unstable economy, a corrupt and overextended state apparatus, and a concentration of resources and political power at the federal center.[5] The need to decentralize and diversify Nigeria's economy has been generally acknowledged, yet economic reform has proven politically difficult. Persistent economic malaise, inequality, and widespread poverty create basic impediments to improvements in governance or national stability.

The crisis that erupted in 1993 reflected these challenges. The proximate source of conflict was the annulment of a widely accepted democratic election and the subsequent reinstatement of military rule. The ethno-regional and religious dimensions of the political struggle revealed long-standing antagonisms within the federation. And the unfolding political crisis was paralleled by a steep decline in Nigeria's already stagnant economy, deepening popular hardship and increasing the country's international marginality.

As in many former colonies, the roots of contemporary problems can be traced to historical features of colonial state creation and decolonization. Nigeria became a single colonial entity in 1914, when Britain amalgamated two separate protectorates (initially created in 1900) together with the colony of Lagos into one country. The rapid growth of anticolonial activism after World War II led to a negotiated settlement between Nigerian nationalists and the British government, heralding a period of gradual transition to independence in 1960.[6]

The new republic inherited a parliamentary system of government and a three-region federal structure. The regional structure, largely congruent with colonial divisions, delineated separate ethnic and religious blocs. Ethnically distinct parties captured control of the separate regions, leading to factionalism and political turbulence. Electoral misconduct and political violence fostered a breakdown of the First Republic, prompting a military coup in January of 1966.[7] This was followed in quick succession by a second coup, widespread ethnic violence, and the attempted 1967 secession of southeastern ethnic Ibo areas under the banner of Biafra. The bitter, destructive civil war ended in 1970, with perhaps a million lives lost to war and famine.

General Yakubu Gowon, head of state for nearly a decade after July 1966, pursued a policy of reconciliation following the civil war. (This was facilitated by the rapid growth of petroleum revenues during the early 1970s.) Gowon also delayed a promised transition to democratic rule, however, and he was ousted in 1975 by General Murtala Muhammed. The new ruler vowed a prompt return to civilian government and expanded the federal system by creating new states and modifying revenue distribution formulas. His assassination in a failed coup attempt the following year did not derail his program, however, and his lieutenant, General Olusegun Obasanjo, supervised the transition to an elected, civilian government in 1979.

The Second Republic adopted a presidential system modeled on the U.S. pattern, including a bicameral legislature and a nineteen-state federal structure. Political parties were required to demonstrate broad ethnic and regional support, and five parties contested the 1979 elections for all tiers of government.[8] Rather quickly, however, the Second Republic came to share many of the corrosive features of the preceding civilian regime.[9] Party strength was rooted in personal and ethnic appeals, and political competition was soon marred by fraud and violence. The Second Republic also straddled the peak years of the petroleum boom, and the availability of copious revenues fueled massive corruption among the country's political elites.

Political disarray and popular alienation rapidly eroded the legitimacy of the civilian regime, and there was scant protest when General Muhammadu Buhari staged a coup at the beginning of 1984. General Buhari's short-lived rule was austere and repressive, although the regime did seek to impose a degree of accountability and probity in governmental affairs.[10] Nonetheless, the government's severity, along with a failure to cope successfully with a declining economy, led to its ouster by General Ibrahim Babangida in August 1985.

Babangida initially displayed greater reformist vigor, as he quickly elaborated a framework for political transition and a far-reaching economic liberalization program. In the early years of his regime, these commitments were advanced by the general's political adeptness, accompanied by fairly consistent and vigorous policy measures. Shortly after assuming power, Babangida implemented a far-reaching Structural Adjustment Program (SAP) with the support of the World Bank and the International Monetary Fund.[11] The government also drafted a democratization schedule and sponsored a revision of the constitution. Renewed economic growth and awakening political activity kindled widespread expectations for constructive change.

Hope soon gave way to disillusion, however, as Babangida retreated from both political and economic reforms, while revealing a growing bent toward corruption and authoritarianism. A failed coup attempt in early 1990, followed by a fresh oil revenue windfall, sharply altered the course of the regime. The political program was subject to meddling and procrastination, as the ruler allowed only two government-created political parties, banned numerous political competitors, and postponed the transition date repeatedly. On the economic front, the Structural Adjustment Program gradually eroded, although a few important policies were retained. Reckless government spending, spiraling corruption, and delinquent debt service led to deteriorating growth, along with a decline in the country's international standing.

As Babangida's reformist project collapsed, the country entered an extended crisis. After the third postponement of his transition program, Babangida eventually allowed presidential elections in June 1993, to be followed by an August transfer of power. The official political parties each nominated a prosperous Muslim business magnate with close ties to the military. The Social Democratic Party picked Chief M. K. O. Abiola, a Yoruba press baron and philanthropist, while the National Republican Convention chose Alhaji Bashir Tofa, a lesser-known business figure from the northern state of Kano. The short campaign was conducted with uncommon decorum and restraint.[12]

The June 12 polls passed smoothly, and unofficial results indicated a solid victory for Chief Abiola. Within days after the election, however, Babangida annulled the exercise, alleging legal and administrative irregularities. Popular protest, sporadic violence, and widespread external censure followed the cancellation. The annulment of the election, which was the culmination of an already artificially protracted process, tapped a wellspring of discontent, most intensely in the southwestern region of the country. The perception of disenfranchisement by a northern Muslim elite—for the third time since independence—incited deep resentments in Abiola's region, home to his Yoruba ethnic group. The country was shaken for weeks by riots, strikes, and demonstrations, concentrated most heavily in the Yoruba states. Many other ethnic groups fled to their home regions, recalling the strife that foreshadowed the civil war. The government sought to quell the unrest, while offering few specific proposals for the transfer of power.

The international response to the transition crisis was ambiguous. The United States and Great Britain censured the Babangida regime for annulling the elections and called for a rapid return to democracy. These countries, along with the European Union and Canada, also suspended most nonhumanitarian aid to Nigeria. Chief Abiola spent several weeks abroad, seeking support in Washington and London. He garnered sympathy, but little in the way of concrete commitments. Nigeria's other leading trading partners, including France, Germany, and Japan, proved diffident. African governments and regional organizations were generally silent regarding the unfolding predicament.

After weeks of intense domestic and international pressure, the general abruptly vacated office on the designated, August 26, 1993, deadline, leaving in place an appointed committee of civilian caretakers. Within ten weeks after Babangida's exit, however, General Sani Abacha, defense minister in the caretaker government, shouldered aside the civilians and reasserted military rule. Abacha quickly dissolved the elected civilian tiers of government, scrapped the transition framework, and discarded the remaining elements of the Structural Adjustment Program.[13] The populist policies of his new regime sent the country into an abrupt economic decline. The moribund economy was linked with massive official corruption and a growing web of international drug trafficking and commercial fraud. The combination of renewed military domination and economic malfeasance prompted a new round of international strictures affecting air links, visas, cultural and sports activities, and assistance from multilateral donors.[14]

Chief Abiola staged a protest on the first anniversary of the electoral cancellation, challenging Abacha to abdicate and announcing the unilateral creation of a transition cabinet. He was promptly jailed and charged with treason. Abiola's arrest sparked a nine-week campaign of strikes and protests involving the strategic petroleum worker unions, along with other civic groups. General Abacha rode out the unrest, curtailing the strikes through repression, intimidation, and inducement. The regime dismissed and jailed the union chiefs, issued a decree exempting itself from the jurisdiction of the courts, and cracked down on the independent media. Compliant union officials and politicians were brought into government forums, usually with generous perks. By the end of 1994, opposition to the military government was largely subdued.[15]

Abacha nonetheless repeated a verbal commitment to eventual democratization, and the government convened a civilian-led Constitutional Conference to ratify the framework for an electoral regime. On October 1, 1995, the regime announced a program for transition to civilian rule, set to culminate in precisely three years. The program was modeled on the agenda set forth by General Babangida, leading many to compare Abacha's plan with his predecessor's machinations to preserve power.

In the meantime, following an announcement that it had foiled an attempted coup, the regime conducted *in camera* trials for more than forty alleged coconspirators.[16] Among those accused were retired generals Obasanjo and Shehu Yar'Adua, Obasanjo's former lieutenant and a recent presidential aspirant. Obasanjo and Yar'Adua were both vocal critics of military rule, having previously supervised the 1979 transition to the civilian Second Republic. The secret tribunal handed down severe rulings, including a death sentence for Yar'Adua and life imprisonment for Obasanjo. The absence of clear evidence or due process elicited protests from the United States, Britain, and a few of Nigeria's other key trading partners.

The government in Abuja responded to international calls for leniency by reducing sentences for most of the alleged coup plotters.[17] Shortly thereafter, however, on November 10, 1995, the regime abruptly executed Ken Saro-Wiwa and eight other activists from the southeastern Ogoni region, who had been convicted on capital murder charges. These leaders were among the most controversial dissidents in Nigeria, as their movement for environmental redress and social equity mobilized an ethnic minority in a strategic oil-producing region. The execution of the "Ogoni 9," after a flawed trial and scant judicial review, provoked a wave of international denunciation.[18]

The executions occurred during the annual meeting of the Commonwealth countries, who suspended Nigeria from their ranks. The United States tightened a range of restrictions on travel, aid, trade, and cultural exchange with Nigeria and declared that it would weigh the merits of a comprehensive oil embargo against the country. The European Union and Canada were also highly critical of the regime, and the United Nations General Assembly promptly began debate on a resolution of censure. Even the traditionally reticent community of African states expressed disapproval, as the leaders of Zimbabwe and South Africa reproached the regime for its authoritarian actions. Nigeria was rapidly becoming a pariah in the world community.

In the wake of the executions, however, Nigeria's domestic and external circumstances stabilized considerably. Internationally, the Abacha government maintained a tense diplomatic standoff with the Commonwealth, the United Nations, the United States, Canada, and South Africa, which had emerged as Nigeria's most vocal international critics. The regime continued to draw criticism and periodic scrutiny of its human rights record and was marked by continuing problems of economic mismanagement, corruption, and drug trafficking. Most of the country's major trading partners, however, were averse to stronger sanctions, and international measures were essentially restricted to verbal and symbolic gestures. International lobbying efforts by the Nigerian government also served to ease external pressures. Commerce and foreign investment proceeded, particularly in the energy sector, although a weak economy and lagging debt service limited the country's access to external markets and discouraged investment in other sectors.

Domestically, opposition to the military government was largely subdued. A variety of human rights groups, prodemocracy organizations, and professional and popular associations continued to protest abuses by the regime and to urge a rapid return to democracy. Substantial elements of the independent press also continued to operate. These activities existed in a gray zone of semilegality, and the government used decrees, detentions, and occasional state terror to intimidate or squelch dissident voices. A spate of detentions and several unexplained murders of prominent political activists (including Kudirat Abiola, the wife of the imprisoned leader) had a chilling effect on opposition activity. When political party organization was authorized in mid-1996 under the official transition program, the regime tightly controlled the registration process. In October the government's electoral commission accredited five parties, conspicuously excluding groups linked to opposition politicians.

Aside from suffering the evident constraints of state repression, the efforts of domestic opposition were blunted by division, demoralization, and opportunism. Two factors have been noteworthy. The first is the lack of resources and unity among the diverse elements of civil society. Much of the democratic movement is centered in the southern states, particularly the Yoruba areas of the southwest; and the leading opposition groups are headed by professionals, business people, and notables, with few links to broader popular constituencies.[19] Even these organizations have limited resources to sustain their activities, and the absence of broad strategic direction hampers their effectiveness. A second factor is the fractious and compliant nature of the political elite. Aspiring civilian politicians make little common cause with elements of civil society, and they have proved amenable to the inducements and opportunities provided by the regime.[20] A substantial number have been willing to participate in the officially sanctioned transition program. There is not presently an independent political bloc to provide the vehicle for a broader democratic movement.

NIGERIA AT RISK

It is important to recognize the enduring and fundamental risks to stability posed by Nigeria's crisis of governance. The cumulative effects of authoritarian rule, political exclusion, and economic mismanagement have eroded the central institutions of government while aggravating social tensions. The recent abatement of overt conflict should not obscure the continuing danger of sudden, large-scale conflict in Nigeria, originating either from divisions within the military or from pervasive civil violence. The continuing sources of instability generally fall within three areas:

♦ **Institutional decay.** In recent years, important governmental functions have markedly deteriorated. The civil service has been buffeted by attrition, declining real wages, delinquent salaries, and pervasive corruption. The legal system has also degenerated, as corruption and demoralization have permeated the police force, while the judiciary has lost independence and professionalism in the face of military intervention. These problems have been accompanied by a virtual collapse of educational and health services. Of greatest concern, however, is the evident dissipation of the military. A succession of purges, reshuffles, arrests, revolts, and executions has reduced the cohesion and integrity of the military, leaving a dangerous residue of mistrust and factionalism. Maneuvers within the upper echelons remain opaque to outside observers, but there is an apparent risk of internal division and violent rupture.[21]

◆ **Ethnic and regional division.** Ethnic, regional, and religious tensions remain high in Nigeria, and the perceived exclusion of certain southern groups from the political process has aggravated general levels of resentment. Southern-based opposition groups and northern elites have demonized one another, and political polarization has fostered an apparent northern monopolization of power, alongside latent southern sentiments for partition.[22] Government efforts to alleviate sectional pressures through the formation of states and local governments have intensified civil violence among rival communities in several areas of the country.[23] Religious tensions, which have attained growing prominence in recent years, have also been evident in periodic outbursts of Christian-Muslim strife and fundamentalist violence.

◆ **Economic malaise.** Economic mismanagement and stagnant performance continue to depress living standards while raising popular frustration. Endemic corruption, decaying infrastructure, and unpredictable policies create basic obstacles to investment and growth. Chronic hardship has further diminished the legitimacy of the government, while inducing officials and politicians to focus on the economic benefits of political power. The result has been a downward spiral of erratic policies, malfeasance, and decline.

RISK SCENARIOS

During the past year, the government has attempted to convince international critics of its seriousness in seeking reform. In October 1996 an extensive program of privatization was suggested, along with the registration of political parties for an impending transition. The credibility of stated commitments to economic and political reform is obviously uncertain, however, in light of the regime's record since coming to power. At least three scenarios are plausible during the next few years:

◆ **The Zaire analogy.** Some commentators have spoken of the "Zairanization" of the regime in Abuja, in the mold of Mobutu's reign in Zaire, as political power has become increasingly personalized, arbitrary, and corrupt. The "road to Kinshasa," as others have termed it, would involve a steady, incremental deterioration of governmental institutions, economic performance, and the social fabric.[24] Under this scenario there would be no immediate large-scale eruption of civic violence or significant political instability, as was the case in Zaire for decades; rather, a stable, predatory regime would preside as the country experienced domestic decay and international isolation punctuated by episodes of local and regional violence.

◆ **The Ghana analogy.** Alternatively, the current leadership may try to stabilize its power by pursuing limited economic and political reform. Jerry Rawlings's economic liberalization program in Ghana and the subsequent civilianization of his regime stand as the model. Improved policies would, it is assumed, lead to renewed investment and external debt relief, and the benefits of growth would presumably mitigate opposition to the regime. The leadership would concurrently play out a political transition, with General Abacha or someone approved by him standing for election in a "transitional" poll. The recent successes of similar exercises in Ghana, Niger, and Gambia, along with signals emanating from the president's office in Abuja, suggest that this is the favored strategy at present.[25] This scenario promises improved economic performance and political stability in the near term, though it fails to address the deep-seated internal fissures in Nigerian society and is unlikely to diminish the country's international isolation.

◆ **State failure.** The prospect of large-scale, catastrophic violence has receded, but there remains a plausible chance that Nigeria could become a failed state. A revolt within the military could lead to splintering and factional conflict, with a possible contagious effect on society. Alternatively, an incident of civic violence—occasioned by Abiola's death in detention, religious violence in the northern states, or clashes over new states or electoral battles—could incite internal divisions in the military. Such incidents of violence have seemed to increase in 1997. In light of the palpable risks inherent in the current situation, there is evident need for a strategy of preventive action to reconcile the political impasse and to alleviate social tensions.

The preceding scenarios offer fairly somber alternatives for Nigeria's future. Some observers, however, have discerned a possible opportunity in the government's transition program. If the military were to definitively exit power and allow a relatively transparent electoral process, then the change of regime could help to assuage tensions while enabling democracy to emerge in the future. Obviously, this result would be predicated upon prompt improvements in human rights and political liberties, as well as tolerance for a wide array of electoral participation. The prospect of civilianization before democratization, accompanied by a partial liberalization of the political arena, provides a clear (though flawed) path out of the present impasse. In order for this opportunity to be realized, however, the military government would have to send clear, unequivocal, and repeated signals of its intention to improve the political environment.

THE CHALLENGE OF PREVENTIVE ACTION

The Nigerian situation offers important lessons about the enabling conditions for preventive action, the array of measures available for effective engagement, and the constraints on various approaches. Strategies for preventive action are conceived in response to an impending national or regional crisis. Such tensions generally arise from deep-seated grievances—whether ethnic, territorial, ideological, or economic—which have become irreconcilable, because of political breakdown or polarization among the principal antagonists. In consequence, competing demands cannot be resolved through existing institutions, and contending groups have little motive for accommodation. The purpose of external involvement, then, is to shift the incentives for leading actors, and to offer new channels for resolving conflicts or satisfying demands.[26] As Michael Lund and his colleagues observed in the previous chapter, situations of conflict are fostered by proximate or behavioral causes, institutional factors, and fundamental or structural conditions. These various causes call for multifaceted policy responses. Some measures focus primarily on influencing the immediate behavior of key actors, while others may be directed toward altering the configuration of important institutions or affecting salient aspects of the social structure. Preventive action embodies both short-term palliative measures and longer-term efforts toward reform.

Several factors influence the prospects for effective intervention. Among the most important conditions are international consensus over the urgency of the problem and a broad impetus for engagement. Nascent crises are commonly neglected until they erupt into serious conflict, so it is important to secure early recognition of the problem and commitment to action. This raises the related challenge of crafting a coherent international response to emergent conflicts. Influential actors must concur on a strategy, including agreement on the tools of engagement. Preventive action can involve various measures, including formal and parallel diplomacy; track-two initiatives on the part of nongovernmental actors; actions by civic, religious, or development organizations; economic inducements; or varying forms of sanctions.[27] Different members of an external coalition may perform complementary roles, but coordinated responses are more likely to be useful than diffuse, ad hoc approaches. A final and decisive question is whether the principal antagonists are susceptible to external pressure or influence. A critical factor affecting external leverage is the degree of dependence on outside resources.

Nigeria's predicament has seemed especially intractable because most of the conducive elements for preventive action have been absent. There has been an ambivalent international response to the country's political travails. In the absence of sustained, violent conflict, the volatile divisions at the heart of the transition crisis have often been discounted by foreign observers. The weakness of the domestic opposition to military rule and the apparent acquiescence of Nigerian politicians to the current transition program also reduce the basis for more forceful external pressure on behalf of democratization and the opening of the political process. Moreover, the country's principal trading partners have concerns with respect to ongoing commercial relationships that preclude confrontation with the government. In consequence, the international response has been halting, uneven, and disparate.

Economic leverage would appear to hold the greatest potential to shift the incentives for Nigeria's rulers, but leading international actors have demonstrated scant influence in this area. The nation's economy has been increasingly isolated in recent years as a consequence of erratic policies and weak performance with respect to external debt. Since aid, loans, and investment have already diminished, threats of additional reductions are of little significance. Given the predominance of oil revenues in Nigerian public finances, sanctions targeted at the petroleum sector might logically be most effective in pressuring the central government. For reasons detailed below, however, there have been few credible external threats to embargo Nigerian oil. Additional suggestions for restrictions on new investments in the petroleum sector, limitations on financial transactions with Nigeria, and the immobilization of foreign assets held by senior officials have prompted equally feeble responses. Consequently, the regime has maintained a stable and abundant revenue base, and external critics have had few means of economic leverage.

THE RECORD SO FAR

Since the electoral crisis of June 1993, a variety of interested groups have debated the appropriate international stance toward Nigeria's military administration. Much of the dispute has centered on official policy, especially the question of oil sanctions. On one side of the dialogue are an array of nongovernmental organizations (NGOs), including human rights and environmental groups, Africa-centered organizations, religious institutions, and community organizations. These groups, joined by many academics, have argued for sustained pressure on the regime to respect human rights and democratic norms. Tactics advocated have included public criticism, sanctions targeted at members of the government, and the possible imposition of a comprehensive oil embargo. The rationale for this policy is that democratization and improved human rights can be brought about only by penalizing the current government for its abuses and inflexibility.

This view has been opposed mainly by representatives of the private sector, as well as by some academics and policy analysts. They argue that confrontation is largely counterproductive, since it is likely to produce a military backlash that could entrench authoritarian rule, while also penalizing U.S. interests in Nigeria. In this view, quiet engagement with the Nigerian government holds the greatest prospect for constructive change, as the carrots of enhanced investment and international legitimacy are likely to be more effective than the blunt stick of sanctions.

The debate between the two approaches has persisted since General Abacha's accession to power, gaining particular intensity during the civil disturbances of mid-1994 and in the aftermath of the hangings of the Ogoni activists in November 1995. Much of the policy discussion, however, has been rendered moot by the evident reluctance of most G-7 countries to consider sanctions. Few of Nigeria's major trading partners (including the United States, Britain, France, Canada, Germany, Japan, and the Netherlands) are willing to discuss any measures more stringent than the current marginal restrictions on military assistance, aid, foreign travel, and cultural exchange.[28] Explorations by U.S. and Canadian leaders for consensus on more assertive action have met with little response from other countries.

Without a broad-based commitment to a petroleum embargo, the United States would be faced with the prospect of imposing unilateral sanctions. There is broad recognition that unilateral action would be ineffective in pressuring the Nigerian government, since oil is highly mobile in international markets.[29] Moreover, unilateral action by the United States would leave American oil companies and other investors vulnerable to forfeiture or pressure at the hands of Nigerian authorities. Thus, neither U.S. policy objectives nor the country's collateral interests would be served by unilateral petroleum sanctions, and multilateral sanctions appear to be precluded at present.

Parallel diplomatic approaches and track-two initiatives have also met with limited success. These have been carried out through a number of channels. Two confidential presidential envoys from the United States, Ambassador Donald McHenry and (then) Representative Bill Richardson, made a series of approaches to General Abacha between 1994 and 1996. Private citizens, including Jesse Jackson and South Africa's Archbishop Desmond Tutu, have also explored dialogue with the military regime. Several fact-finding panels and special delegations have organized missions to Nigeria, including groups from the United Nations, the Commonwealth, and nongovernmental organizations from the United States. Such undertakings have not yielded conspicuous progress on fundamental political issues, especially human rights practices. The record of these efforts suggests that Nigerian political leaders have regarded informal diplomacy as a useful tactic for fending off external pressure while buying time for the consolidation of their programs.

TOWARD A BALANCED STRATEGY

Alternative prescriptions for policy toward Nigeria grow out of different analyses of the current situation. If the crisis is diagnosed simply as a transient leadership problem, then pressure on the present government, or engagement with senior officials, might be sufficient to promote change. Over time, and with the proper combination of incentives, the regime could conceivably be induced to move in a less repressive and predatory direction. From this perspective, a change of rulers or a shift to civilian government would be sufficient to alleviate the present impasse, and to restore equilibrium in political and economic affairs.

If the current situation is viewed as symptomatic of a broader systemic crisis of governance, however, then more varied and extensive approaches are warranted. Many observers, both within Nigeria and abroad, ascribe the country's travails to a basic set of structural problems affecting the society, the economy, and the political system. Foremost among these are the divisive effects of ethno-regional competition; the malign impact of excessive economic centralization; and the debilitating legacy of regime instability and military intervention. These features of the Nigerian syndrome cannot be adequately addressed by a shift of regime. In this view, political transition is a necessary but insufficient condition for long-term change.

The diverse challenges to development and stability in Nigeria suggest that international responses should be framed more broadly to encompass aspects of social and economic restructuring as well as political reform. As noted earlier, external initiatives may be directed mainly at the conduct of elites, or toward alterations in institutions or social structure. The current policy debate in the United States—concerned mainly with the balance between pressure and engagement—focuses on measures affecting the short-term actions of political leaders. While this is obviously a crucial dimension of the problem, such an approach overlooks opportunities for engaging other segments of Nigerian society, notably nongovernmental organizations and the business community. These groups may be instrumental in fostering more permanent changes in national institutions and behavior.

An essential component of long-term political reform can be addressed through a strategic focus on Nigerian civil society. This approach entails two aspects, the first being direct assistance to Nigerian NGOs and the second comprising efforts to preserve or enhance opportunities for popular participation. This strategy would combine track-two initiatives to enhance political rights and aid conflict resolution at the nongovernmental level with capacity-building initiatives to strengthen the role of civic organizations.

Civil society encompasses a broad array of autonomous nongovernmental organizations: trade unions, professional and business associations, women's and student organizations, religious institutions, community associations, and ethnic solidarity societies.[30] The lessons of international experience illustrate the importance of a vigorous civil society for democratic development. The dispersal of social power (notably in the private sector and the professions) provides an essential check on excessive centralization of political authority. This is an especially important consideration in Nigeria's pluralistic society. Civic associations also offer an important foundation for participatory government and a potential deterrent to the arbitrary uses of power. Pressures from organized social groups can be a catalyst for democratic transition, and the process of negotiation and accommodation within civil society offers an important arena for conflict resolution in divided societies.

There are compelling reasons for a strategy in Nigeria that focuses on civil society. The current political configuration in Nigeria suggests the need to take a long view with respect to the problem of political change. There are few immediate levers for bringing about rapid political reform, yet there are outlets for affecting the capacities of political actors over the longer term.

A more vigorous and autonomous realm of civic associations could hasten the onset of democratic rule in Nigeria. In comparing global instances of democratic transition, it is evident that independent pressures from societal groups are often instrumental in persuading authoritarian regimes to exit. Even when the departure of rulers is effected mainly through negotiation between opposition elites and incumbent leaders, popular participation is usually influential in shifting the balance of forces. In the absence of countervailing influences from domestic society, authoritarian incumbents have few inducements to abdicate power. Thus, civil society is an important catalyst in the process of democratic change—one that has been largely overlooked by external actors.

The development of resources within civil society can encourage an environment conducive to democratic politics. This is not the sole (or even primary) condition for democratic change in Nigeria, yet it is an essential element in the process of political development. Compacts between civilian and military elites and problems of institutional reform must also be addressed if Nigeria is to achieve a durable democratic settlement.[31] But the foundations of popular participation and social accord must be reinforced in order to strengthen the basis of civilian electoral rule and discourage abuses of power by politicians or military leaders.

An additional function of civil society pertains to conflict resolution. Nigerian society embraces a number of incipient conflicts in which nongovernmental actors can play a constructive role. Any lasting compact for the reform of civilian-military relations, for instance, is likely to involve some participation of civic organizations in negotiations with the military establishment. Moreover, direct contacts among representatives of the country's major ethnic, religious, and cultural blocs offer a necessary supplement to governmental policies of state creation and revenue allocation. The inclusion and engagement of civil society can play a vital role in resolving the quandary of governance and averting major ethno-regional strife.

Initiatives directed toward capacity building among Nigerian NGOs constitute only one part of a comprehensive strategy. Action to support civil society is unlikely to be effective in the absence of a favorable domestic environment for political activity. Consequently, international initiatives to enlarge and protect political space for Nigerian NGOs should be pursued in tandem with direct assistance to such organizations. The expansion of an open arena for political activity in Nigeria could provide the most important enabling condition for long-term development. Current pressures on the government of Nigeria to respect human rights and enlarge political liberties are important components of this strategy. International advocacy might entail increased pressure on the military regime, if existing channels of engagement and inducement prove fruitless.

— 5 —

CARROTS, STICKS, AND COOPERATION
ECONOMIC TOOLS OF STATECRAFT

David Cortright and George A. Lopez

The use of economic sanctions and incentives has become increasingly common in the conduct of international policy. Sanctions have been imposed recently to contain military aggression in Iraq and the former Yugoslavia, to restore democracy in Haiti and Burundi, and to advance human rights in South Africa. Inducement strategies have been used to prevent nuclear proliferation in North Korea and the former Soviet Union, to encourage peace processes in El Salvador and the Middle East, and to facilitate military demobilization in Africa and Eastern Europe. Sanctions have been used as a means of pressuring abusive regimes to cease aggression or human rights violations, while incentives have been employed to encourage disarmament, military demobilization, and conflict settlement.

Both approaches have direct relevance for conflict prevention. Sanctions tend to be imposed in response to acts of aggression or abuse that have already occurred, while incentives are often used to head off a crisis or prevent a recurrence of violence. Much has been written about sanctions and incentives separately, but few attempts have been made to analyze the two approaches together.[1] In this chapter we examine the uses of sanctions and incentives and compare their respective costs and benefits. We elucidate the factors that account for success or failure and the conditions under which sanctions and incentives are likely to be most effective. We pay particular attention to the political context of each and their impact on internal dynamics within target/recipient states. We conclude with a discussion of the advantages of incentives over sanctions in building the long-term foundations for international cooperation.

THE RISE OF ECONOMIC STATECRAFT

Sanctions and incentives have always been part of international policy, but their prominence and the frequency of their use have increased in recent years. The changing nature of economic sanctions policy in the post–cold war world has been particularly pronounced. Prior to 1990, when East-West cooperation was rare, sanctions episodes were predominantly unilateral, in most cases involving the United States acting alone. Multilateral sanctions were imposed by the United Nations only twice, against Southern Rhodesia (1965) and South Africa (1977). Since the end of the cold war, a new pattern of sanctions use has emerged: The number of episodes has increased, and nearly all of the major cases have been multilateral, usually under the auspices of the UN Security Council. Comprehensive or partial multilateral sanctions have been imposed against Iraq (1990), the Federal Republic of Yugoslavia (1991), Libya (1992), Liberia (1992), Somalia (1992), Haiti (1993), parts of Angola (1993), and Rwanda (1994). In July 1996 the nations of eastern Africa imposed sanctions against the military government of Burundi, with backing from the Organization of African Unity (OAU) and the United Nations.

Although the trend toward multilateral sanctions is unmistakable, unilateral sanctions have remained an option for the United States. Some argue that the United States has the economic and political power to impose unilateral sanctions and should use them, while others caution that such unilateral action can cause diplomatic frictions and impede the prospects for cooperation on other matters. U.S. sanctions against Cuba were tightened following the March 1996 destruction of two private American airplanes by Cuban fighters; unilateral sanctions against Iran have also been strengthened. In both cases, secondary sanctions and extraterritoriality measures have been mandated against nations or companies that continue to trade with the target country. These measures have aroused hostility and resentment among U.S. allies in Europe and elsewhere, however, adding weight to the argument that multilateral sanctions are the preferable form of economic coercion.

The use of inducement strategies has also become more prevalent. One of the most prominent examples has been the use of incentives to prevent nuclear proliferation in North Korea. In response to Pyongyang's announced intention to withdraw from the Nuclear Nonproliferation Treaty in March 1993, the United States joined with South Korea and Japan to craft a set of economic and diplomatic incentives that persuaded North Korea to abandon its apparent nuclear ambitions. In the Agreed Framework of October 1994, the United States and its partners offered to provide North Korea with fuel oil; new, less-proliferation-prone nuclear reactors; and the beginnings of diplomatic recognition. In exchange, North Korea agreed to accept international inspections and controls on its nuclear program. As of this writing, the agreement is holding, and North Korean production reactors and reprocessing facilities remain shut down under international inspection.

In the former Soviet Union, Ukraine and Kazakstan were persuaded to give up the nuclear weapons on their soil in exchange for economic assistance, improved diplomatic relations, and security assurances from Russia and the West. Small arms disarmament has also been aided by incentives policies (as observed by Edward J. Laurance in this volume), mostly through weapons buyback and turn-in programs linked to peace settlements. In Bosnia, pledges of economic assistance from bilateral donors and international financial institutions have been used to encourage implementation of the Dayton accords. In the Baltic Republics and Germany, housing construction assistance for Russian army officers helped speed the withdrawal of the Soviet army and cleared away some of the last vestiges of the cold war in Eastern Europe. In El Salvador, the United States offered economic incentives to both the Salvadoran government and the guerrilla forces of the Farabundo Martí National Liberation Front (FMLN) to facilitate peace negotiations and assure implementation of the resulting agreement.

These and other examples demonstrate the relevance and increasing importance of incentives in the prevention of international conflict. They also illustrate some of the complexities and difficulties involved. In the North Korea case, critics charged that the Agreed Framework could be interpreted as a reward for wrongdoing that would encourage other states to engage in similar transgressions in the hope of obtaining like rewards. The greatest concern about inducement strategies is that they may inadvertently become a form of appeasement. One way of mitigating this danger is to package incentives in a step-by-step reciprocal process that conditions the delivery of rewards on specific concessions from the recipient. This model is followed in the Agreed

Framework accord with North Korea, with each incentive from the United States and its partners tied to clearly delineated, observable steps toward denuclearization by North Korea. This approach can help to overcome the "moral hazard" of incentives and allow for the constructive use of inducement strategies.

Mixing Carrots and Sticks

Carrots (incentives) and sticks (sanctions) are spoken of separately, but they are closely related. Ending a negative sanction may be considered a positive incentive, while removing an incentive can be a sanction. In economic theory, incentives and sanctions are often interchangeable. An incentive is a positive sanction; a sanction is a negative incentive. Each is designed to influence the recipient and bring about a desired change of behavior.

In diplomatic practice, carrots and sticks are usually combined. Incentives may be offered to increase the attractiveness of a preferred course of action, while sanctions are threatened if objectionable behavior is not halted. As Alexander George has emphasized, coercive diplomacy often requires offers in addition to threats to achieve success. According to David Baldwin, the use of negative sanctions can lay the groundwork for the subsequent application of positive incentives.[2] In the former Yugoslavia, the promise to lift sanctions was an effective incentive in gaining the participation of the Milosevic regime in the Dayton peace process. The United States has maintained an "outer wall" of sanctions (for example, blocking Belgrade's membership in international financial institutions) and has made the removal of these restrictions dependent on, among other things, cooperation in preventing conflict in the South Balkans, especially Kosovo. In North Korea, the offer of economic and diplomatic incentives was accompanied by the threat of sanctions and the movement of U.S. military forces in and around the Korean Peninsula; this simultaneous coercive message no doubt enhanced the appeal of the proposed inducements. As Alexander George has emphasized, deterrence is most effective, especially with respect to crisis prevention, when it includes inducements for cooperation as well as punishments for resistance. What the stick cannot achieve by itself may be accomplished by combining it with a carrot.[3]

Combining sanctions with incentives can help to avoid moral hazards. Researchers have found that incentives work best when they are offered from a position of strength rather than out of weakness. If conciliatory gestures are made pusillanimously as a substitute for decisive action, the recipient may indeed attempt to exploit the situation and engage in further aggression. According to Martin Patchen, incentives work best when they flow from strength and are accompanied by a latent threat capacity. Russell Leng has similarly observed that offers "are more likely to be effective when the influencer has the requisites for the effective use of negative inducements as well."[4] When carrots are mixed with sticks, or at least the threat of sticks, the danger of appeasement and of encouraging wrongdoing can be diminished.

The decision whether to emphasize incentives or sanctions in a given situation depends on the nature of the problem and the objectives being served. When the issues involved have a long-term horizon and do not pose an immediate threat to peace, incentive policies will be more effective. When there is a more urgent crisis, especially a conflict involving mass suffering or posing a great danger to international security, a more coercive response may be necessary. Michael S. Lund suggests in this volume that a more forceful international involvement in Burundi at an earlier stage of the crisis might have been more effective than the attempts that were made at mediation. When the policy of the targeted regime is perceived as exceptionally heinous (e.g., apartheid in South Africa) or the transgression is a threat to international peace (as with Iraq's invasion of Kuwait), incentives must give way to a more coercive strategy. Coercive measures are more appropriate and effective for addressing crises involving overt aggression and deadly conflict. Inducement strategies are preferable for creating the long-term foundations for peace and cooperation and for ameliorating conflict situations before they reach the crisis stage. One approach addresses an immediate crisis of violent conflict, while the other seeks to create the long-term conditions for reducing the likelihood of such conflict.

The mix of carrots and sticks also depends on the relationship between the parties. When relations between initiator and recipient are distant or highly conflictual, it may be difficult to craft an effective incentives policy; the communication and bargaining aspects of an inducement process are more uncertain when the two sides are hostile and distrustful of one another. At the opposite end of the spectrum, where the relationship is more cordial and offers promise of cooperation, incentives will be easier to initiate and sustain. As Arnold Wolfers has noted, inducements tend to be more effective in cooperative contexts, when relations between the actors are friendly.[5] In hostile environments, achieving cooperation is more problematic.[6]

Even when there are troubled political relations, however, incentives can be successful. Few countries were more hostile and distant from one another than the United States and North Korea prior to 1994, yet the two were able to negotiate a successful compromise to the nuclear crisis with the aid of incentives. The negotiations fared poorly at first, as the two sides traded ultimatums and threats, but a more constructive atmosphere eventually emerged. The bargaining that led to the Agreed Framework was greatly aided by the mission to Pyongyang of Jimmy Carter in June 1994, which helped to break the diplomatic ice between the two countries and opened the door to high-level dialogue. It may be hard to get started when relations between two countries have been adversarial, but once the process of dialogue begins, mutual accommodation becomes possible. Even in the most contentious circumstances, skillful, incentives-based diplomacy can bring success.

HOW SANCTIONS WORK

Although sanctions have become increasingly common, many doubt their effectiveness. Some view sanctions as an ineffective bromide intended to placate public demands for action but incapable of achieving real results.[7] Eminent scholars share this skepticism. Margaret Doxey, whose work on sanctions has appeared in multiple editions, states that "sanctions will not succeed in drastically altering the foreign and military policy of the target."[8] If the goal of sanctions is defined in purely instrumental terms, their effectiveness is indeed limited. Gary Hufbauer and his colleagues at the Institute for International Economics (IIE) have concluded that "sanctions are seldom effective in impairing the military potential of an important power, or in bringing about major changes in the policy of the target country."[9] Sanctions serve multiple purposes, however, and these must be assessed as well when calculating impact. As Alan Dowty has argued, "The 'success' of sanctions depends on what goals they are measured against."[10] Sanctions can serve symbolic or expressive purposes, such as reinforcing international norms. Sanctions can send a message of disapproval to an abusive regime or of solidarity to its domestic opposition. Sanctions may also serve as a deterrent to future wrongdoing by the target regime or others. These symbolic purposes of sanctions can have important influence on international affairs, especially in upholding standards of democracy, human rights, and nonproliferation. Sanctions also may have implicit goals that are not stated in Security Council resolutions or official documents but are widely shared by the major powers. This is the case with sanctions against Libya and Iraq, which have been maintained on a long-term basis, primarily at U.S. and British insistence, as a form of political and military containment.

Although sanctions traditionally have been considered tools of interstate policy, many of the recent uses of the instrument have involved intrastate disputes. This is most clearly illustrated in South Africa and Haiti, where sanctions were used to advance human rights and democratic rule. The case of South Africa is widely considered a success, while sanctions in Haiti proved ineffective and gave way to U.S. military intervention. The case of Bosnia represents more of a hybrid, with sanctions imposed against the newly distinct state of Yugoslavia as a means of halting aggression by Serbs within Bosnia. In this case sanctions were considered at least a partial success in moderating the behavior of Serbian authorities in Belgrade. Sanctions have been used within states against armed factions that violated initial peace settlements. In Cambodia, sanctions were imposed against the Khmer Rouge, and in Angola sanctions were applied against territory controlled by the National Union for the Total Independence of Angola (UNITA). The enforcement of these measures was problematic, however, and their contribution to the settlement of conflict in the two cases is uncertain. There seems to be no discernible pattern regarding the effectiveness of sanctions in intrastate as opposed to interstate conflicts.

The most important empirical study of sanctions, conducted by the Institute for International Economics, necessarily focused on officially declared goals. The IIE study examined 116 sanctions episodes between 1914 and 1990 and found an overall success rate of 34 percent: sanctions made a significant contribution toward achieving the purposes for which they were imposed in one-third of the cases.[11] This effectiveness rate compares favorably with that for the use of military force.[12] The IIE study found that sanctions are most effective when economic costs are high for the target but low for the initiator, when the initiator is much larger than the target, and when the target and initiator have extensive trade relations. Sanctions also take time to achieve their political effects, on average nearly three years.[13]

The effectiveness of sanctions depends greatly on swift and comprehensive implementation and rigorous enforcement. Cooperation among the states capable of trading with the target is essential. In many cases, however, sanctions have been either poorly implemented or ineffectively enforced. In Haiti sanctions suffered from inconsistency (the initial Organization of American States embargo left gaping loopholes) and flawed implementation (the Governors Island agreement lifted sanctions before the actual return of exiled President Aristide). Many nations lack the legal, administrative, and institutional capacity for implementing and enforcing multilateral sanctions. In the case of sanctions against the Federal Republic of Yugoslavia, implementation steadily improved during the course of the sanctions regime as regional European institutions made important and innovative contributions to enforcement. The European Union and the Organization for Security and Cooperation in Europe established Sanctions Assistance Missions to monitor commercial traffic, and NATO and the Western European Union created a "Sharp Guard" naval interdiction force in the Adriatic Sea. These innovations made the sanctions against the former Yugoslavia the most effective in history, according to a UN report.[14] As a result, sanctions helped to moderate Belgrade's war policies.[15] The Yugoslav example suggests that the active participation of regional security institutions may be crucial to enhancing sanctions' effectiveness.

The case of Nigeria illustrates the problems that result from a lack of consensus among international actors. Following the annulment of the June 1993 election results and the November 1995 executions of Ogoni activists, the United States barred all military sales to Nigeria and broadened its ban on U.S. visas for junta members and supporters. The European Union imposed an arms embargo, travel restrictions, and a sports boycott. The Commonwealth Ministerial Action Group suspended Nigeria from membership but stopped short of outright expulsion. The Organization of African Unity, however, has been reluctant to condemn its most populous member. As Peter M. Lewis notes in this volume, Nigeria's leading creditors and trading partners in Western Europe want to preserve ongoing commercial interests and have parried proposals to impose tougher sanctions. An oil embargo against Nigeria could be readily enforced and would have a major impact on the regime in Abuja, but the lack of international consensus so far has precluded the effective use of sanctions.

One of the most important empirical findings from the IIE study is that financial sanctions have a higher success rate (41 percent) than do the more widely imposed general trade sanctions (25 percent).[16] Financial sanctions include such measures as the freezing of foreign assets, the cancellation of debt rescheduling, the withholding of credits and loans, and restrictions on travel, commerce, and communications. These forms of financial pressure are often found in combination with trade sanctions and add powerful leverage with respect to a target regime. Carefully crafted financial sanctions allow coercive pressures to be targeted against the economic and political elites responsible for wrongdoing. Financial sanctions also tend to have a multiplier effect within the target country. When external governments or multilateral institutions freeze assets or ban lending and investment activities, financial institutions abroad and at home may be prompted to reconsider their commitments as well. Banks are acutely sensitive to uncertainty and the perception of risk, and they may be reluctant to make commitments in nations facing financial sanctions. Because financial sanctions are more focused and exert pressure primarily on elites, their humanitarian consequences for vulnerable populations may be less severe than those associated with broader trade sanctions. This has important significance for the moral legitimacy and political effectiveness of sanctions and can help to ensure that economic coercive measures achieve greater political gain with less civilian pain.

The conventional theory about how sanctions are supposed to work assumes that political change is directly proportional to economic hardship: the greater the economic pain caused by sanctions, the higher the probability of political compliance. Johan Galtung has termed this the "naive theory" of sanctions, because it fails to account for the efforts of the target state to adjust to or counteract the impact of sanctions.[17] Rather, this theory assumes that the population in the target state will react to the pain of sanctions by forcing political leaders to change policy. As Baldwin has observed, however, "the economic effects of sanctions do not necessarily translate into political impact."[18] There is no direct transmission mechanism by which social suffering is translated into political change. This is the case even in the most democratic of countries and is especially so in the authoritarian or dictatorial regimes that are the usual targets of sanctions.

In fact, economic sanctions may actually strengthen a target regime and generate a "rally-round-the-flag" effect. A regime may adopt defensive measures that enable it to withstand the pressures of economic coercion or that redirect the hardships onto isolated or repressed social groups while insulating power elites. The latter form of adjustment is especially evident in Iraq's response to UN sanctions. Rather than causing political disintegration, sanctions may evoke nationalist sentiments and generate autarchy in the target country. In some cases, sanctions may enrich and enhance the power of elites who organize and profit from smuggling and illicit trade activities. In Haiti, military and business elites close to the regime of Raoul Cedras controlled the black-market trading of oil and other vital commodities. In the former Yugoslavia, hard-line militia groups used their control of checkpoints and smuggling routes to enrich themselves and consolidate political power. Some amount of leakage is inevitable in the course of a sanctions regime, as shortages and rising prices create opportunities for profiteers, but when these operations become large-scale and fall under the domination of the political elites who are the target of sanctions, policy objectives are often undermined.

While sanctions sometimes cause a rally-round-the-flag effect, they can also generate internal opposition to the target regime. Sanctions may empower internal political forces and render more effective their opposition to a regime's objectionable policies.[19] As a report of the U.S. General Accounting Office has observed, "if the targeted country has a domestic opposition to the policies of the government in power, sanctions can strengthen this opposition and improve the likelihood of a positive political response to the sanctions."[20] In the case of South Africa, the opposition African National Congress actively encouraged stronger international sanctions and gained moral and political support from the solidarity thus expressed by the international community. Sanctions did not have a huge economic impact on South Africa, but the combination of external sanctions and the civil resistance campaign of the United Democratic Front helped to bring about a sweeping political transformation.[21] In Nigeria the lack of a strong, coherent domestic opposition has been a major constraint on the potential effectiveness of sanctions. As Peter Lewis notes, opposition efforts within Nigeria have suffered from division, demoralization, and opportunism. The absence of a powerful and united democratic movement has clouded the prospects for effective sanctions against Nigeria.

The prospects for an internal opposition effect depend substantially on the degree of support for sanctions within the target nation. When credible civil organizations and human rights movements within the target country support international sanctions, the moral legitimacy and likely political effectiveness of those measures are enhanced. In its 1993 study, *Dollars or Bombs*, the American Friends Service Committee argued that sanctions are morally justified when there is "significant support for sanctions within the target country among people with a record of support for human rights and democracy, or by the victims of injustice."[22] In her review of the ethics of sanctions, Lori Fisler Damrosch emphasized the importance of internal opposition in both the South African and Rhodesian cases: "I attach great significance to the fact that the authentic leadership of the majority populations called for the imposition, strengthening, and perpetuation of sanctions."[23]

In the case of very poor countries such as Burundi, the effects of sanctions may be subject to a natural targeting. As Lund, Rubin, and Hara point out in this volume, the vast majority of Burundi's population is engaged in subsistence agriculture, with little connection to external markets. The impact of the regionally imposed sanctions on this rural population has been less severe than for city dwellers, who include the military leaders who staged the July 1996 coup and their elite supporters. The economic effects of the sanctions have been more severe in Bujumbura than in the countryside, generating relatively greater pressure on elite wrongdoers.

A greater use of targeted financial sanctions may be a way of reinforcing internal opposition effects while minimizing the prospect of a rally-round-the-flag effect. By avoiding harmful impacts on vulnerable populations, targeted measures deny political elites the opportunity to rally broad political support. Instead of punishing the general population, financial sanctions apply pressure primarily on the political and military elites responsible for wrongdoing. While there are limits to how much sanctions can be fine-tuned, attempts to focus coercive pressures on elites can yield positive dividends. Targeting economic pressures against decision makers is the strategy that is most likely to produce the desired political changes within target nations. Combining this approach with support for democratic opposition movements offers the greatest opportunity to achieve the desired policy change within the target nation while minimizing adverse humanitarian consequences.

HOW INCENTIVES WORK

Incentives can be either conditional or unconditional. Cooperation theorists have emphasized what might be termed the power of positive reciprocity, the ability of cooperative gestures to induce similar behavior in others. Robert Axelrod and others have found that the simple tit-for-tat process, in which one party responds in kind to the gestures of the other, can be a highly stable form of cooperation.[24] Incentive policies, however, go beyond the concept of narrow reciprocity. Inducements are sometimes offered as part of a long-term process in which no immediate response is requested or expected. This is the so-called pure form of incentives, in which there is little or no explicit conditionality.[25] The purpose of incentives in such instances may be to establish the basis for cooperative relations in the future, or to help rebuild a society ravaged by war in the hope that this will prevent a renewal of bloodshed.

There are many forms of incentives, but the most powerful inducement for peaceful relations in the world today is access to the emerging system of political cooperation and economic development among the major states. A zone of relatively prosperous democratic peace now stretches from Japan and Australia to North America and through much of Europe. The states in this zone are characterized by economic cooperation and development, democratic governance, and peaceful relations with one another. While one can be critical of the inconsistencies and inequalities within and among these nations and their exploitation of others, the fact remains that access to this system of peaceful cooperation is an attractive inducement for many countries. The promise of improved political and economic relations with the major powers, especially the United States, has often served as an inducement for cooperation. For the countries of Central and Eastern Europe, including Serbia and Montenegro, the lure of integration with the European Union and NATO is a powerful incentive. Steven L. Burg notes that both sides in the Kosovo dispute have sought to please the United States in the wake of the Dayton accords, and that this gives Washington potential leverage for preventing conflict in the region. Conditioning access to the system of peaceful cooperative development on the observance of civilized rules of behavior can be an effective inducement for the prevention of conflict. Paul Schroeder has described this process as "association-exclusion," contrasting it with traditional "compellence-deterrence."[26] The greatest hope for a more cooperative future lies not in the power to punish, according to Schroeder, but in the creative use of association to reward those who abide by civilized standards of behavior while excluding those who do not.

The history of the cold war illustrates the potential of incentives to generate a positive response. Lloyd Jensen found in his review of U.S.-Soviet arms negotiations that concessions by one side tended to be reciprocated by the other.[27] William Gamson and Andre Modigliani examined eight episodes in which the West made conciliatory gestures toward the Soviet Union from 1946 to 1963; in seven out of the eight cases, the Soviet Union reciprocated with cooperative behavior. By contrast, when faced with hostile actions, each side tended to respond with "refractory" actions and increased belligerence.[28] Perhaps the most dramatic recent case of positive reciprocity occurred in September 1991 when President George Bush announced the unilateral demobilization of U.S. tactical nuclear weapons from ships and submarines and the removal and dismantlement of nuclear artillery and short-range missiles in Europe. This bold initiative was promptly reciprocated by Soviet president Mikhail Gorbachev, who announced a similar and even more sweeping withdrawal and dismantlement of tactical nuclear weapons from Soviet land forces and naval vessels.[29] The Bush initiative was prompted by a desire to rein in the far-flung Soviet nuclear arsenal at a time of rapidly disintegrating Soviet authority and thereby limit the danger of de facto nuclear proliferation. The reductions were highly effective in reducing the nuclear danger and constituted the largest single act of denuclearization in history.

The Bush-Gorbachev nuclear reductions and other mutual concessions at the end of the cold war were a partial reflection of Charles E. Osgood's important concept of GRIT (Graduated and Reciprocated Initiatives in Tension-Reduction). The GRIT strategy goes beyond simple reciprocity and proposes a sophisticated series of conciliatory measures designed to reduce tensions and distrust.[30] The initiating side announces a series of accommodating steps and continues these actions even in the absence of a reciprocal response. If the other side exploits the situation or acts in a hostile manner, the initiating side responds in kind, although only to the limited extent necessary to restore the status quo. If the other side reciprocates positively, the pace of conciliatory action is accelerated. The point of the strategy is to foster a sense of common identification and mutual interest in further cooperation and to reduce distrust and animosity.

The nature of the objectives sought is one of the most important variables affecting the potential effectiveness of incentives. Just as sanctions are more successful in achieving modest or limited policy changes, incentives are more likely to achieve small-scale change than sweeping political transformation. Arnold Wolfers has argued that incentives are more likely to be effective in the area of "low politics," where national sovereignty and territorial integrity are not at stake.[31] It is extremely difficult to persuade a state to trade territory or national security for economic benefits. On the other hand, if security assurances and the rewards of political association are included in the inducements package, even far-reaching political change may be achievable. Denuclearization successes in Ukraine and Kazakstan were facilitated not only by economic inducements but also by broader security and political assurances. The pursuit of major political objectives may be possible through incentives, but in such cases larger and more comprehensive inducements will be necessary.

The experience of attempting to use incentives for intrastate conflicts has been uneven. In El Salvador, the promise of U.S. aid and recognition was used effectively to induce both the government and the FMLN to implement the 1992 peace accords. Each side found greater advantage in accepting the benefits offered by the United States than in continuing the armed conflict. In Bosnia the use of inducements has been less successful. Despite major commitments of financial assistance from the European Union, the World Bank, and other international actors, Croats and Muslims have refused to cooperate in Mostar, while Serbs and Bosnian government representatives have made little progress in creating a genuine federal structure. Because of the deeply rooted nature of the conflict in Bosnia, even large-scale inducement efforts have been unable to overcome local hostilities.

The most successful incentives strategies are those that are focused on a single objective and consistently sustained over time. When there are multiple or conflicting objectives, the inducement process is likely to be confused and ineffective. U.S. policy toward Pakistan offers a classic case of conflicting and inconsistent purposes. In the late 1970s nonproliferation was the major priority, and sanctions were imposed against Islamabad. In the 1980s, however, Islamabad's cooperation was needed in the struggle against the Soviet invasion of Afghanistan—so U.S. aid and arms poured into Pakistan. The Reagan and Bush administrations certified, despite evidence to the contrary, that Pakistan did not have a nuclear weapons program. In 1990, as the Soviet army withdrew from Afghanistan, and Pakistan's assistance was no longer needed, nonproliferation resurfaced as the priority, and aid was abruptly canceled.

Competing interests and agendas are a particular problem in the application of aid conditionality by international financial institutions.[32] The World Bank has emphasized "structural adjustment" policies, which often require reductions in public sector spending, but the bank has also made commitments to alleviating poverty, which may necessitate major public investments in infrastructure, job creation, and social welfare. Structural adjustment policies may also conflict with military demobilization programs, such as those in Mozambique and Uganda. The joblessness and economic hardship caused by adjustment policies can make it more difficult for demobilized combatants to find employment.

The perception of value is one of the most important variables in the success of incentives. In economic theory, an incentive is calibrated to increase the value of the option preferred by the initiator over what the recipient would otherwise choose. An incentive seeks to raise the opportunity cost of continuing on the previous course of action by changing the calculation of costs and benefits. The scale of the incentive depends on the magnitude of the desired change in behavior: the greater the change, the larger the required inducements. Leonard Spector and Virginia Foran have applied the concept of "reservation price," a standard notion in economic theory, to the bargaining situation of nuclear weapons control; the reservation price means the lowest price a potential proliferator will accept for giving up its nuclear program.[33] The reservation price takes into account the sunken costs already invested in a nuclear program. For a country such as India, which has invested a vast quantity of scarce economic resources and a huge amount of political capital in its nuclear program over a period of more than thirty years, the reservation price is likely to be spectacularly high. In the case of North Korea, on the other hand, where the nuclear program was only partially completed when the crisis broke in 1993, the sunk costs were much lower and could be matched by the United States and its South Korean and Japanese partners.

Access to advanced technology is a highly valuable incentive. This is especially true for developing countries but applies to industrialized nations as well. William Long has found that access to technology raises the perceived value and utility of an incentives offer and is highly effective in encouraging bilateral cooperation.[34] Because technology is so crucial to both economic development and military capability, it has value in terms of the most fundamental objectives of government. The lure of military technology is especially great, although an overemphasis on weapons transfers can have counterproductive economic and political consequences. The World Bank and other international financial institutions now recognize excessive expenditures on weapons as an impediment to sustainable development. Edward J. Laurance notes in this volume that small-arms proliferation can also lead to a decline in aid from development donors, while contributing to a host of other adverse political and security consequences. Arms sales and an emphasis on military inducements may also reinforce a bias toward the use of military force to solve complex political problems and devalue the search for more nonviolent, civilian-oriented approaches to conflict prevention. Offering access to civilian technology carries none of these risks and is the preferable means of offering technology inducements.

The effectiveness of incentives also depends on credibility, which requires that the sender have a reputation for fulfilling pledges and a demonstrated ability to deliver the promised reward. Promptness in delivering a reward is especially important. The swift fulfillment of a pledge increases the influence of the promised reward and raises the likelihood of positive reciprocation.[35] Delays in the implementation of an incentive may impede cooperation. In Gaza and the West Bank, the failure of international lenders to deliver on the financial pledges made at the time of the 1993 Israeli-Palestinian accords has contributed to political problems and delays in the implementation of the peace process. Promises fulfilled far in the future are less effective in encouraging compliance. Cooperation theory emphasizes the importance of a quick response to conciliatory gestures as a way of assuring additional cooperation. According to Axelrod, the shorter the response time, the more stable the relationship and the more enduring the cooperation.[36]

Incentives can be offered by either a single state, such as the United States, or a multilateral institution, such as the Council of Europe. Each approach has advantages and disadvantages. A single nation usually can decide upon and implement an incentives strategy more effectively than a coalition. A single actor may also be better able to deliver on a promised reward and communicate a coherent objective. On the other hand, coalitions or multilateral institutions have more market power and a greater potential for offering security assurances. Multilateral participation is especially important in peace implementation and postconflict reconstruction. The enormous costs associated with rebuilding countries such as Bosnia or Angola make it impossible for any single country to shoulder the burden alone. A disadvantage of multilateral actors, however, is that sustaining a coherent policy commitment over time is more complex, especially if the inducement strategy involves security commitments and the provision of financial assistance. Differences among the senders may also send confused or contradictory messages to the recipient.

Economic and military power are important to the effectiveness of inducement strategies. The larger the market power of the sender or senders, the greater the potential for offering economic incentives. Military capabilities obviously influence the capacity for providing security assurances. These factors help to explain the leadership role of the United States and other major industrial nations. While these considerations of power are important, however, they are not sufficient. Reliability, political will, and the soundness of the underlying policy are more important to success than raw capabilities. The United States plays a leading role as both an individual initiator and a major player in multilateral coalitions and institutions. Most of the major cases of incentives policy involve the United States acting either alone or in partnership with others. Many argue that leadership from the United States is indispensable. Whether in fashioning the incentives package for resolving the nuclear crisis in North Korea, initiating and sustaining the Dayton peace process for Bosnia, or attempting to keep a lid on simmering disputes in Macedonia and Kosovo, American leadership has been decisive.

As with sanctions, the effectiveness of inducement strategies depends on how they affect internal political dynamics within the recipient nation. External attempts to change policy must be able to influence the political preferences of important actors within the recipient country. In his analysis of trade policy, Long has demonstrated how commercial preferences and technology transfers appeal to particular groups and constituencies within the recipient nation who are willing and able to mobilize on behalf of the reforms sought by senders.[37] By targeting benefits to stakeholders and potential allies within the recipient country, senders are able to use incentives with maximum political effectiveness. Etel Solingen has observed a linkage within some developing countries between support for trade liberalization and acceptance of cooperative security and nuclear nonproliferation goals. The political constituencies committed to economic globalization, according to Solingen, are less inclined to favor overt nuclearization and assertive nationalism. Solingen recommends using trade preferences to encourage these political dynamics: "Coalitions favoring steps toward denuclearization could be rewarded with a variety of trade benefits, investments, selective removal from export control list[s], debt relief, and the like."[38]

Attempting to achieve targeted influence in this way is a delicate matter. It is always better to frame incentives as assistance rather than "compellence." Overt influence attempts can backfire if they are perceived as interference or manipulation. Offering incentives that influence domestic politics requires finesse and aplomb, and a keen sensitivity to the traditions and culture of the recipient nation. Just as sanctions can generate a "rally-round-the-flag" backlash, inducement efforts may spark nationalist resentment and denunciations of attempts to "bribe" the recipient nation. Seemingly irrational concerns about national pride can override utilitarian calculations of costs and benefits. As with sanctions, incentive policies must consider the possibilities of unpredictable responses within the recipient nation.

Ultimately the success of an inducement strategy depends on subjective factors. As Denis Goulet has observed, "an incentive system can only sway a subject who is disposed to respond."[39] Moral and cultural considerations can be as important to the success of an incentives offer as purely material factors. David Baldwin has made the same point in noting that the value of an incentive depends on a recipient's perceptions of the situation and the baseline of previous expectations.[40] The intended beneficiaries of an incentive offer will always be the final judge of its effectiveness, which makes the assessment of a recipient's subjective feelings crucial to the prospects of success. Incentive policies can have unanticipated negative consequences if senders are insensitive to internal political dynamics. Incentives delivered to military elites or to corrupt political leaders can weaken the standing of constituencies seeking democratic reform and undermine the long-term prospects for cooperative behavior.[41] Understanding the likely internal consequences of inducements and targeting benefits to empower the supporters rather than the opponents of reform are key elements in the strategic design of incentives policy.

Goulet has proposed an approach to incentives policy that encourages popular participation as the key to mobilizing political support within the recipient nation.[42] This approach differs from strategies that target rewards to elites; the distinction lies in the nature of the recipient's internal political dynamics. If there is popular concern about selling out to foreign influence, or if there is a recalcitrant leadership that refuses to reform, a nonelite strategy may be preferable. Making an offer that is appealing to popular forces can help to minimize concerns about external interference.[43] Crafting proposals that benefit popular movements rather than narrow elites may empower such constituencies to overcome obdurate leaders. By enhancing the involvement of nonelite groups and empowering them to acquire political and economic rights, this approach targets assistance to those who often need it most, while providing concrete inducements for domestic constituencies to mobilize on behalf of reform and cooperation. This model of directing incentives to popular movements rather than governments is relevant to the alternative strategy for Nigeria proposed by Peter Lewis. Given the limitations of previous domestic opposition efforts and the profound crisis of governance in Nigeria, Lewis has recommended a strategic focus on empowering civil society. This approach would include direct assistance to reform-minded NGOs and greater efforts to enhance opportunities for popular participation in the political process. Lewis's strategy would de-emphasize short-term efforts to influence the Nigerian government and focus instead on a longer-term process of building effective and independent civic associations as a counterweight to corrupt elites. The prospects for achieving genuine and long-lasting political reform in

Nigeria depend on the empowerment of a stronger autonomous, democratic opposition movement. This can be achieved, according to Lewis, through a strategy of targeted engagement with and assistance to key sectors of civil society.

COMPARING SANCTIONS AND INCENTIVES

We conclude our essay with a series of direct comparisons of sanctions and incentives and an assessment of the relevance of these instruments to the challenge of preventing deadly conflict. One important difference between sanctions and incentives is in their cost to the initiator. In narrow accounting terms, a sanction is not a cost. When countries impose an embargo on an offending state, this does not show up as a line item in the national budget. As a result, some policymakers naively consider economic sanctions a kind of "foreign policy on the cheap."[44] In reality, sanctions impose significant costs on private companies and local communities, but since these losses do not appear as specific government expenditures, they are easy for political leaders to overlook or ignore. By contrast, foreign assistance, loan guarantees, and other forms of financial aid are listed as specific budgetary allocations, which can make them easy targets for budget cutters, especially in an era of fiscal austerity.

Trade preferences and technology incentives, however, appear to be relatively cost-free to governments and have become a favorite tool of economic statecraft. While trade incentives do not require budgetary allocations, they do have financial implications. U.S. budget legislation mandates that reductions in revenue from any source, including the lowering of tariffs, must be offset by tax increases or compensating budget reductions. Since trade incentives increase the overall level of commerce, however, they usually result in *greater* government revenues. Trade incentives also open up new opportunities for commerce that can benefit domestic constituencies.[45] Whereas sanctions impose costs on particular industries and communities, trade incentives can bring benefits to these groups. As a result, domestic constituencies in the initiator state may gain a stake in maintaining trade preferences and provide political support for sustaining the incentives policy. As noted earlier, incentives can create similar dynamics within the recipient country. In contrast to sanctions, which cause hardships for both initiator and recipient, trade incentives bring benefits to both. They are a classic win-win proposition.

A related advantage of incentives is that benefits can be designed and targeted to ameliorate the root causes of conflict. Whether the primary needs are economic, political, or security-related, inducement strategies can be packaged and delivered to meet those needs and lessen the likelihood of conflict. In the case of Ukraine, security assurances were added to the package of economic benefits offered to Kiev as a way of addressing concerns about Ukrainian vulnerability vis-à-vis Russia. In Germany, officials fashioned a targeted economic assistance program to pay the housing costs of Soviet army officers, thereby helping to overcome political obstacles in Russia to the rapid withdrawal of Soviet forces. This targeting of resources to meet specific political objectives is an important way in which incentives differ from sanctions. Where sanctions take away resources or deny benefits to contending parties, incentives add resources. When these rewards are targeted strategically to address the sources of conflict, the effectiveness of incentives is enhanced.

Incentives also differ from sanctions in their relationship to market forces. When incentives are offered, there is no natural tendency, as with sanctions, for black marketeers or third-party actors to step in and circumvent trade restrictions. As Eileen Crumm has observed, "Where market forces work against negative sanctions, they can reinforce positive ones."[46] Many scholars have noted that economic sanctions generate countervailing pressures that can undermine the effectiveness of such measures. A tightly enforced embargo will raise the price of imports in the target country and in the process create powerful motivations for cheating.[47] By contrast, an offer of incentives such as foreign assistance or concessionary loans will not create market pressures for another party to do likewise. Competing offers of assistance may result from political motives, but they are not generated by market forces. During the cold war the United States and the Soviet Union vied to provide incentive offers, but such competition is less likely now. Positive incentives work in harmony with the natural forces of the market and thus have a significant economic advantage over negative sanctions.

Sanctions and incentives also have differing impacts on international trade and the prospects for economic cooperation. One of the most significant, some would say most hopeful, characteristics of the post–cold war world has been the widespread expansion of free markets and the substantial increase in international commerce. Richard Rosecrance has spoken of "the trading state" phenomenon as a powerful antidote to war and armed conflict.[48] Expanding trade and economic interdependence can establish a long-term foundation for peace and enhanced international cooperation.

The use of economic sanctions runs counter to this trend. Peter van Bergeijk has argued that the increased use of negative sanctions may threaten the expansion of trade, thereby weakening the incentive for political cooperation that comes with increasing economic inter-dependence.[49] A related point is made by Jeffrey Garten, who fears that sanctions serve as a much-too-easy, common-denominator tool for poli-cies in international labor standards, human rights, and environmental protection—each of which can be better influenced by other means.[50] By contrast, positive measures encourage trade and international coop-eration and thereby contribute to long-term prospects for peace. Incentive policies provide a basis for long-term cooperation and under-standing and create the foundations for international stability.

Perhaps the greatest difference between sanctions and incentives lies in their impact on human behavior. Drawing on the insights of behavioral psychology, David Baldwin has identified key distinctions between the two approaches. Incentives foster cooperation and good-will, while sanctions create hostility and separation. Threats tend to generate reactions of fear, anxiety, and resistance, while the normal responses to a promise or reward are hope, reassurance, and attraction.[51] Threats send a message of "indifference or active hostility," according to Baldwin, while promises "convey an impression of sympathy and con-cern."[52] Incentives tend to enhance the recipient's willingness to coop-erate with the sender, while negative measures may impede such cooperation. Roger Fisher has argued that "imposing pain may not be a good way to produce a desired decision" or influence another's actions.[53] Whereas threats and punishment generate resistance, promises and rewards tend to foster cooperation.[54]

These differences have important implications for the conduct of political communications. One of the drawbacks of sanctions is that they close off channels of commerce and interaction, which can inten-sify misunderstanding and distrust. Inducement strategies do not carry this burden. Because incentives create less resentment and obstinacy in the recipient, communication is clearer and more precise, and negoti-ations are more likely to succeed. Punitive measures may be effective in sending a message of disapproval, but they are not conducive to con-structive dialogue. Sanctions may generate communications gridlock; incentives open the door to greater interaction and understanding.[55]

Our conclusion from the foregoing analysis is obvious. On bal-ance, incentives are preferable to sanctions as a means of attempting to influence the behavior of other states. We agree with Roger Fisher's conclusion that "the process of exerting influence through offers is more conducive to international peace than the process of exerting influence through threats."[56] While inducement strategies are not appropriate in every setting, and may be counterproductive if employed in the face of overt military aggression and gross violations of human rights, they have many advantages over punitive approaches. Incentives have the ability to generate positive reciprocity and can establish the basis for enhanced cooperation and trust. A diplomacy that employs carrots more often than sticks offers hope for transforming the international system and creating a more cooperative and peaceful world order.

The appropriateness of sanctions or incentives for preventing a specific conflict depends not only on the characteristics of the tools themselves but also on the nature of the conflict and the overall effectiveness of external involvement. Michael Lund suggests in his model of the multiple sources of conflict that when violent behavior and attitudes are deeply embedded and institutionalized, as in Burundi or the Balkans, attempting to bring about change is extremely difficult, especially in the short run. On the other hand, when violence results from the actions or words of specific leaders, with less systemic or institutional grounding, the prospects for influencing the course of events may be greater. Sanctions and incentives, like other tools of influence, will be more effective in changing immediate behavior than in erasing the underlying structural or systemic causes of violence. However, because of their unique ability to supply resources in situations of need and to create a climate of reassurance and cooperation between previously distrustful parties, inducement strategies offer greater promise for addressing the long-term sources of conflict. While sanctions will continue to be necessary as an immediate response to violent and abusive behavior, incentives can build the long-term foundations for greater peace and understanding.

— 6 —

SMALL ARMS, LIGHT WEAPONS, AND CONFLICT PREVENTION
THE NEW POST–COLD WAR LOGIC OF DISARMAMENT

Edward J. Laurance

The rise in ethnic and communal conflict since the end of the cold war has captured the attention of the international community. Most often a response has come after conflict has occurred. Recently an effort has been made in the direction of prevention. Conflicts that have died down or not as yet erupted have increasingly been the target of national governments, international organizations, and in particular those nongovernmental organizations (NGOs) that normally represent the most prevalent presence in these areas. The Center for Preventive Action (CPA) of the Council on Foreign Relations is one such effort, with the goal of averting or ameliorating conflict by promoting effective early attention.

Such an effort naturally evolves into a "comparative tools" exercise. What are the methods that work best in preventing conflict? The answer to this question revolves on how one assesses the causes of conflict. Such an analysis very quickly reveals a host of "root" causes—inequality among groups, relative deprivation, poverty, etc. And just as quickly these causes are seen as intractable in the short term. It is at this point that those focused on prevention turn to those methods that can have some effect on the outbreak or amelioration of conflict. This chapter discusses one such method, disarmament of light weapons and small arms.

Before devising methods for dealing with the weapons used in these conflicts, one needs to acknowledge the existence of an age-old debate: Do people kill people or do weapons kill people? Perhaps Albania can provide a relevant example. Ethnic Albanians live in both Macedonia and Kosovo and are one of the parties to ethnic tension in that region. In Albania itself, visited by members of CPA's South Balkans Project, we have seen the recent destabilization of the entire country due to armed violence. How did this happen? The "root" causes are known: the failure of the government to meet the needs of its people, economic crisis, corruption, fraudulent elections, and, in the short run, a failed pyramid scheme that caused a large segment of the people to lose their life savings. These conditions created significant grievances, as reflected in growing demonstrations and pressure on the government. Overnight, however, the situation changed from tension to massive armed violence owing to one factor: the almost unlimited supply of weapons available to all segments of the society as a result of the opening up of arsenals full of small arms and light weapons. The effects of this supply are clear for all to see. And not only in Albania. Should tensions rise in either Macedonia or Kosovo, Albanians in these countries are markedly more likely to be supplied with weapons from supporters in Albania as a result of recent events.

In other areas of concern to CPA, especially the Great Lakes region of Africa, the supply of arms to the participants in these conflicts has exacerbated the situation and frustrated the many efforts of NGOs, the OAU, and the UN to resolve the conflict and prevent the outbreak of additional violence. Kathi Austin, a field researcher for the Human Rights Watch Arms Project, highlighted the role of weapons in this conflict. "There has been an attempt to portray this crisis as a local, clan-based rivalry, but there are external actors engaged in the militarization of the region."[1] These include actors in South Africa, the People's Republic of China, several countries of Western Europe, the former Yugoslavia, and Bulgaria. More recently, the situation in eastern Zaire revealed major supply activity by private dealers bringing in surplus weapons from the former Soviet Union.[2]

The effect of all these weapons pouring into the Great Lakes region was seen quite clearly when the international community was considering a rescue force for the hundreds of thousands of refugees who had fled Rwanda and were now in eastern Zaire. The magnitude of armaments possessed by the militants among the refugees was such that the NGOs in the region attempting to deal with the humanitarian problems were calling for an international force to conduct a disarmament campaign. The major powers who would have supplied the troops for a humanitarian mission to open up corridors for refugees to return to Rwanda balked at the prospect of disarming the militants—"too dangerous." But without such disarmament, humanitarian assistance was becoming impossible. "It is ridiculous to think that the guys with the guns are going to stand aside for the guys with the soup pots. To imagine that you can do anything else if you don't disarm these guys is illogical, to put it mildly."[3]

As a general approach, then, doing something about the armaments available to participants in a conflict is essential to prevent and mitigate conflict. But how? This chapter addresses this question by first laying the groundwork for a new logic of disarmament, focusing on the shift in the nature of conflicts being addressed by the international community, the use of weapons (small arms and light weapons) whose characteristics and effects present unique problems, and the rise of a variety of sources of supply that defy previously developed attempts to control weapons transfers. With this as background, we then describe new approaches to dealing with weapons so as to prevent or mitigate conflict, which are described as a typology of disarmament techniques practiced in varying phases of conflict. The chapter concludes by summarizing these developments as a new logic of disarmament, a set of principles for using disarmament as a policy tool in preventing conflict.[4]

THE NEW POST–COLD WAR ERA ENVIRONMENT

In the post–cold war era, the nature of the conflicts dominating the international landscape has changed, as has the class of weapons used to fight them. Intrastate conflict has gained partial recognition as a global problem, which was not possible during the cold war. These conflicts are deadlier than ever, owing to the increased destructiveness of more easily available weapons.

A NEW TYPE OF CONFLICT, WITH GLOBAL CONSEQUENCES

Five years after the end of the Gulf War, the international community has begun to deal more effectively with weapons of mass destruction. The discovery that Iraq was in the process of building a nuclear weapon applied some shock therapy in support of those promoting international collaboration in nonproliferation. The Chemical Weapons Convention opened for signature in January 1993 and became operative as a treaty in April 1997. This released the international community from the constraints of the cold war, freeing it to deal with conventional weapons as a primary factor in conflict for the first time.

There were many policy options proposed to prevent the recurrence of a Gulf War type of conflict. The United Nations Register of Conventional Arms and the Wassenaar Arrangement as a successor to COCOM (Coordinating Committee) are both attempts to deal with the negative effects of conventional arms buildups.[5] There has also been good news in preventing and mitigating conflict featuring major conventional weapons. Five years into this new era, the threat of interstate conflict carried out with major conventional weapons, with the possible exception of the Korean Peninsula or between India and Pakistan, is lower than it has been since 1945. Even the often-cited "arms race" in East Asia is a pale imitation of the action-reaction cycle that dominated the cold war era in places like the Middle East.

But in place of threats of interstate war are more than fifty intrastate conflicts, fought almost exclusively with small arms and light weapons. The dominant type of warfare in this new era is defined by insurgency, terrorism, and a heavy emphasis on the psychological aspects of warfare. The combatants rely on being aggressive and mobile, are often nonmilitary in nature, and have few traditional supply lines. The conflicts usually occur in countries or regions where the state cannot provide adequate security for its citizens. In such an environment, small arms and light weapons are the weapons of choice. As a result of the fluidity of such conflicts, a significant percentage of these arms are "supplied" through capture from opposing fighters, raiding of government arsenals, and such means.

This new type of conflict situation is also more global, attracting the significant involvement of multilateral institutions. First, United Nations peace operations face daily the consequences of this unchecked accumulation of small arms and light weapons, whether they are engaged in preventive diplomacy, peacekeeping, peace enforcement, or postconflict reconstruction. Such operations now include disarmament in order to create a more stable environment, with fewer weapons in the hands of those who threaten peace efforts. Second, the acquisition of these weapons often occurs across national boundaries. Multilateral actions are often the only approach that can achieve success in stemming this traffic. Third, a major cause of these conflicts is the inability of affected states to cope with the influx of these weapons into their territory. Conscious of international organizations' traditional responsibility for capacity building, the UN, the World Bank, and other institutions have begun to respond to states who request assistance in dealing with these arms buildups. Whereas in a previous era disarmament focused on arms held by specific "enemies," the new type of conflict often focuses on halting or reversing arms accumulations within the society and the state. This has been the goal of operations in central and southern Africa, the former Yugoslavia, Guatemala, and El Salvador.

THE NEW FACTOR OF SMALL ARMS AND LIGHT WEAPONS

Availability. Since 1990, small arms and light weapons have become more easily available to groups and individuals who have used them to destabilize governments and social systems. The end of the cold war saw a large surplus of new and used light weapons left over from the inventories of the major military powers—a surplus due in part to their lower defense budgets and lower levels of forces armed with such weapons. Additionally, some newly independent states of the former Soviet Union with a large surplus of this class of weapon experienced a short-term collapse of their export control systems, resulting in an outflow of the weapons to regions of conflict. Ironically, many of these weapons found their way onto the open market as a result of incomplete disarmament mechanisms that were part of the otherwise successful resolution of several major conflicts in Central America (El Salvador) and Africa (Mozambique).

This increased availability of light weapons coincides with the aforementioned rise in intrastate conflicts and a concurrent loss of control over these conflicts by the major powers. The surplus of light weapons, whose export is much more susceptible to the control of, and covert supply by, private parties, has had little difficulty finding its way into these zones of ethnic and intrastate conflict. The problem is further exacerbated by an additional development—the adoption of trade in light weapons by the illicit networks developed for drugs and laundered money. These smaller conflicts do not need the high-technology weapons produced and traded during the interstate wars of the cold war era. While some of the atrocities in these intrastate conflicts were carried out using weapons such as tanks and heavy mortars, most were carried out using lighter weapons that went undetected by both governments and the news media covering these conflicts. This spiral of weapons accumulation and violence has the tragic consequence of creating fear among previously secure populations, who often respond by acquiring small arms for their personal protection and security.

In such an environment, where supply is often effectively unlimited, disarmament efforts must focus on demand. Most of the traditional ways of preventing the escalation of arms buildups into conflict, such as supplier cartels, export controls, and transparency (the public availability of information), can do little in the face of this new type of supply system.

Unique Characteristics. Small arms and light weapons are conventional weapons, in that they are not weapons of mass destruction. They have, however, an additional set of characteristics that set them apart from major conventional weapons, characteristics that have an impact on the possibilities of conflict, the destabilization of societies, and the efficacy of disarmament efforts in ameliorating their effects. (See Table 6.1 for a list of weapons dominating today's conflicts.)

TABLE 6.1
INVENTORY OF SMALL ARMS, LIGHT WEAPONS,
AND THEIR REQUIRED AMMUNITION

Small Arms

Revolvers and self-loading pistols
Rifles and carbines
Assault rifles
Submachine guns
Machine guns

Light Weapons

Hand-held under-barrel and mounted grenade launchers
Portable antiaircraft guns
Portable antitank guns, recoilless rifles
Portable launchers of antitank missile and rocket systems
Portable launchers of antiaircraft missile systems
Mortars of calibers up to 82 mm inclusive

Ammunition and Explosives Required

Cartridges (rounds) for small arms
Shells, missiles, and mines for light weapons
Mobile containers with missiles or shells for single-action, antiaircraft and antitank systems
Antipersonnel and antitank hand grenades
Antitank mines

Weapons in this class are typically smaller, weigh less, cost less, and are more portable and less visible than major conventional weapons. This enhances the capability of nonstate groups and criminals to acquire and transfer them. Furthermore, the lighter and smaller the weapon, the more likely it is that there are provisions for its legitimate use by citizens for personal security, hunting, and other culturally acceptable purposes. As a result, disarmament and arms control are made much more difficult. For example, the international community and the United Nations are attempting to use transparency as a tool to deal with the negative effects of excessive armaments. Transparency refers to the belief that the greater the public knowledge about weapons production, transfer, and accumulation, the greater the opportunity to avoid their negative consequences. But in the case of this class of weapon, transparency is notably lacking.

Weapons in this class do not require an extensive logistical and maintenance capability. Their prominence in current conflicts stems from the fact that these conflicts are waged by nonstate groups that require mobility and independence to achieve their objectives. These weapons can be carried by an individual combatant or in a light vehicle; they are weapons normally assigned to infantry units operating on land; and training is less important than in the case of major conventional weapons.

Small arms are essentially any means of causing lethal damage except by unarmed physical force. For example, machetes have been used in some of the conflicts being dealt with by the United Nations. While a machete is a culturally acceptable tool in many states, recent history has shown that this type of weapon can be accumulated in such numbers that, with the appropriate intentions, it can be used to destabilize a state and cause significant casualties, especially to civilians. Pistols, whose possession by an individual is often legitimate and justified, can also be destabilizing if accumulated in large numbers by nonstate groups that advocate and use armed violence.

New Modes of Acquisition. There is another dimension of this issue which sets the present era apart from previous arms control and disarmament actions. During the cold war, all classes of weaponry, even those now called small or light, were under the control of states. While not much was accomplished in the way of multilateral arms control during the cold war, a great deal of arms control occurred unilaterally, through export denials and other measures. Although production of and trade in arms is legal, states normally have policies and regulations controlling exports and a greater level of transparency than do private traders. In the case of small arms and light weapons, however, these restraints often do not apply.

There are a variety of ways to acquire small arms and light weapons:[6]

- **Indigenous production.** Unlike major conventional weapons, many developing countries manufacture high-quality armaments in this class, eliminating the necessity to rely on industrialized states for such weapons. Countries seeking more sophisticated weapons technology may import the technology and/or manufacture the weapon under license.

- **Legitimate import.** Countries that manufacture small arms and light weapons continue to legitimately export them, along with their surplus of used weapons. As a result, such weapons continue to be imported legally by countries in regions of conflict. This can take place as a grant (i.e., as foreign aid), particularly when a large army is decreasing in size and wishes to export its surplus weapons. Government-to-government sales take place as well, but the dominant mode of legitimate transfer is the commercial sale.

- **Illicit import.** The first variant of this mode is the covert or secret transfer of arms to a government from another government. This mode is less prevalent in the post–cold war period but continues to be an option for those states supporting guerrilla forces outside their borders. A second type occurs when a government, to bolster its own security and political power, arms subnational groups that support its political or social policies and act as a supplement to government security forces. This often takes the form of arming "self-defense" forces that retain the weapons when the need for such forces diminishes at the end of a peace process. A third variant of illicit imports is the black market. As United Nations arms embargoes have increased, and more and more conflicts involve nonstate groups, black-market suppliers have become the only source of arms for countries under embargo. Additionally, underground political organizations and criminal organizations, such as drug cartels, are forced to rely on this means of acquisition. The portability, low cost, and concealability of small arms and light weapons makes this mode of acquisition and transfer particularly effective.

◆ *In-country circulation.* One of the major differences between this class of weapons and major conventional weapons is that a significant amount of the supply is already in the region and sometimes in the country where it is in the greatest demand. It is more feasible, economically, militarily, and politically, to obtain the needed weapons without complicated export and import procedures. In many cases cross-border acquisitions are not required. The first such type of acquisition is theft from government arsenals and citizens. Second, the fluid nature of conflicts typical today ensures that ambushes and other tactics will be employed for the purpose of seizing weapons from opponents. In the conflict in El Salvador, the disarmament process revealed that both sides had significant quantities of weapons originally supplied to the other. Third, it is now common for subnational groups to conduct mutual arms deals. This has been prevalent in Liberia, where several groups were armed by others participating in the conflict. Fourth, arms transfers can take place between subnational groups and criminal organizations, especially when the former are used by the latter to protect their illegal activities. And a fifth mode can be termed the leaking pipeline: While one or more of the above modes of acquisition is being employed, weapons are siphoned off by either government officials or subnational groups.

THE CONSEQUENCES OF THE SMALL-ARMS EXPLOSION

Negative Consequences. Since the dawn of modern weaponry, reducing the negative effects of weapons has been primarily focused on military outcomes. In the type of conflicts now present in the international system, the effects are economic, social, and political as well as military. These effects are of four basic types.

First, the increase in the use of this class of weapons has heightened the destructiveness and lethality of conflicts. Individuals and groups who disagree politically can more easily resort to violence instead of resolving conflicts peacefully. Large accumulations of light weapons, especially assault rifles and hand grenades, increase the lethality of conflicts as compared with less capable weapons such as handguns and knives. This leads to greater numbers of civilian casualties and refugees, overwhelming health care systems and, in general, disrupting the economic development of the country.

The second basic effect is the increase in criminal or nonpolitical acts committed with these military-style weapons—armed robberies, hijacking, terrorism, stealing of livestock, drug trading, and smuggling. The criminal elements in some states are in some cases better armed, in quantity and/or quality, than the legitimate security forces. This also enhances the proliferation of agents of violence, including drug dealers and criminal gangs. Rival groups within a state compete to maintain inventories of equally capable equipment.

Third, the level of violence produced by these weapons is so high that it forces citizens to arm themselves, either personally or through private, nongovernmental security organizations. Additionally, the availability of military-style weapons has emboldened the disaffected in many parts of the world. Faced with little or no economic or social development, desperate citizens opt for acquiring a weapon for individual survival, to satisfy basic needs, or for commercial purposes. The end result is an overall increase in the number of weapons in the society.

Finally, the increased availability and use of this class of weapons threatens peace-building efforts. Recently reformed or reconstituted security forces in states undergoing transitions to democracy have reverted to repression when faced with increased criminal activity or intrastate violence. It has become more difficult to conduct development projects and programs, leading to a decline in economic aid from donors who question how their funds can achieve goals in a violent environment. Even when a UN peacekeeping operation is successful, the postconflict reconstruction process is imperiled by violence from small arms and light weapons. Eliminating the root causes of the violence would require socioeconomic development, effective democracy, and a credible judicial system—but these developments take time and are more difficult to sustain in an environment of indiscriminate access to the tools of violence.

Unique Challenges for Arms Control and Disarmament. Small arms and light weapons present some unique problems that require more difficult remedies than those devised for weapons of mass destruction and major conventional weapons.

First, in any arms control and disarmament effort, it is critical to recognize that there are underlying or root causes of intrastate conflict, regardless of the weapons involved. In hostilities dominated by small arms and light weapons, it is inherently more difficult to directly link the accumulation of weapons to the outbreak, conduct, exacerbation, and termination of conflict.[7] Second, most efforts at disarmament take into account the principles and purposes of the UN Charter, especially the right to self-defense, noninterference in the internal affairs of states, and the affirmation of the right to self-determination of all peoples. In the case of this class of weapon, these principles are more sensitive since the conflicts are often within a state's jurisdiction. In many instances, citizens can legitimately own and use small arms for personal security against crime, which may be difficult to distinguish from warfare.

Third, solving the problems caused in part by this class of weapon requires going beyond traditional arms control approaches. Solutions will require a broad scope of policy options involving such areas as development, human rights, judicial systems, and police work. The response must go beyond supply-restriction efforts, which dominate the approach to security problems created by weapons of mass destruction and major conventional weapons.

Fourth, this issue is challenging because this class of weapon is found in the inventory of every state's legitimate armed forces. Pistols, rifles, automatic weapons, hand grenades, and the like are manufactured for military purposes and are the mainstay of every army in the world. Although weapons of mass destruction and major conventional weapons can also be justified as legitimate tools of self-defense, not every state possesses them. Each state, however, possesses small arms and light weapons—with few international norms restricting such possession—and participates in the legitimate trade of these weapons.

Awareness. Despite these challenges, the casualties of the violence from small arms and light weaponry engaged in brush-fire wars have moved the international community to focus on the weapons themselves as a causal factor.

During the cold war, the arms control debate revolved around two competing hypotheses: People kill people versus guns kill people. At the nuclear level, solving the problem of the nuclear arms race between the United States and the USSR proceeded along one of two basic approaches: eliminating or transforming an evil Communist dictatorship (people kill people) or slowing, freezing, or eliminating the weapons seen as the cause of the problem (guns kill people). At the conventional arms level, attempts at arms control were normally condemned from the start, with the dominant view being that states have a sovereign right to defend themselves, and that arms control should follow conflict resolution, not the reverse. But now, the words and actions of the citizens, governments, and international organizations that work on conflict resolution point to a new emphasis on the weapons themselves.

In a September 1996 workshop held by the United Nations Experts Panel on Small Arms in South Africa, governmental witnesses from several countries, especially South Africa, made it very clear that the influx of AK-47s and hand grenades from both Mozambique and Angola was destabilizing the region and threatening to undo the progress made in the years since the end of the apartheid government.[8] In Rwanda, the scheduled delivery of light weapons by the government of South Africa to the government of Rwanda in October 1996 was suspended as a result of complaints from those in the region dealing with the conflict. In Haiti, the first priority for the U.S. Army troops entering the country under a UN mandate was to take action to buy or seize as many weapons as possible so as to enhance the success of the mission. Irrespective of the success of such a weapons-first approach (the results were mixed, as will be seen later in this chapter), the peacekeeping effort recognized that despite the obvious root causes of conflict, lowering the levels of armaments in the region was a required first step. In Northern Ireland, despite centuries of sectarian conflict and root causes that are known to all, progress will depend on resolution of the issue of decommissioning of weapons by both the IRA and the Protestant paramilitary forces.

The United Nations is turning its attention to the problems stemming from the proliferation of light weapons. Since 1993, the UN has been involved in assisting several countries in West Africa with problems resulting from light weapons. The UN Disarmament Commission produced a consensus report in 1996 that established guidelines for states that must deal with illicit trade in arms. In January 1995, the secretary-general reviewed the experience of the past three years and issued a *Supplement to an Agenda for Peace*. After reviewing the progress made in limiting proliferation of weapons of mass destruction, he called for "parallel progress in conventional arms, particularly with respect to light weapons." He introduced the concept of micro-disarmament. In the conflicts dealt with by the UN, he wrote, light weapons are those "that are actually killing people in the hundreds of thousands." He went on to refer to the "enormous proliferation of automatic assault weapons, anti-personnel mines (APM), and the like." He also identified the negative consequences of such proliferation, including the economic costs of acquiring such weapons, the dissipation of resources that could be used for development, and the human cost in casualties. In regard to small arms other than antipersonnel landmines, he noted that the "world is awash with them and traffic in them is very difficult to monitor, let alone intercept."[9]

As a result of Boutros-Ghali's call for action, a panel of experts was formed to prepare a report on small arms for submission to the General Assembly in the fall of 1997.[10] It is the most developed initiative to date by the UN to deal with light weapons and disarmament issues. The panel is addressing the following issues: (a) the types of small arms and light weapons actually being used in conflicts being dealt with by the United Nations; (b) the nature and causes of the excessive and destabilizing accumulation and transfer of small arms and light weapons, including their illicit production and trade; and (c) the ways and means available to prevent and reduce the excessive and destabilizing accumulation and transfer of small arms and light weapons, in particular insofar as they cause or exacerbate conflict.

This work will continue, as key states are preparing a resolution in the 1997 UN General Assembly to use the report of this panel to develop practical disarmament measures.

USING DISARMAMENT AS A CONFLICT PREVENTION TOOL IN THE POST–COLD WAR ERA

In the previous section of the paper, we have argued that arms control and disarmament in the post–cold war era are qualitatively different tasks than they were during the cold war. The dominant mode of conflict and the effects of such conflicts, the availability and type of weapons used (small arms and light weapons), the sources of supply—all pose new challenges. Some conditional generalizations may be drawn to guide policy in this area—keeping in mind that the effective use of disarmament is influenced by the phase of conflict in which it is employed.[11]

PRECONFLICT DISARMAMENT

Assume a scenario in which violent conflict has not yet occurred in a country or region. The root causes of conflict begin to emerge and create tensions, and various groups and/or governments begin to arm themselves, anticipating that tensions might lead to armed conflict. One way to reduce tensions is by lowering the levels of armaments.

Several characteristics of this scenario, however, will make such an approach difficult. First, as outlined by Michael Lund, there are significant challenges to effective early warning in such a situation. Conflicts in the current era are "messy," and indicators are hard to find, let alone interpret. In addition, Lund argues, "in a world full of national transitions from one kind of economic and political system to another, change, tension, and political turmoil can have positive as well as negative results." Furthermore, in the cold-war days, the link between early warning data and the policymakers was much clearer than now, when the warning is often coming from news reports or humanitarian NGOs with no accountability to either national governments or international organizations such as the United Nations.[12]

In regard to early warnings of arms buildups, it is interesting that Lund does not include any reference to arms in his list of factors that analysts have identified as local antecedents of possible genocide.[13] Also, in his table listing tasks and tools for each of his stages of conflict, no tasks or tools relating to arms are mentioned until the "near crisis" stage of unstable peace is reached.[14] This omission may reflect sovereign states' protection of their right to acquire and control arms within their borders, but it also demonstrates a need to focus more attention on what can be done to restrain the tools of violence prior to the outbreak of bloodshed.

As Lund develops his schema for matching tools with problems on the ground, however, he does begin to stress the importance of arms control in preventing disputes from becoming violent. His research indicates that disputes become violent or peaceful depending on one or more of the following six deficiency or need factors: (1) lack of restraints on violence; (2) lack of a process; (3) lack of resources; (4) lack of solutions; (5) lack of incentives; and (6) lack of trust. He goes on to point out that intervenors often do not deal with the most dangerous of these factors. He cites the example of Yugoslavia in 1991, where the international community ignored widespread evidence of the arming of ethnic militias in the republics.[15]

Later in his assessment, Lund proposes tools to respond to each of the six deficiencies. For the lack of restraints on violence—there are few limitations restricting hostile parties from resorting to armed force—he sees the task as depriving parties of arms, and providing protection against the use of arms. The tools include enforced demilitarized zones and military assistance. Preventive diplomacy at this stage can "reduce, restrain, or regulate the weapons that might be used in the future through some form of disarmament, arms control, and/or nonproliferation enforced by international agreements."[16] As previously mentioned, such efforts are hampered by the particular characteristics of the class of weapons used by the combatants—small arms and light weapons; their acquisition may be more easily concealed than a buildup of major conventional weapons, especially given the post–cold war supply networks. Furthermore, in the preconflict phase, little blood has been shed, and no war-weariness has set in. A call to disarm at this time is least likely to be heeded.[17] And in a situation where a state's authority has collapsed but conflict has not yet occurred, multilateral intervention accompanied by some sort of international mandate to disarm the warring parties will not likely occur. Even if the international community succeeds in deploying a preventive force, any mandate to disarm actual or potential combatants is less likely to be approved by the receiving state(s).

While the challenges are significant in the preconflict phase, there are several arms control techniques that can be effective. First, the international campaign against land mines has demonstrated the power of transparency and publicity. A norm is developing against the use of antipersonnel mines in any scenario. This is not yet the case with respect to the assault rifles, grenades, and mortars so popular with today's combatants. Constant public focus, however, can have an impact. In regard to Rwanda, for instance, the Security Council voted in May 1994 (Resolution 918) to embargo the sale or supply of arms and related material to Rwanda by states or their nationals. Media reports about the Hutu forces fleeing Rwanda caused the Security Council (in Resolution 997, dated June 9, 1995) to expand the 1994 embargo on Rwanda to include the Hutu camps in neighboring countries.[18] Human Rights Watch publicized a major shipment of arms from the Seychelles to Hutu forces in Zaire during this period; the result was a UN commission that verified the charges, brought attention to the matter, and, in their view, could have made a difference in the actual supply if they had been given some personnel to oversee the embargo.[19] The public outcry that accompanied the exposure of a British company's involvement in the transfer of weapons to these groups also supports the importance of transparency and publicity.[20]

Transparency itself, however, does not guarantee that action will be taken. Lund's account of the 1993–94 period in Rwanda concludes that the 500 UN military observers were "insufficient to be able to detect the efforts being taken by the Hutu authorities not only to avoid the implementation of the [Arusha] accords but also to recruit and arm militias ready to retake the country at the first opportunity."[21] Other accounts, however, conclude that transparency was there but political will was not. Alison DesForges has made a strong case that the international community knew that dealing with the arms buildups was crucial to resolving the conflict. Early versions of the UN Security Council mandate for the force being assembled in support of the August 1993 Arusha Accords provided that the force would "assist in tracking of arms caches and neutralization of armed gangs throughout the country" and would "assist in the recovery of all weapons distributed to, or illegally acquired by, the civilians." In the final mandate, these provisions were completely eliminated. The final version included only the simple mandate to "investigate and report on incidents regarding the activities of the gendarmerie and police."[22]

But even with this weak mandate, UN officials in Rwanda detected the impending genocide and reported it to their superiors in New York, including information on the arming of militias and the stockpiling of arms caches. The UN force asked permission to preempt the disaster by raiding these weapons caches, a request denied as being beyond the mandate. UN observers monitored and, in some cases, intercepted arms flows into Rwanda but were again denied permission to take action. The resulting catastrophe did shift significant attention to a similar situation in Burundi; the aforementioned UN Commission of Inquiry was formed as a result of Human Rights Watch's exposure of arms flows to Hutu militias in Zaire. In mediation efforts, former President Nyerere of Tanzania also insisted that no further arms be allowed to compound the already violent situation in Burundi. Although no solution is in sight, a catastrophe on the scale of Rwanda and an all-out civil war has been averted. To the extent that the fall of Mobutu and the closure of Hutu bases in eastern Zaire diminish the capabilities of Hutu armed forces to conduct raids in Burundi, some hope remains that the violence can be reduced to a level that will allow the root causes of this conflict to be addressed in earnest.

Where stable peace prevails, providing more security for weapons stocks is another approach. In Albania, the tools of violence were provided by government arsenals that were opened when major defections occurred in the armed forces. South Africa and countries of the former Soviet Union have also had similar problems. Perhaps a more concentrated effort could be made to safeguard such obvious sources of the tools of violence, either through an international capacity-building effort or an international control regime.

Another armaments-specific measure that has seen little development focuses on ammunition. The post–cold war surplus assures that weapons will be available to fuel conflicts for some time to come, but ammunition is a different story. For one thing, it requires fairly high technology to produce reliable ammunition. Most ammunition manufacturing equipment has been built by the industrialized countries. Where did they export such machinery? Can it be located and monitored, or perhaps acquired and destroyed? Furthermore, ammunition in quantities that make a difference is heavy and bulky, which makes it easier to detect. Although assault rifles are highly lethal, their rapid-fire capability also requires a constant supply of ammunition.

Another preconflict scenario is that of crime and lawlessness in a country or region that has recently undergone major democratic reforms, such as South Africa or El Salvador. Both of these countries are suffering from a massive diffusion of military-style light weapons into the hands of criminal elements and have identified their high availability as the primary cause of violence. The problem is exacerbated by the absence of a sufficiently large, well-trained, and noncorrupt police force to combat the increase in armed violence. What begins as apolitical crime can soon be met with a vigilante-style response by the police, leading to organized centers of violence—centers that can then be co-opted by drug traffickers.

A more dangerous situation would be the politicization of such criminal groups and the outbreak of civil war. In this scenario, disarmament action must be taken prior to escalation. States in Southern Africa have begun to discuss the coordination of weapons collection programs, border policing, and other disarmament tools to stem the cross-national flow of weapons.[23] In El Salvador, community groups, with support from the government, have been conducting voluntary weapons collection programs and publicizing the dangerous effects of these weapons.[24]

As these examples illustrate, preconflict disarmament should not be restricted to those situations in which the parties are moving from stable to unstable peace for the first time. Congo and Rwanda, Southern Africa, and El Salvador have each lived through a period of armed violence and can arguably be put in the postconflict category. At least in South Africa and El Salvador, however, peace created by elections and a move toward democracy is now being disrupted by increased diffusion of weapons. Neither state has the capacity to deal with the situation, but as long as the situation of crime and violence remains short of civil war, multilateral intervention and disarmament approaches are politically unlikely options.

DISARMAMENT DURING CONFLICT

The focus of this volume is on prevention, which naturally points toward lessons learned in the pre- and postconflict phases; however, recent history has revealed that even during conflict, disarmament is frequently practiced. It is briefly reviewed here so that the challenges may be highlighted and compared with those applying to the other phases.

Until 1990, the concept of disarmament during conflict was not really an option. In Vietnam, for example, anyone with a weapon was a member of either the government or opposition forces. The idea that citizens would have their own weapons for protection—a situation faced by many peacekeepers today—was out of the question. Turning in a weapon was tantamount to surrender, with all the accompanying consequences.

For a variety of reasons, however, disarmament is regularly practiced while today's conflicts are still being waged. First, conflicts today are marked by fluidity and the absence of front lines, in a classic military sense. A lull in fighting provides a natural occasion for a cease-fire and perhaps disarmament and demilitarization. Second, parties to the conflict are rarely dominant, and the fighting and level of violence vary significantly by time and place; the parties are more likely to accept temporary cease-fires and even disarmament while they shift their attention elsewhere. Third, many of these conflicts are monitored by the international community. This monitoring has an impact on the combatants, who despite their legal right to reject any advice or actions of a multilateral body, rarely do so completely. Cease-fires and lowering the level of violence are normally the immediate goals of such multilateral interventions. Hence, there is a combination of such disarmament efforts in the middle of what is, on a larger scale, a war.

The conflict in the former Yugoslavia provides several examples of temporary disarmament during conflict, as well as of disarmament as a function of providing humanitarian aid.[25] But, as is well known, despite the temporary lull in the fighting and the opportunity provided the participants to reach a more lasting end to the conflict, fighting, massacres, and ethnic cleansing resumed. While such disarmament actions may be defended on moral grounds, it appears that such actions during conflict may not be effective, and much more needs to be learned about disarmament during this phase.

POSTCONFLICT DISARMAMENT

Disarmament efforts have the best chance for success in the post-conflict environment. In this phase, the parties are experiencing war-weariness. In some cases, the conflict has overwhelmed civilian structures and services. In most cases no one has won the war, and both sides have agreed to accept a peace of some kind. The root caus-es of the conflict, while still present, have taken a back seat to the immediate humanitarian conditions. It is in this type of environment that disarmament is likely to be more acceptable and more effective. The nature of the effort made, however, will vary according to the situation confronted.

Civil War between Well-defined Groups and a Working Govern-ment. In this case, disarmament is part of the overall resolution of a conflict between identifiable groups with leaders and a government with some semblance of legitimacy, authority, and capacity to gov-ern. Because a peacekeeping force, UN or otherwise, is not present, the emphasis is on capacity building. The case of Mali illustrates this type of disarmament effort.

In the 1980s, civil strife between the Mali government and the Tuareg nomads resulted in a mass exodus of the Tuaregs from the north, fleeing both conflict and severe drought. They settled in Algeria and Libya. Libya armed and organized them as part of a larger Islamic Legion fighting force. Their weapons included AK-47s, machine guns, rocket launchers, and mortars. In 1990, owing to the failure of the Libya-sponsored Islamic movement in North Africa, they were forced to return to Mali, bringing their weapons back with them. Almost imme-diately, serious conflict once again erupted between the Tuaregs and the government. In 1992, a peace pact was signed by the Tuaregs, set-ting up an interim government that would integrate some 3,000 Tuareg fighters into the Malian army and 4,000 others into the government's civilian sector. The accord also called for the demilitarization of the north, with joint Tuareg-government patrols to ensure security. But the implementation proved problematic for several reasons: a change in government in Mali, a shortage of funds for the promised develop-ment projects in the north, a rise in banditry due to insecurity and the need to survive, a ready supply of weapons, and the self-arming of law-abiding citizens to defend themselves against the increased vio-lence. Overall, there was a breakdown in law and order.

During this period, the Malian government requested assistance from the United Nations in collecting light weapons. Assistance was provided in the form of an Advisory Mission in August 1994, which documented the presence of significant quantities of light weapons and the existence of very little security or customs apparatus to deal with the influx. This led to another UN mission to Mali's neighbors, in recognition that the light weapons proliferation problem could be solved only regionally and multilaterally.

Mali has taken steps to deal with these surplus weapons on sev-eral fronts. Domestically, it has outlawed the possession of military-style weapons; internationally, it has established joint commissions with Niger and Burkina Faso to prevent smuggling. The states in the region have begun to exchange information on illegal weapons traf-ficking, with some positive results. But clearly, the most important action was the successful demobilization and disarming of the five rebel groups, which precipitated the end of the civil strife. Repatriation camps have been set up, with one of the primary require-ments for repatriation being the turning in of one's weapon. Approximately three thousand of the nine thousand combatants have come in from the field to surrender and are now receiving assistance from donor countries such as the United States, Norway, the Netherlands, and Canada.

At the conclusion of the first phase of demobilization, the col-lected weapons were burned publicly in a bonfire. The destroyed arms consisted of 2,642 light weapons and small arms, of which 95 percent were in working condition: They included mortars, assault rifles, grenade launchers, machine guns, and pistols. Many of these weapons were in better condition than those in use by the army of Mali.[26] In attendance were Presidents Alpha Oumar Konaré of Mali and Jerry Rawlings of Ghana, along with the former foes from the Tuareg and government forces and United Nations officials. The two presidents appealed to the warring parties in all African countries gripped by civil war to do likewise—to destroy these weapons of war.[27] President Konaré also stated that "the people of Africa are tired of war. The warlords should know that their time has passed."[28] For their part, the Tuareg rebel groups pledged to dissolve their movement but empha-sized the importance of following through with all aspects of the pact.

In a press conference upon his return from the weapons burning ceremony, the director of the United Nations Centre for Disarmament

Affairs, Prvoslav Davinic, called the burning a "politically courageous" act on the part of the government and the rebels, since the opportunity to bear a weapon was often considered a right. He also emphasized the dual-track approach of disarmament and development. "We realized that we had to deal first with the demand for the weapons. We still have a lot of work to do and hopefully the demand for weapons will decrease when the combatants engage in productive activities. You cannot stop the traffic of small weapons and solve the problem of rebellion in that part of the country without development, and you cannot invest in development until you have some security in the region."[29]

United Nations Peace Operations. Some recent wars, including those in Cambodia, Nicaragua, El Salvador, Guatemala, and Mozambique, have ended through peace accords brokered by the United Nations and other international organizations. Typically, these agreements contain provisions for demobilization, disarmament, and the reintegration of combatants into a peaceful society with an elected government.

One of the more successful disarmament operations occurred in El Salvador. In a phased schedule designed to promote trust among the parties, the leftist guerrillas of the Farabundo Martí National Liberation Front (FMLN) and the government forces disarmed on a similar timetable. The FMLN deposited its weapons in a locked container, guarded by unarmed UN personnel; the UN and the FMLN had the keys to the lockers. The FMLN would continue to turn in its weapons as long as it was assured that the government had met its commitments, including demobilizing and withdrawing its forces to agreed-upon levels and locations. When the FMLN was assured by the UN that the government had met its commitments, the UN destroyed the weapons and the FMLN ceased to exist as a fighting force.[30] At that point, given the two to three hundred thousand weapons still remaining unaccounted for in El Salvador, it was possible for the FMLN to rearm. But the disarmament process had been tightly linked to the development of a political process that allowed the FMLN to pursue its goals in a nonviolent manner.

It is well known that many of the other UN disarmament efforts in this category did not fare as well. In Mozambique, a poorly executed disarmament plan resulted in more than 800,000 AK-47s remaining available for use and/or export; these are the very weapons destabilizing South Africa today. In Cambodia, the Khmer Rouge refused to participate in the demobilization process. In Angola, a host of factors, including land infested with mines, is making the collecting of weapons very difficult. Most importantly, conflicts of this type suffer from an over-supply of weapons—an outcome of the nature of the warfare, in which armed groups are constantly ambushing each other and stealing from government arsenals. These losses are neutralized by importing more supplies from outside the region, creating a supply far above what the combatants could ever use. When such a conflict is resolved, the result-ing surplus is available for recirculation and diffusion in the region. This is exactly the situation in southern and central Africa, Central America, and other conflict zones.

Formal Disarmament and Arms Control Agreements. The cur-rent situation in Bosnia is an example of the type of disarmament process in which a formal agreement has been reached that contains well-defined guidelines regarding who should be armed and with what type of weapon. The agreement also identifies the appropriate author-ity to enforce the agreement, in this case the International Force (IFOR). This is not to say that situations do not occur for which no guidance exists, as happens frequently in Bosnia; but this type of dis-armament is noted for its capacity to be enforced.

The Dayton Accords established specific timetables for turning in weapons, after which all discovered caches and seizures from persons would be the property of IFOR. A November 1996 incident typifies this mandate. Fighting broke out when Muslims who saw Serbs destroying their homes in the demilitarized zone took up arms from previously hidden caches and attacked the Serbs; the Serbs respond-ed. After separating the parties, the U.S. Army troops in that zone destroyed the Muslims' weapons.[31] Interviews with recently returned IFOR officers reveal that this and similar incidents are commonplace and require ingenuity and patience. Apparently, there are no proce-dures for the disposal of weapons seized, as was demonstrated when an IFOR unit seized Serb weapons being used to threaten the unit. The commander requested disposal instructions and a week later was told that the Serbs had made a formal complaint about the seizure and the weapons were to be returned. The commander crushed the weapons with a tank and then returned them; he was court-martialed for his disarmament fervor.[32] There is no specific list of weapons autho-rized to be carried by police in the demilitarized zone; in one case they requested permission to carry hand grenades, since they regular-ly did so prior to the accords, but this request was denied.

As is the case in many conflict zones, massive quantities of arms were distributed prior to the conflict. In Yugoslavia, the defense plans required arming the Territorial Forces in each village; when the country disintegrated, the caches and supplies remained for peacekeepers to deal with as they tried to create a secure environment. This was also the case in Guatemala and in Mozambique, where over a million AK-47s were distributed to citizens by the government.

General Mandate to Bring Security and Stability. In contrast to the mission of IFOR in support of the Dayton Accords in Bosnia, the UN mandate in Haiti was more general. The United Nations Mission in Haiti was to help maintain security and stability, aid the return to constitutional rule, assist in the training of a new national police force, and assist in the holding of elections. In this type of scenario, disarmament policy varies according to the interpretation of the mandate. In Haiti, the U.S. Army, operating with a mandate to create a "secure and stable environment," conducted a weapons collection program as a part of the UN's Multinational Force.[33] Cash was paid for functional weapons voluntarily turned in; those holding arms caches that were discovered and confiscated received no remuneration. The initial prices being paid for weapons were high: $100 for handguns; $200 for semiautomatic weapons and grenades; $400 for fully automatic weapons; and $600 for heavy- and large-caliber weapons. Prices were to increase to higher levels in later phases.

Types of weapons collected included machine guns, assault rifles, submachine guns, rifles, shotguns, handguns, pistols, flare guns, mortars, howitzers, high explosives, CS (tear gas) grenades, and heavy weapons, including several tanks. Modern weapons in good condition were passed on to the U.S. Department of Justice International Criminal Investigative Training Assistance Program (ICITAP) for use by the Haitian police; weapons with historical value were set aside as museum pieces. The remainder of the weapons were inventoried, boxed, and shipped to be melted down at a destruction facility in the United States.

By March 1995, the total number of weapons and munitions collected (both bought and seized) was over 33,000. As of January 1995 the total amount paid for weapons collected through the buyback program was $1,924,950. The United Nations chose not to associate itself with this operation, because the large sums of money involved had resulted in several middleman operations that did not fit with the UN approach. Similarly, when Canada succeeded the United States, its troops did not conduct any weapons collection. In addition, despite the large number of weapons collected and the arguably more secure environment created, President Jean-Bertrand Aristide remained unhappy that the United States had not confiscated weapons from his enemies. This illustrates the limited nature of the disarmament tactics used by the U.S. troops. As they often told the citizens in their areas of operation, the rules were only that you could not carry these weapons *in public*. Another feature of the U.S. program was that it was imposed quickly and without advance notice. Normally, villages and towns had three days to turn in their weapons for cash, after which they were seized if seen or discovered. The program became less effective over time as middlemen organized weapons collection as a business.

Crime and Armed Violence with Military Weapons. In this type of situation, the violence is mainly apolitical crime carried out with military weapons. In El Salvador, for example, a very successful peace process is threatening to come undone as a few hundred thousand light weapons are increasingly being used by criminals to hijack cars and trucks, make public transportation too dangerous, and make life risky for civilians caught not only in crossfires but also at the wrong end of shrapnel from rockets and grenades. In South Africa, the standard weapon for criminals is the AK-47, readily available in marketplaces. Many people trade AK-47s for food.

In both of these countries, the escalation in violence carries with it the threat of political instability. In both, peace and democratization processes had as a major component the reining in of police forces and an army that had used excessive force. There is, accordingly, great reluctance to call on these forces to contain the violence. In these situations, a variety of disarmament tools can be and are being used, with a focus on banning either specific types of weapons or specific types of users. High-crime zones are targeted for special seizure tactics. All of these approaches, however, are problematic in places like El Salvador and South Africa, since security provided by the state is not adequate, and genuine fear has prompted citizens to arm themselves. In such an environment, there are very few supply-side solutions, and the emphasis must be on lowering the demand for such weapons.

Voluntary Weapons Turn-in and Collection Programs. One policy tool becoming more prominent in postconflict situations is the voluntary weapons collection program, often referred to as a "gun buyback" program. These programs provide incentives for those possessing weapons (legal or illegal) to turn them in for money or in-kind benefits. They also involve amnesty for those turning in the weapons, the goal being to get the weapons off the street and out of homes. The goals of such programs are to publicize the connection between weapons and violence, to develop norms against the violent use of weapons, and to lower the number of weapons available for crime and violence. Normally, hardened criminals do not turn in their weapons, so these programs are seen more as leading to changing attitudes and norms. As a result, they rely critically on the participation of the community and can have the spin-off effect of enhancing community-police relations and social development programs.

Voluntary weapons collection programs have been conducted extensively in American cities for the past five years and continue to be a popular approach to both collecting guns and addressing gun violence by emphasizing the negative consequences of gun possession and use. In Central America and the Caribbean this method has been used in Panama, Haiti, Nicaragua, and, most recently, El Salvador. In Africa it has been used in Somalia, Mozambique, and South Africa, and smaller-scale programs have been initiated in the former Soviet Union. Those programs that have been successful are characterized by incentives appropriate for the locale, adequate funding and publicity, and the integration of weapons collection efforts with other social, economic, and law enforcement programs.

In 1991, a weapons collection program was conducted in Nicaragua by the Special Disarmament Brigade (BED), created by the government of Nicaragua expressly for this purpose and made up of government officials and ex-combatants from both sides of the conflict. Following the demobilization, disarmament, and reintegration of guerrilla forces at the end of the war, some of the ex-combatants had rearmed; the sources of the arms were caches left from the war. The BED was created to develop and implement a buyback program.

In the first buybacks, conducted in January 1992, the BED would approach groups known to have rearmed and offer them several incentives to hand in their weapons. First, approximately $100 cash and $100 worth of food was offered for individual weapons. Eventually, the Italian government sponsored a microenterprise program that offered $300-500 to each participant for use as seed money for a development project. In addition to weapons, information—on arms caches or on other individuals and groups that had rearmed—was also exchanged for money and goods.

The operation ran from January 1992 through the end of 1993. During that time, approximately 78,000 weapons were confiscated by police and army personnel, while 54,000 weapons were bought back in rural areas and 10,000 in Managua; in addition, more than 250,000 pieces of munitions and ordnance were collected. The buyback process did not distinguish between functional and nonfunctional arms; both were remunerated. The weapons were destroyed by fire in an open pit in a public space. The total cost of the program was $6,000,000, including funding from the Italian government for the microenterprise project.

In September 1996, a Salvadoran nongovernmental organization, El Movimiento Patriótico contra la Delincuencia, conducted a two-phase weapons collection effort in three cities in El Salvador; the Catholic Church provided turn-in locations and the private sector provided money and goods worth $170,000 as incentives for citizens to turn in weapons. As of October 1, 1996, the program had collected 375 small arms, 601 large arms, 736 grenades, 9 grenade launchers, 84 rocket launchers, 73 pounds of TNT, 35 pounds of C4, 970 ammunition clips, and 31,324 rounds of ammunition. The weapons were turned in to the Division of Arms and Explosives of the National Police and will be melted down and made into a monument. The weapons collection program may have sparked a larger effort that is now resulting in information on larger caches of weapons.

Voluntary weapons collection programs can be used in conflict scenarios other than armed criminal violence. Haiti provides a good example, although it should be remembered that citizens had only a few days to turn in their weapons for cash, after which weapons were seized. An interview with an IFOR officer in Haiti revealed that in IFOR's attempt to retrieve more of the weapons that it knew were out there, it was suggested that IFOR organize a voluntary weapons collection program. It was rejected, not on the basis that it would be unsuccessful, but rather because it was likely to be *too* successful. IFOR was mainly concerned with the safety of citizens handling weapons and explosives. One technique that IFOR did use was to provide a pit outside each garrison for those weapons that were turned in.

It should also be noted that in October 1996 the United Nations and the Croatian government launched a weapons collection project in Eastern Slavonia: They agreed to pay $120 per working automatic rifle, $150 per machine gun, and $20 per hand grenade. "Serbs say the deal will not work," the Open Media Research Institute reported, "because they do not trust the Croats and the offers are too low."[34] But the latest information from the gun buyback program reveals that within three months, UN peacekeepers in Croatia collected 100,400 rifles, 253,000 reusable antitank rocket launchers, nearly as many disposable rocket launchers, 6,271 hand grenades, and more than 250,000 rounds of ammunition. The program is funded by Croatia and administered by the United Nations, which stockpiles some of the weapons for use by the Croatian army and destroys the rest.[35]

THE NEW LOGIC OF DISARMAMENT

The basic conclusion from this overview of the new international security environment, and the actual practice of disarmament, is that there exists a new logic of disarmament. This logic has even produced a new set of principles to guide policymaking related to conflict prevention, management, and resolution.

Match the Tools of Disarmament to the Phase of Conflict. The specific disarmament instruments employed will vary with the phase of conflict in which they are used. Forcible disarmament may work in the midst of conflict, but it would be inappropriate in a postconflict stage. Conversely, voluntary weapons collection programs may be effective in a postconflict situation but more difficult to implement during conflict.

Expand the Range of Expected Outcomes. The objectives of disarmament must cover a wide range of outcomes beyond simply lowering the amount of arms possessed by persons and groups participating in the violence. In many cases, reducing the visibility of arms can contribute significantly to bringing stability to a local situation, which will in turn enhance other conflict resolution initiatives. Even temporary possession of weapons by a neutral party can have positive effects.

Value the Symbolic and Political Importance of Disarmament. Although disarmament can lower the capability of the parties to conduct armed violence, an equal amount of emphasis should be given to the symbolic and political nature of disarmament actions. In the case of Srebrenica, turning in weapons did not alter the military balance, but it did mean that the parties accepted the deal: no visible guns, no slaughter. In Northern Ireland, where the decommissioning of weapons is a principal issue, a commentator partial to the IRA explained:

No one has convincingly argued that decommissioning is a decisive security measure, however desirable it might be.

Indeed security personnel are clear—mostly in private, some in public—that this is essentially a political issue. Secondly, it is a voluntary exercise, which logically and necessarily requires the cooperation of those holding the weapons. The governments and their vast security apparatus have been pursuing a decommissioning policy for years, seeking out and confiscating illegal weapons wherever they can be found. Unionists should not confuse their public by conflating two entirely different exercises.[36]

A political focus is also appropriate with respect to voluntary weapons collection programs, which are often criticized as ineffective because the drug dealers and the gang or guerrilla leaders do not participate. These programs continue to be popular expressly because the drug dealers and the gang or guerrilla leaders do not participate. These programs continue to be popular expressly because of their political and symbolic importance.

Develop Norms against the Possession and Accumulation of this Class of Weapons. The norms that evolved with regard to weapons of mass destruction, and some major conventional weapons such as surface-to-surface missiles, do not exist for the small arms and light weapons that dominate today's violence. This means that an important aspect of any disarmament policy is the promotion of norms against accumulation of weapons that can seriously complicate the prevention or resolution of conflict. (The multitude of policy actions against antipersonnel land mines might serve as a guide.) For this class of weapons, however, the task is harder because of a norm in favor of possessing light weapons, either as part of every country's army or by individuals who fear for their safety. One technique that is being used more often is the public destruction of weapons that have been collected. Another is making public the damage from this class of weapons.

Postconflict Demobilization and Reintegration Are Critical. It is becoming clear that a successful demobilization process in those countries where wars have ended is a critical link to preventing the recurrence of conflict. The new logic calls for emphasis on preventing former combatants from taking up their guns because of a failed demobilization and reintegration effort. Such a process is a holistic exercise, in which disarmament is only the initial step to success. Disarmament in postconflict situations has to be conducted in cooperation with development experts, the police, and judicial personnel; it is much more than a matter of too many weapons, as we see from the increased role of the World Bank and other lending institutions in demobilization programs.[37] This also means that experts from outside the region must become more interdisciplinary—the usual suspects from the cold war arms control and disarmament effort are not enough.

Develop Cross-Cultural Sensitivities. Coping with weapons of mass destruction, and in most cases with major conventional weapons as well, has been done in a monocultural fashion—as a missile is a missile regardless of context. This has allowed the International Atomic Energy Agency and supplier regimes like the Missile Technology Control Regime and the Nuclear Suppliers Group to act on the basis of a set of globally applicable procedures. This is not possible with small arms and light weapons. Disarmament in this realm requires a more sensitive awareness of the role of these weapons in the history and culture of a region. Even if agreement is reached that such weapons must be taken out of the hands of combatants and citizens, the disarmament approach taken should be appropriate to the culture.

Explicitly Fund Disarmament. Preventing conflict through disarmament is not cheap; the world has now learned that a disarmament plan will not accomplish its goal without resources. Too often the disarmament "annex" to a peace operation has been an afterthought. The conflict and failed disarmament in Liberia from 1989 through 1996 is testimony to a totally unrealistic plan, made even worse by incompetent and corrupt execution by the responsible parties. In Rwanda in 1993 and 1994 the arming of militias for genocide was known to the UN, but a restrictive mandate and a lack of resources resulted in no action. It is encouraging that the IFOR mission in Bosnia has the resources to execute the critical disarmament and arms control components of its plan.

THE ROLE OF DISARMAMENT IN PREVENTING CONFLICT: CAN ANYTHING BE DONE?

The examples given in this short treatment demonstrate that a great deal is being done to disarm individuals and groups. In some cases disarmament has succeeded in lowering the temperature to a point where the critical political issues can be discussed and resolved. But in many other cases no attempts were made, or the attempts that were made failed. This is especially true in the stable peace (refer to Michael Lund) or early preventive diplomacy (Kalypso Nicolaidis) phases of conflict. The conflicts selected for attention by the Center for Preventive Action and described in this volume—Nigeria, Burundi and the Great Lakes region of Africa, and the South Balkans—are in such a stage. All have great potential for armed conflict and are the subject of multiple types of interventions by national governments, NGOs, and international organizations, but few of these efforts address the tools of violence that would be employed should hostilities escalate. Why? What can be done?

Transparency. Transparency (the public availability of information) remains critical, with respect not only to the suppliers of tools of violence but also to the users. There should be no letup in the adverse publicity that increasingly accompanies the human carnage resulting from the use of these weapons—which should include pictures of the weapons. In Burundi, much of the violence is committed with machetes, clubs, and knives, but the most lethal attacks are with military weapons such as grenades, rockets, assault rifles, and mortars, used by all sides to the conflict. Where did these weapons come from? Are they under the control of responsible military units, or have they been distributed to militias? Those who use such weapons should be consistently condemned, in the hope that lower levels of violence at least will allow negotiations on the root causes of conflict to proceed.

Increase the Involvement of Humanitarian and Development NGOs. In their effort to be neutral, humanitarian and developmental NGOs have a bias toward not being involved in things military. (The increasing casualties suffered by these NGOs have begun to change this orientation.) In many cases these NGOs are in place on the ground and could be a source of early warning, not just with respect to the factors related to starvation and health epidemics, but in connection with arms buildups as well. In Albania, neutral observers of the black market in arms observe fluctuations in the price of an AK-47, one of several indicators of how many such weapons are on the market and how large the demand is. Appropriate training could improve NGOs' reliable analysis and collection of such information, which is often hampered by their lack of familiarity with weapons and their means of transfer into potential conflict zones.

Even a Few UN Observers Can Make a Difference. The Great Lakes region and other places have demonstrated that even a few UN observers on the ground can have an impact. We should not succumb to those who say that it is no use intervening unless there is enough force to control the entire situation. Observers, such as blue helmets at airfields, can be especially effective in the early stages of unstable peace.

Prevent or Delay the Arming of Oppositionist Forces. There are many examples of nascent conflicts not escalating into armed violence simply because the would-be combatants could not obtain weapons. The most recent case is in the Xinjiang province of China, where many Uighurs (a Muslim, Turkic-speaking group that accounts for two-thirds of Xinjiang's 16.6 million people) want increased autonomy or even independence. While some violence, such as bus bombings, has occurred even in Beijing, for the most part this group is stymied by a lack of weapons. An official of the separatist group just across the Chinese border in Kazakstan stated recently that "if we had weapons, we would already be in Xinjiang. If we had weapons, we could raise 10,000 men here in Kazakstan overnight."[38] This example and many others testify to the role of weapons as a causal factor in armed violence: Provide the arms and they will come.

In the case of Nigeria, the question that needs to be asked is, would we be better off if the opposition were armed? This central question has prompted some to hold the firm view that intervention that prevents conflict is unnatural, that in many cases it is better that some armed violence take place; conflicts need to be intensified, according to this view, before they can be resolved.[39] But others working on this issue recognize that access to the tools of violence must have some limits. "In some cases, the challenge is to let a conflict emerge and unfold, while guarding against its most violent expressions and dealing with its side-effects."[40]

In some conflicts the international community has stigmatized one side as responsible for the armed violence. It is understandable that some single out support for oppositionist groups as the major factor in the escalation of tension to violence, especially when that support is in the form of weapons. "Oppositionist groups should instead be encouraged to use nonviolent means to keep pressure on the regime, thereby allowing their cause to retain the moral high ground and thus international support."[41] This approach puts a moral responsibility on the international community to publicize such restraint and reward the oppositionists in some way. But the international community has a way of neglecting spots unless they are hot. How has Ibrahim Rugova, the leader of the Albanians in Kosovo, been rewarded for his restraint?

This approach also violates one of the basic principles that have shaped the actions of the international community since the advent of the United Nations — that the oppressed have an inherent right to rise up against their oppressors. Recently, President Museveni of Uganda called for drastic action in support of the rebel SPLA forces in the south of Sudan against the government. He admitted that he gives moral support to the SPLA, but "until the OAU defines south Sudan as a colonial question we are inhibited from supporting them."[42] Museveni is calling for the civil war in Sudan to be declared a colonial conflict, so that Uganda and other countries in Africa would be allowed to provide arms, equipment, and material supplies to the rebels.

Every UN effort to deal with armaments faces this hurdle. In 1996, the United Nations Disarmament Commission produced a set of guidelines for states to deal with illicit arms trafficking. Before a consensus was possible, language was inserted that has now become the standard phrasing for all subsequent disarmament efforts:

> States should respect the principles and purposes of the Charter of the United Nations, including the right to self-defense; . . . and should continue to reaffirm the right of self-determination of all peoples, taking into account the particular situation of peoples under colonial or other forms of alien domination or foreign occupation, and recognize the right of peoples to take legitimate action in accordance with the Charter of the United Nations to realize their inalienable right to self-determination.[43]

This is not to say that attempts to control the supply of arms to oppositionists are not warranted. The issue of what constitutes "colonialism" or "domination" has hardly been settled. Rather, expanding such ad hoc efforts to some type of international or even regional regime will prove difficult. What is desired is that often sought after consensus that the government being opposed is a "good" government.

CONCLUSION

Replacing the supply of arms is not necessarily the impossible task that many make it out to be. It is true that people have taken up arms—to defend their person, their home, their community, or their nation or to overthrow oppressors—since the beginning of history. But, just as true, humankind has been quick to realize that the accumulation of armaments can have negative effects that counter the security that arms are designed to produce. Isaiah was one of the first to call for disarmament, prophesying to the people of his time, "They shall beat their swords into plowshares and their spears into pruning hooks," a call emblazoned on the wall of the United Nations Plaza across from UN headquarters in New York. In the twentieth century, the advent of modern and lethal weaponry has put the concept of disarmament to the test. But as this chapter has shown, the growing consensus that something should be done about guns is beginning to generate practical tools in the pursuit of peace.

— 7 —

RELIGION AND VIOLENCE PREVENTION

Donald W. Shriver, Jr.

What is the best regime? Within this question is that of how a person should live. And with this question, we are at the point of so raising the gaze of parties to a conflict that all things become possible. For now, these questions that were tossed out the back door by the Enlightenment sneak back in through the windows of the minds and souls of the men and women who may be found at, or brought to, the negotiating table.
— Stanton Burnett[1]

Peace is not Utopia, it is just better than the alternatives.
— Robert L. Rothstein[2]

O n the lawn in front of the United Nations building in New York City stands a statue, donated by the USSR, of a strong man beating a sword into a plowshare. The original of this statue is in the courtyard of the Tretyakov Museum in Moscow. On neither version does an inscription appear referring the viewer to the source of this image in writings now some 2,500 years old: Isaiah 2:4 and Micah 4:3. (And compare Joel 4:10.)

Official modern versions of the relationship of religion to international conflict are likely to assume that religion regularly beats plowshares into swords while being powerless to reverse its own role in generating, or intensifying, conflict. Illustrations crowd the front pages:

♦   If not a cause of the Bosnian war, the religions there were skillfully mobilized by politicians seeking their own ends.

♦   Tutsis and Hutus in Rwanda, largely Catholic and Anglican in formal religious affiliation, fell into active or passive collaboration with the armed fomenters of mass murder in 1994.

♦   Fifty years after the founding of Pakistan and the Republic of India, Hindus and Muslims seem just as unable to contribute to a peaceful solution to the question of who owns Kashmir.

♦   Buddhism and Hinduism seem more cause than cure of the violence that still afflicts Sri Lanka.

♦   Try as their leaders may to claim that the Northern Ireland problem is political rather than religious, their constituents usually identify themselves as "Protestant" or "Catholic."

Revive our received memories of the long history of religion and war, and the list lengthens ad infinitum: militant seventh-century Islam, equally militant Christian Crusades, the Thirty Years War, the "Presbyterian Revolution" of 1775–83, the religious ardor of all combatants as they marched out in 1914, the Nazi mobilization of Martin Luther in the cause of killing Jews. . . . Iran, Algeria, Cyprus, Jonestown, Waco, Aum Shinrikyo, Hebron: the names rattle through our rough index of incidents in the grim history of religion and violence. Add to all these sins of commission the numerous omissions of silence that have tarnished religion's reputation as a source of timely verbal outcry against organized atrocity: the deflection of world Christian and Muslim attention from the Armenian massacre of 1915, the sluggish delay in Western church protest against Nazi anti-Semitism, tardy public response to murder in Bosnia, forgetfulness about the slaughter of Tutsis in 1959 and passivity in the face of its repetition in 1994. . . . The list goes on and on. Much shorter, for most of us, is any listing under the title: Religion and Violence Prevention.

THE PERIL AND PROMISE OF HUMAN SOLIDARITY

Were this a longer essay on the actual and potential contributions of religion to "peace," one might pause a while to wonder at the power of religion to quell enough "normal" conflict *within* a polity or community to enable its members to identify with those huge collective efforts called wars. Long ago, Augustine noted the irony that any band of successful criminals must effect a certain peace and justice among themselves. Ordinary among politicians is the strategy of uniting a conflict-prone populace around an external enemy. From the Crusades to the Gulf War, the uses of religion for effecting this political solidarity multiply. Though publicly proclaimed religious enthusiasm for going to war tended to erode in the United States from 1917 through 1991, it is still rare for any president to call the country to arms without some invocation of the God who will "bless America." Skeptical social scientists are likely to concede that religion can be a useful tool for fortifying political power, a "dependent" yet assisting variable not to be totally neglected amidst political crisis. Stalin's prudential, temporary truce with the Russian Orthodox Church in World War II is a salient example.

Less amenable to this easy secularist analysis are those incidents in political history when religious belief, leadership, and loyalties generate collective protest against tyrannical power, challenge its legitimacy in whole or in part, and form a countercollectivity that ranges from loyal opposition to revolutionary enemy. A recent example, producing much admiration in the West, was the role of Nobel Prize laureate Bishop Carlos Felipe Ximenes Belo in East Timor. Under his leadership, Catholics in that former Portuguese colony, occupied by Indonesia over the past twenty years, increased their numbers to become a majority religion, an attraction generated in large part by the church's championing of the cause of East Timor's independence from the Jakarta government. The alliance of Korean Protestants who protested against Japanese colonialism in the 1910–45 era displayed similar movement-generating power. Both the East Timor and the Korean cases illustrate the classic Weberian "elective affinity" between strictly religious appeals and the interests of certain groups in a society.

Perhaps the most puzzling of these phenomena are those in which religion helps generate conflict and then helps to resolve it. Bishop Belo and his colaureate José Ramos-Horta were the successful organizers of large protest rallies in Dili, but by managing to keep the demonstrations nonviolent in the face of the central government's violence, they became violence preventers as well as protest organizers.

When religiously motivated people function so, they embody a form of power distinct from dominant economic, political, and military forces. Those analysts for whom "political power" in society is always something simple and coercive, or who dismiss human "values" as always the dependent variable in human behavior, ought to be puzzled by such incidents.[3]

To unravel some of the puzzle, it is important to distinguish among levels of those historical phenomena labeled "religion." Religion is a many-dimensioned thing. It comprises (1) a set of ideas, symbols, and rituals; (2)institutions with more and less social power; (3) communities united by shared beliefs; (4) personal attitudes that help to define an individual's sense of internal identity and external reality; and (5) an alleged transcendent source of criticism of all human constructions, including of religion itself. The contradictions in the relationship of religion to political violence stem in part from incoherence within and among these levels. For example, pacifism can draw on one section of Scripture and the case for "just war" from another, and institutional religious leaders may be bought off by the political elite with rewards for guiding their constituencies to "Be subject to the authorities" (Romans 13), only to be opposed covertly by some constituents who find in Revelation 13 a reason to despise government as demonic. As will be evident in several places below, the strength and the weakness of religion as an influence on human social behavior is this characteristic appeal to "ultimate concern," as Paul Tillich put it.[4] Like the U.S. Supreme Court, religion may lay down a law it cannot enforce, and it may appeal to different principles of its "constitution" in different historical contexts; as in secular jurisprudence, ultimates may acquire new interpretations over time, especially among subsequent generations of believers. In their very experience of history, religious people can change their beliefs and politics and the relationship of one to the other. Their intellectual and moral leaders may make the crucial difference. A classic example is the Hebrew tradition of the prophet, who calls the people to traditional loyalties that mandate loyalty to the king in one era (Isaiah 37) and disloyalty to him in another (Jeremiah 27).[5] A complex modern example is the interaction of religious belief and political stances represented by Desmond Tutu, F. W. de Klerk, and Nelson Mandela. Each mobilized constituencies with appeals to religion, while also acquiring Nobel peace prizes for thus far preventing their conflicts from escalating into a civil war.

The body of this short paper will attempt to scan religion's contribution to violence prevention in the recent histories of nations. Two problems afflict the method in such a selective analysis. One concerns questions of timing. Like other contributors to conflict resolution, religious persons and groups can become agents of conflict prevention prior to such conflict, in the midst of it, and after it has died down. The challenge of preventing the repetition of old conflicts, as well as the eruption of new ones, would seem to belong to all agents, so that "preventive action" is one potential at every stage of peacemaking. Indeed, as Harold Saunders has recently written, participants in a peace process "move back and forth between stages in a circular rather than linear fashion as they revisit assumptions or tackle new problems."[6]

A second unavoidable problem, implicit in the literature on "preventive action" but not much mentioned therein, is how to identify convincingly the influences behind "nonevents"—things that did *not* happen. The political roots of the recent Rwandan massacre went back at least as far as 1959. Who can be sure of the reasons it erupted massively in 1994 and not before? The paradox of preventive action is that violence sometimes has to erupt before the potential "preventers" know that there is something to prevent.

In what follows I am greatly indebted to the recent book quoted in the epigraph, *Religion: The Missing Dimension of Statecraft*, which enumerates the real, often modest achievements of religiously oriented catalyzers of peace in the past fifty years. The various concrete historical illustrations mentioned here will attribute only one range of powers to religion alongside other sorts of power that may induce human beings to restrain, patch up, or otherwise discontinue their violence-prone quarrels. At the end of a violent century, we find ourselves wanting to bring to bear every possible resource for delivering the twenty-first century from the legacies of our wars. Religion is, and ought to be, one such resource.

CONCEPTUAL LEVERAGES

Preliminarily, let me identify some ideas that the major world religions have sponsored as counters to the propensity of Homo sapiens to inflict violence on its own kind.

The Concept "Human"

A colleague at Union Theological Seminary reports that in instructing him for Christian baptism in 1942 in Tokyo, his Japanese pastor said, "The God of the Bible loves all people, including the Americans." The notion of such a deity has not characterized every historical religion. Scholars have pointed out that the roots of a law, faith, and ethics that expanded tribal religion to a humanity deemed "universal" seemed to emerge in several regions of the world in the period between the sixth and third centuries B.C.E. This was the era of Second Isaiah, the Buddha, Confucius, Alexander the Great, and the Stoics. Imperfect and often denied in practice, the concept "humanity" was a great cultural breakthrough, as each of these religious innovators eroded the wall of alleged superiority that separates "us" from "them." Implicit in this breakthrough was an attack on ever-ancient-and-modern racism, a weapon of great power in most wars of the twentieth century.[7] To define an enemy as a nonhuman species is to prepare a constituency for killing him or her (or "it") with a clear conscience.

A "Higher Authority," the Transcendent

Conscience can be shaped in contrasting directions. Imprisoned by the Gestapo in Norway, resistance member Leif Hovelsen later testified, "At the very moment I decided to say, 'No,' I experienced the inner freedom that conquered the Nazi ideology. A force within me speaking through my conscience made me resist."[8] Strictly considered, Hovelsen's logic and language mark him as different from many advocates of "conscience" as arbiter of morality—a "force" spoke "through" his conscience. He believes in a Higher Power.

The psychological power of dependence on "higher authority" is well known in the literature of conscientious resisters. Once united in a collective, such resisters can exert public leverage for change—or for fortifying the status quo. For example, the Roman Catholic Church in the Philippines seemed solidly allied—along with the United States government—with the Marcos regime for many years. Led by Cardinal Jaime Sin, that church gradually withdrew public support from Marcos and finally became the galvanizer of the People's Power Revolution of February 1986. A formal parallel is the Iranian revolution of 1979, effected through an ayatollah living in Paris. He was external to the shah's government in a double sense: Not only was he safe for a while in France, but he could tell the Iranian faithful that God commanded an obedience that transcended their current government.

Illustrated here is the potential of religion for generating conflict in advance of quelling it. As Cardinal Sin remarked in 1983, "a minister of reconciliation must first be a prophet of denunciation"— a remark that suggests how the roles of religion as conflict arouser and conflict resolver are sometimes intermixed.[9] Both potentials grow out of religion's ability to call upon its adherents to obey a standard of behavior that transcends every other authority. In Rhodesia as in the Philippines, the role of Catholic leaders changed. They first supported white patriotism and the Ian Smith revolt but finally (together with the Quakers and Moral Rearmament) helped turn Rhodesia away from war and toward the political founding of Zimbabwe. In that process some observers on both sides came to believe, with Ron Kraybill, that "a sense of transcendent calling is more sustaining than pragmatic ambition."[10] As a Korean Christian dissident once said to me, "If you have a cause you can last about five years; if an ideology, maybe ten or fifteen. But if you have a faith, you can last until you die for it."

But "dying for it" reintroduces the ambivalent capacity of religious faith for legitimating turns toward both peace and violence. Will my Korean friend die in violence that he initiates or in violence that his nonviolent protest evokes from official or unofficial antagonists? How did Gandhi, Desmond Tutu, Martin Luther King, Jr., and Bishop Belo turn their protesting constituents into practitioners of organized nonviolence? It is an age-old question, akin to the question politicians must face when some high ideal in national culture is threatened by internal or external enemies. Are ideals ever worth fighting for? Warmakers assume that they are. Legal scholar Robert Cover images this ambivalence of religion as its capacity to be both "sword and shield"—aggressive in its mission to change the world; protective of its inner integrity against all external forces whatsoever. The former is often compatible with idealistic legitimation of violence, while the latter has often endorsed an equally idealistic pacifism.[11]

CAPACITY FOR SELF-CRITICISM AND REFORM

There is a long history of debate within religious communities over these alternate stances toward violence. The "just war" versus pacifism debate is the most famous example. The unresolved conflict between these two views met a circumstantial complication in 1945 with the beginning of the nuclear era. In the fifty years since, the existence of humanity has been at stake in the prevention of nuclear war, and theologians in the Christian community worldwide have turned increasing attention to the attainment of "just peace" as pre-venting our having to engage in a "just war." Careful students of the "just war" doctrine have always conceded that war involves grave injustices. Better, as diplomats might say, to prevent World War III by refusing to write a peace treaty like Versailles; by far better to help an enemy recover from war, as with the Marshall Plan. Uniquely, in the era of nuclear arms, many theologians perceive that there is no just use of such all-destroying weapons, unless one posits an ironic form of justice that says, "The only just use of such weapons is to prevent their use"—as in the doctrine of Mutually Assured Destruction. Less ambiguous, some now say, and more forthright is "nuclear pacifism," the abandonment of ethical justification of the use of these weapons.

This is just one illustration of the capacity of changing historical circumstance to send religious leaders back to a reassessment of ancient theological norms of interpretation. Juxtaposing the imme-diate and the transcendent in mutual influence is the dynamic here. Without such mutuality, change is unlikely in either religion or sec-ular law. The antigovernment role of the Catholic Church in Zimbabwe in 1979 and in the Philippines in 1986 was shaped in part by the reforms of Vatican II in 1965, especially in its turn toward reli-gious liberty and concern for justice for the poor. As Arvind Sharma comments with respect to the evolution of Sikhism, ". . . [A]ny com-parative study of religions in the interest of drawing upon them for conciliatory values must avoid a kind of 'functional fundamentalism' that overemphasizes canonical sources at the expense of religious his-tory. The values of a [modern] tradition arise from both."[12]

Speaking out of the recent South African context, Charles Villa-Vicencio observes that "the amazing thing about religion is that it has the capacity to renew itself" as well as to critique all human construc-tions whatsoever—a capacity that Paul Tillich called the Protestant Principle. Religious vision is an ultimate horizon for its affirmers, and that is one reason for its vulnerability to forms of absolutism; but, notes Villa-Vicencio, "to acquire a horizon" may also mean "that one learns to look beyond what is close at hand—not in order to look away from it, but to see it better within a larger whole and in truer proportion."[13] For the religious imagination it is easy to believe, as Samuel Huntington does, in "the contingent character of social and political structures."[14] Deep down, religion knows itself to be contingent. Put simply, religious believers and religious establishments, on their own grounds and at their best, must be learners.

To be sure, there is a crucial conceptual-practical divide between those religious people who bring absolute views to bear upon society and those who know that at most they have a view *of* the Absolute. The former deserve the title "fundamentalist"; the latter, the designation "liberal." A famous entreaty of Oliver Cromwell to a contentious Scot regiment captures the liberal stance: "I beseech you by the mercies of Christ, think that you may be wrong!" Learned Hand voiced virtually the same sentiment: "The spirit of liberty is the spirit that is not too sure it is right."

Absolutism in all forms—political, ideological, religious—is immune to second thoughts; it is the functional equivalent of idolatry. But one reason world religions persist across generations is their inner capacity for acknowledging that the Divine is greater than all its human interpreters. Israelis may say that it is better to negotiate with Yasir Arafat, the politician, than with the Koranic text in the hands of fundamentalist Hamas. But Islam, too, has its interpreters who know (with the Puritan preacher John Robinson) that "God has yet more light to break forth from the Holy Word." Though he does not represent mainstream Islamic thinking, Islamicist scholar Abdullah A. An-na'im exemplifies this when he explores the meaning of *ijtihad* —the "effort" required for interpreting the Koran in relation to matters not specifically treated in the text. Over the centuries, says An-na'im, Islamic jurists have applied *ijtihad* to the text itself, relying on their own judgment of how the letter of law might be reasonably interpreted in a new way, given new circumstances. "[S]ince *ijtihad* was defined and regulated through human reason in the past, rather than being the direct product of divine revelation as such, it can be re-defined and re-regulated through human reason today and in the future."[15]

The First Crusade started in Europe with the cry, "God wills it!" Latter-day Christians have mostly retreated from that presumption. Sooner or later, even in Hamas, interpreters of the Koran may find therein reasons for a similar retreat. Both Arafat and the Israelis have to hope so.

OLD AND NEW RELIGIOUS STRATEGIES FOR CONFLICT RESOLUTION

The above bases for hoping that religion can make a positive contribution to peacemaking worldwide are necessarily conceptual and abstract—but they are no less powerful than other abstractions in political conflict such as "national honor," "just cause," and "manifest destiny." More down to political earth are certain contributions that contemporary religiously motivated persons and groups have made to actual conflict prevention and conflict resolution in various parts of the world in the last decade or two. Let us consider some of these.

PROVIDING SAFE "SPACE" FOR PEACEMAKING

Over the centuries, religious conviction and religious communities have exhibited extraordinary resistance to obliteration at the hands of government. Catacomb Christians, ghettoized Jews, Santeria devotees, French Protestants, Nagasaki Catholics, and Chinese house churches long ago demonstrated that. And it goes beyond sheer survival: once spread organizationally throughout a society, a religious organization may acquire powers that politicians envy.[16] Recent history suggests that, if not envy, *frustration* has been the lot of politicians who have had to deal with religion's power to reach and to influence growing numbers of people in a society, sometimes in defiance of government.

Huntington was not far from the sociological reality when he called the Philippine Catholic Church a "latent national political machine," able to influence and communicate with members in every village of the country.[17] Different but equally dramatic was the role played by Protestant churches in *die Wende* (the "change") in the German Democratic Republic (DDR) in the 1980s. Beginning in 1981, a secular, grassroots peace movement focusing on the nuclear arms crisis was taking shape in the DDR. Among the few institutions with affinity for this cause were the churches: local and national assemblies of the antinuclear movement met in church-controlled spaces. So churches offered sanctuary for these secular group meetings; but, at the same time, its leaders often sought to moderate the radical leadership of the movement—while using their access to government to warn against violent suppression of the protesters. Ironically, one of the movement's early confrontations with the DDR government centered on the use of Isaiah's "swords into plowshares" symbolism, suggesting that the Communists knew about the power of symbols and liturgies for coalescing an opposition.

The East German story has been told in a growing body of literature, and it is clear that *die Wende* occurred out of a complex of forces, of which religion was only one. External migration of East Germans to the West, at first permitted by the government as a way to get rid of some dissidents, along with the "internal migration" of other dissidents, combined to move masses of citizens from passive obedience to public demand for change. By 1988 the Protestant churches were holding conferences throughout the DDR calling for a full range of political reform in the areas of law, elections, limits on state authority, media, energy, and the environment, all as part of a newly vigorous demand for private and public discussions which should "not exclude any areas of life."[18] As Protestant church assemblies expanded to include Roman Catholics, ecumenical support was also coming from outside the DDR, especially through the World Council of Churches. The growing pressure on the DDR government, intensified by the momentous, Gorbachev-related changes in the USSR, warned Chinese Communist leaders that religion might become a focus of opposition in their situation, too. Christian Bishop K. H. Ting, in fact, cautioned his foreign visitors not to put the small Chinese Christian community in renewed jeopardy by comparing Tiananmen Square and the East European "velvet revolutions."

An often neglected dimension of conflict resolution is that between governments and dissidents whom political leaders wish to destroy or imprison. Whether with respect to accused criminals in medieval Europe or political refugees from Central America in the 1980s, "sanctuary" has been a right claimed by churches in the name of supralegal justice. Tragically and horribly, the exercise of that ancient right in Rwanda in 1994 made the churches a collection point for Tutsi victims of Hutu machetes. But by claiming the right to control its own "sacred space," religious bodies have sometimes saved lives, entering into conflict with the state in the name of protecting the innocent from state violence. C. M. Kao, Stated Clerk of the Presbyterian Church in Taiwan, supplied sanctuary for one critic of the government in the 1970s; and the rabbi of the principal synagogue in Buenos Aires, the late Marshall Meyer, was probably the chief protector of the life of Jacobo Timerman long before the latter came to international prominence.[19] Not yet written is an adequate history of what local religious bodies have done to save the lives of some of the potential victims of totalitarian governments.

Opinions will differ as to when religion or any other agency has actually prevented violent conflict. The problem, again, is identifying causes of events that did not happen. In East Germany, peaceful candlelight processions streaming out of churches could have been met by the bullets of the DDR military. Without question the churches generated conflict, short of violence, and provided space in which civil dialogue could occur. The word of a Kurt Masur from Leipzig to Berlin had its role, but it would not have been a necessary word without the public demonstrations.

Important to note here is the democratic culture that was evolving in East Germany in the 1980s. In the course of survey research there between 1989 and 1990, sociologist Mary L. Gautier came to the strong conclusion that church attenders in the DDR "report higher levels of support for democratic values than non-attenders." In the early 1980s peace groups did push the church toward debate and confrontation with government policies, coexisting with church congregations inside the congregations' physical spaces. "At the end, though, the church was quite influential in the democratic reform movement," which by any definition of "democracy" mandated the resolution of conflict by shared talk rather than coercion. "This experience of coming together, usually within the protective confines of the church, in order to recreate civil society, caused church members to become the carriers of democratic values." Gautier believes that the peace protesters and the church members learned together "how to be democratic citizens." She expects that the churches in the former DDR will continue this same learning as they multiply their "network of horizontal linkages between people that are so important to the success of democracy." Indeed, these very linkages were "carefully preserved by the churches during the years of totalitarianism."[20] It is hard to avoid the conclusion that the churches in East Germany discovered—or stumbled into—a unique mix of contributions to the drama of the "change": They hosted the protests, they cultivated its nonviolent character, and they furnished a social context hospitable to a cross-section of both its own members and others.

The East German experience exhibited other roles that religious leaders and constituents can play in the simultaneous generation of peaceful conflict and of new levels of social justice and peace. A second role was advocacy of negotiation as an alternative to killing, and a third was training in the practice of nonviolence.

ADVOCATING NEGOTIATION

The combination of protest with negotiation is difficult for any person or organization to bring about in situations of potential and actual violence. But the Philippine, Rhodesian, East German, and American civil rights movement cases illustrate how different actors in the same movement can consciously collaborate in effecting such combinations. As Harold Saunders observes, peacemaking is a complex process requiring a great variety of actors and roles.[21] In the civil rights movement of the 1960s, it was common for some protesters to break the law and get arrested, while others protested within the limits of law and still others were offering to sit at negotiating tables with their adversaries. Getting opponents to such tables is, of course, a major step toward the resolution of many a political conflict. Often the role of religious leaders in these conflicts has stopped short of joining the negotiations or trying to determine their agenda. In other cases, religious leaders sometimes do move toward advocating policy—as did British Quakers, who, while trying to get the warring parties in Rhodesia to the negotiating table, were advising members of Parliament not to lift economic sanctions too soon, lest the Ian Smith government be tempted to prolong the war. At the same time they made British officials aware of the universal rejection by African governments of the Abel Muzorewa-Smith "Internal Settlement."

Moral Rearmament leaders in Rhodesia are probably to be credited with the crucial personal meeting of Robert Mugabe with Ian Smith as the results of the 1980 election hung in the balance; and Catholic bishops simultaneously kept stressing the need for major changes in the economic and political structures of the country. Processes leading to negotiation, personal contact between adversaries, and advocacy of structural change thus became the respective specialties of the Quakers, Moral Rearmament, and Catholics in the Rhodesian conflict. These three ingredients helped achieve a peace that some observers of Rhodesia in the 1970s deemed impossible.[22]

URGING NONVIOLENT RESISTANCE TO VIOLENCE

Gene Sharp has enumerated 198 kinds of nonviolent action that brought about social change in the past three thousand years. Selecting from this list some seventy-three twentieth-century instances, Walter Wink documented "the exponential increase in the use of nonviolence in just the last few years" before his study.[23] Among the instances he cites are:

◆ Gandhi campaigns against British colonialism, 1919–47.

◆ Martin Luther King, Jr., adopts Gandhian principles in the civil rights movement of 1955–68.

✦   Solidarity in Poland, after nine years of nonviolent struggle, wins a parliamentary election without violence in spite
of a hundred violent deaths of its members.

✦   Throughout the 1980s the South African Council of Churches
(SACC) offers one of the few sanctuaries for discussion among
African National Congress (ANC) leaders. Some leaders consider the SACC the exiled ANC's stand-in presence inside
the country. South African security forces eventually bomb
SACC headquarters in Johannesburg, but the SACC never
asks its ANC friends to retaliate with counterviolence.

✦   Ukrainian Catholics—in 1989, the largest banned religious
organization in the world, with five million members—hold
a protest mass to call for restoration of their legal status.

✦   Rev. Laszlo Tökes, Reformed Church pastor in Timisoara,
Romania, "speaks the truth" about Nicolae Ceausescu from
his pulpit in 1989. When police try to arrest him, 200 people,
mostly parishioners, surround Tökes, jam the streets, light
candles, and refuse to move. Fifty thousand people converge
on the city center, and "the public continues nonviolent
demonstrations while the army battles the secret police."[24]

The last illustration is a reminder that, combined with other forces
in a turbulent political time, nonviolent religious protest can spark
violence among both friends and foes of political change. It has to be
remembered that not all religious traditions are particularly supportive
of nonviolent resistance to evil, as the classic Western "just war" doctrine makes clear, along with some expressions of the Islamic *jihad*.[25]
The notion that peaceful *means* are a close complement to
peaceful *ends*, however, seems almost an idea whose time has come in
both religious and secular circles, given the sheer magnitude of violence that governments can now mobilize and the new tools for organizing collective nonviolent protest now available in most parts of
the world. To an extent never before seen, instruments of communication make governmental violence against its own and neighboring
peoples less secret—and less palatable for many outsiders. The deaths
of 200,000 East Timorese at the hands of the Indonesian military in
1975 and the murder of Steve Biko in 1977 were not kept secret for
long. For a while, at least, in Tiananmen Square a lone student

stopped a tank, and the fact that he was being televised was one reason for his temporary success.[26] "The Philippine revolution was orches-
trated by transistor radios, the Iranian one by cassette tapes, and the
nonviolent Thai revolution of 1992 by portable telephones," explains
Walter Wink. "A Polish priest commented prior to the victory of
Solidarity that he thought the outcome in Poland would more likely be
nonviolent thanks to television coverage of the Philippine revolution," which soon roused hopes among Korean students that they could
duplicate the Philippine feat.[27] The fact that churches owned and
controlled some of these instruments of communication was significant. That the efforts of religion were either aided or frustrated by
other forces (e.g., this new technology) is equally significant. One
occasional fruit of worldwide religious networks has been the protection of political prisoners through the pressures of the Vatican and the
World Council of Churches, sometimes working together with
Amnesty International. Along with science and business, religion is
among the great globally organized social entities; many of its leaders
are old hands at collaboration across national boundaries.

Nonviolence may not be a uniquely religious tactic for fending off
massive violent death; alone, it is no master strategy for social change.
But the achievements of both Mahatma Gandhi and Martin Luther
King, Jr. suggest that the twentieth century might have been yet more
violent if these leaders had not discovered in their own religious roots
the need for a profound complementarity between the means and
ends of political protest. Politics may be war by other means, but the
change from war to politics is often the shift from death to life.
Moreover, close study of the successes and failures of nonviolence as
an alternative political "weapon" underscores the fact that sheer violence is often a very blunt political instrument. The military of the
DDR might have killed thousands in the streets of Leipzig and
Dresden in 1989, but they might have thereby hastened the demise of
their power, too, something the British had discovered to their sorrow
after their April 13, 1919, massacre of Indian National Congress
protesters in Amritsar. In the end, in Leipzig and Dresden candle-
power had an effect, and the fact that the candles were lit inside of
church buildings was not coincidental.[28]

CREDIBILITY, TRUST, TRUTH-TELLING, TRUTH-LISTENING

Edward Laurance relates in the preceding chapter how, in
September 1996 in El Salvador, as part of a weapons turn-in effort,

"the Catholic Church provided turn-in locations and the private sector provided money and goods worth $170,000 as incentives for citizens" to do so. Both the incentives and the location were important in this exchange, and one judges that the church was chosen to offer sites because it enjoyed a measure of popular trust exceeding that of other institutions.

Especially in situations of violent conflict, "truth" can take a battering. In the early 1980s two branches of the American Presbyterian Church sent delegations to Central America to probe the complex issues of revolution in El Salvador and Nicaragua. Among their conclusions from interviews with leaders on many sides of the conflicts was that official U.S. State Department policies in the region were based on very selective interpretations of fact. Delegation reports to the denomination's general assembly were full of statements like: "This is what our ambassador said, but this is what we saw and heard."[29]

Ambassadors deal with different interests and dynamics than "independent" sources may have to, and no church leader—even a missionary after twenty years in a foreign country—has a corner on the market of political truth anywhere in the world. But alternative means of communication can be a vital resource of organized religions for limiting conflict, for on occasion theirs may be the channels most accorded popular trust. A clear example is the Catholic Church's Radio Veritas in the Philippines, virtually the only source of mass communication apart from Marcos-controlled media during the February 1986 crisis. The rule in that situation seems to have been, "If Cardinal Sin says so, it must be so," and, "If the bishops and the Cardinal say we should come out to EDSA, we should come." In El Salvador, up to his assassination, Archbishop Oscar Romero had the same credibility in his public criticism of government. Not only did the church give him organizational support for his public voice, but also his assassination only amplified that voice through the uses that his constituents made of his death. Death in service of a cause can sometimes undergird that cause with increased public credibility. Indeed, the term *martyr* ("witness") is religious in origin. For many believers it carries an increment of authority not available to mere ideologues.

In some recent conflict situations, religious organizations have established their credibility not so much via claims to know and tell "the" truth, but by their demonstrated readiness to *listen* to stories and facts that government and other media have paid little attention to. Both Catholics and Quakers contributed tangibly to the outcome of the Rhodesian conflict by their use of "disciplined listening." There, in the early 1970s, the Justice and Peace Commission set up by the Rhodesian Catholic bishops attracted testimony about the civil war from far out into the countryside:

"Africans grew to see it as a major means at their disposal to speak of their oppression." Villagers trekked long distances to Salisbury to tell the commission of their plight. "Often there was no thought of redress, simply the quest for someone who would listen, see the wounds, and understand what was happening in the guerrilla war. It was strangely not so much a quest for justice and peace as a quest for truth. And it was ultimately truth, rather than justice and peace, that the Commission achieved and will be remembered for."[30]

Later, in the Geneva conference that led to the final, decisive Lancaster House negotiations, Quakers practiced their traditional arts of listening so consistently that "increasingly the parties became eager to know what the Quakers were hearing from *other* parties. Theirs was the politics of transformative listening."[31]

Such transformation, when it occurred, grew as much out of understanding the emotions and experiences of war as it did out of the "facts" of the situation. Emeka Ojukwu, Biafran head of state, testified that in the various attempts at ending the Nigerian civil war, "We saw [the Quakers] as a religious people but [also] as friends. Only a nonpolitical actor would have a chance of bringing the two sides together or giving the necessary type of assurance—not of security, but rather an umbrella under which you go in and you don't lose anything." Most decisive of all was the Quaker capacity for empathy. Rugged political negotiators, said Ojukwu, "are likely to dismiss the deaths of fifty people with an 'Oh, well, that happens.' But when you say to the Quakers, 'this is what happened,' there is a silence for a bit. There is a fellow human feeling for the tragedy, which is fully understood, and they then take that into consideration in their responses."[32]

That there is some goodness in every human being—Christian, Muslim, traditional religionist—was a doctrine that Quakers brought with them to Nigeria and Rhodesia. Listening long enough to locate that goodness was their regular practice, honed in their own traditional forms of worship and prayer. It became the essence of their procedural contribution to the peace process in those two countries.

A kindred contribution came from the Evangelical Church in the DDR, as the government in the 1970s and 1980s painted the face of the West as inherently hostile, inhuman, and threatening. "They are human, like us," the publicity of the Kirchebund kept insisting. In the cause of credible truth telling, the current Truth and Reconciliation Commission in South Africa is evoking similar perceptions. The tears shed during some of its sessions to date tell an eloquent story about the importance of paying attention to the emotional and psychological levels of peacemaking—an attention that careful listening makes possible. As Robert Rothstein says: "For hard-nosed realists or for analysts content to stress an interest-based approach to peacemaking, the psychological aspects of reconciliation may appear irrelevant or naive. But there is an important psychological or emotional component of protracted conflicts and there is likely to be an equally important psychological or emotional component to their resolution."[33]

Out of his own career as a diplomat, Harold Saunders makes similar claims: "Approaches to these tasks may call on some of the skills of mediation and negotiation, but they also require the insights and the art of those who think deeply about why human beings fear, hate, kill, and change their relationships." Religious leaders, at their best, can be among those who "think deeply" about these very things. In particular, as these cases illustrate, they can help bring about some of Saunders's empathetic "milestones": "when one party includes the other's definition of the problem in its own," and when together they "gradually learn to see those in their dialogue as human beings" and "to understand the other side's human and political needs."[34]

CATALYZING CROSSCUTTING CLEAVAGES

The indispensable aim of every effort of political conflict resolution is that parties to the conflict learn to live together "civilly." In his paper for this volume, Steven L. Burg distinguishes between two major approaches to the theory and practice of conflict resolution: segregation and integration.[35] Thomas Friedman images the difference in his opinion that "coexistence begins with barbed wire, not block parties."[36] The context of his view is the Israeli-Palestinian standoff. Robert Rothstein, in a lecture at Hebrew University in May 1996, rejected Friedman's rule as politically "untenable and dangerous." Build a fence between Israel and a Palestinian state, he notes, and it will have to be patrolled; furthermore, those who would "outflank it" will have to be "outwitted," a difficult prospect when two such nations can hardly avoid economic dependence on each other. Rothstein would agree that barbed wire at best temporarily halts war, giving the combatants time to consider how to organize the equivalent of block parties—a civil society that structures the competing as well as complementary interests of the former enemies.[37]

One can contrast here the violence-punctured politics of the South Africans and the Northern Irish with the current prospects for peace and war in Bosnia. In the former two situations, there is a history of encounters between individuals belonging to opposing camps in institutional settings that, over time, have helped diminish stereotypes and paranoid perceptions on all sides. One Belfast academic has recently made the wry observation, "The very fact that the Northern Irish conflict has spread over thirty years implies that these people have decided that somehow they have a common future. Even the three thousand deaths suggest a collective will to contain and not expand the violence."[38] Anthony Lewis quotes Ehud Barak, former foreign minister of the Peres government, now leader of the Labor Party in opposition, to the same effect: "The prerequisite for a stable Middle East is that we recognize the needs and sensitivities of our inevitable partners. They're going to be there forever. You don't choose your parents, and a people cannot choose their neighbors."[39] Even in South Africa in the apartheid era, whites and blacks made similar statements, backed up by relationships established over time in businesses, labor unions, universities, and churches.

"Crosscutting cleavages," says Burg, "contribute to the moderation of conflict only when they become the basis for political identity, electoral competition, and participation in representative institutions and decisionmaking processes." Almost all observers testify that nothing is more lacking in Bosnia today than just such moderating identities. Currently, an international military force is keeping the parties to the war separated, but the elements of civil society remain primitive. The same can probably be said of Nigeria; and in both countries the principal religious institutions offer both despair and hope with respect to the development of the much-needed civil society: despair because ethnic identity has for so long been associated with religious identity; hope because each of the major religions has supraethnic principles as part of its self-definition. Each of the major religions in Bosnia considers itself part of an international religious body, and external members of that body therefore have influence to bring to bear upon their local constituents. And they have an interest in exerting that influence. Furthermore, the local religious bodies have some freedom, if they want to use it, to begin building civil relations among their leaders and ordinary members.

Both the Bosnian and the Rwandan tragedies demonstrate that people who merely live alongside each other are not necessarily incapable of murdering each other. The breakdown of trust between long-time neighbors is one of the fearful phenomena in the recent history of these two societies. Interestingly enough, however, according to research by Marc Sommers among refugees from Rwanda stranded in Tanzania, the one organizational attachment that many seem most likely *to* trust is their local Christian congregation back in their home villages. In spite of the failure of Catholic, Anglican, and Muslim leaders to stem the violence of 1994, the refugees express more confidence in the promised help of those remote village congregations than in on-site international agencies like the Red Cross, UNHCR, and foreign church aid groups.[40] In late 1996, Sommers found that the local churches and mosques were locations of "religious identities . . . that Rwandan Hutu and Tutsi people share"—which, added to their mutual share in great suffering, promises "to advance the reconciliation process by reducing defensiveness among returnees." On the whole, he believes, "targeting local groups and locations that appear to have the best chance for successful reintegration would provide Rwandans with lessons learned" from their recent traumatic past.[41] In Bosnia and Nigeria as well, the freedom of Christians and Muslims to talk with each other would seem to provide one of the few opportunities for civil bridge building in the current life of the two countries. In each, however, the freight of recent, religion-tinged political violence makes the promise of dialogue very fragile. Nonetheless, dialogue among local and national religious leaders and congregants may constitute one of the few real openings for the emergence of civil societies there.

SUMMARY

THE PRAGMATIC MIX OF VISION AND ACTION IN RELIGION'S CONTRIBUTION TO VIOLENCE PREVENTION

Precisely because vigorous religions tend to spread a broad umbrella over human life as a whole, they are sometimes doubly invisible to empiricist observers: by claiming to relate to everything, they are hard to pin down to any one thing. And when they are involved in certain concrete activities, religious actors may or may not wear the formal badges of religion. Most theologians are little worried about this latter phenomenon; they readily accept the old principle, "You can do a great deal of good in the world if you don't care who gets the credit." Occasionally the genuinely self-effacing religious actors in some conflict situations have made their contribution in their very willingness to remain catalytically invisible in the process and outcome. Until it was concluded, the same catalytic function was at work in the Oslo meetings that led to the 1995 accord between the Israelis and the PLO.

History subverts most attempts at a comprehensive summary of what any set of actors do to prevent violent human conflict, but the concepts and cases in this paper suggest some generalizations about how religion hinders or helps the arts of peacemaking. On the negative side, religion seems *least* effective in conflict prevention:

◆ when it is so solidly allied with powerful political elites that it has to endorse the latter's resort to violence, sometimes offering unambiguous legitimization thereof;

◆ when it is content with a theology that calls for a "two kingdom" or otherworldly preoccupation among believers, leaving the powers that be to their own unchallengeable designs—when its leaders are unwilling, in short, to distance themselves from civil authority on grounds of allegiance to a more ultimate authority;

◆ when its leaders become alarmed at the onset of violence only when the guns and machetes, so to speak, are already raised; so, as war explodes, its cries for peace get drowned out;

◆ when it allows myths and symbols of the "inhuman" enemy to meet with silence or sanction in the internal rhetoric of the religious community; and, in so speaking (or not speaking), it hinders the development of a postconflict civic culture, which will require a restoration of the human image of the enemy;

◆ when it refuses to take conflict seriously enough to allow the parties access to its own "neutral ground," out of fear that verbalization of the conflict and attention to great clashes of interest inside the religious community will destroy that community; when, ironically, the religion is so used to shunning conflict in its own ranks that it lacks capacity to contribute to the lessening of conflict outside.

Alternatively, religion may contribute *most* to conflict resolution and violence prevention:

◆ when its articulate leaders keep prominent before their constituents the assurance that even in their commission of dehumanizing acts, the "enemy" belongs to the human community, even though the theological vision of that human community is suffering great political-ideological assault;

◆ when, in the service of opening up possibilities of realistic negotiations, it supplies political actors with alternative factual information about the culture and interests of the "enemy"; when, for example, missionaries and other religious personnel knowledgeable about the enemy's culture help alleviate popular stereotypes and make known the enemy's view of what is at stake in the conflict;

◆ when, in its liturgies, preaching, and public rhetoric, the religious community acknowledges its own partial responsibility for the violent state of things, refusing to provide even the "good" side of the conflict with unambiguous religious justifications of killing (Reinhold Niebuhr: "It may be possible for Christians to carry a gun, but they must carry it with a heavy heart.");

◆ when its leaders and constituents are schooled enough in awareness of their own and others' vulnerability to violence to understand the benefits of organized nonviolent resistance to injustice in advance of its victims' resort to violence; when its religiously grounded *ethics* propel its constituents into hearing from the "oppressed" soon enough to provide voice and remedy for their complaints before they believe violence is their only recourse;

◆ when its leaders and members do a lot of listening to all sides of a conflict, seek to interpret the interests of one side to the other, remain suspicious of propaganda, and acquire a public reputation for truth seeking and truth telling; when—as required for the effective performance of a number of the very activities we are enumerating—religious leadership refuses to identify with only one side of a conflict.

Hardly any of the contributions enumerated here are the exclusive prerogative of religion. We may argue that a religious—or transcendent—basis "is more sustaining than pragmatic ambition"; but the cause of peace is so important, and human capacities for peacemaking so diverse, that religious people should rejoice whenever *any* party to violence-prone conflicts practices "the art of those who think deeply" about the many dimensions of human existence.

But a religious orientation to human affairs will have its own definition of what constitutes deep thinking about human capacities for violence—which, as it happens, has been on the religious agenda since time immemorial.[42] My own view is that religion's most vital contribution to the question of violence in our time is a steady erosion of the conceptual and cultural connections between violence and the *sacred*. Sacralized violence is the bane of politics and the corruption of religion: wars are bad, but the worst wars are crusades.

In the service of across-the-board desacralizing of violence, there are two other dimensions of a religious worldview to be commended to political adversaries: the call to repentance and the transcendent valuation of human life. Both are commonly associated with the ethics of certain religions. Both ought to be regarded as pragmatic contributions to conflict resolution and not dismissed as merely idealistic. Kurt Lewin said that "nothing is so practical as a good theory." But the sad truth is that bad theories are practical too, as the history of warfare abundantly illustrates.

BEYOND TRAGEDY: FORGIVENESS, REPENTANCE, RECONSTRUCTION

In their paper in this collection, David Cortright and George Lopez speak of "the power of positive reciprocity." One side of a conflict makes a tentative offer to help the other, without, for the moment, demanding a return offer, in the hope "that this will prevent a renewal of bloodshed, or encourage a process of dialogue and negotiation." Such offers, they say, "are central to the art of diplomatic persuasion." They go on to observe that such initiatives were highly effective in seven out of eight arms negotiations between the United States and the Soviet Union in the past thirty years.

Among other things, to refrain from strict reciprocity is to forswear revenge and all strict adherence to the norm of retributive justice. In the aftermath of wars, religious organizations have counteracted impulses to revenge by offering to millions of enemy victims impressive arrays of economic, medical, and other aid. Such charity seems to come naturally to most religions. Often they have saved millions of lives by prompt response to material devastation in ways parallel to programs of government (e.g., the Marshall Plan) and other NGOs (e.g., many refugee resettlement agencies). One might surmise that religious forces are better equipped to deal with the devastation left after violent conflict than with conflict prevention.

In line with Harold Saunders's cyclical theory, however (see note 6 of this chapter), genuine recovery from a past devastation means taking those steps that will prevent a repetition of similar devastation in future political relations. The peace settlement that strips away reasons for *resuming* a conflict is the only true peace settlement. Many a settlement deteriorates because the debris of past evils done or suffered has never been dealt with.

The notions of forgiveness and repentance have not often been integrated by religious thinkers into their own ideas about these matters—and, a fortiori, secularists are apt to regard such notions as utterly irrelevant to politics. In the last ten years there has been a noticeable reassessment of this assumption, however, in some secular quarters. Peace may have to begin with apologies for the excesses of war on all sides. Robert Rothstein, for example, in his May 1996 lecture delivered in Jerusalem, said that he is now impressed with the importance of "collective expressions of guilt, apology, and reconciliation." He goes on to observe:

One reason for this is because I have been struck in dealing with Israelis and Palestinians how frequently each will begin denunciations of the other with reference to one atrocity or the other that the other has failed to acknowledge or apologize for.

Thomas Scheff has argued that in any prolonged conflict a cycle of insult, humiliation, and revenge destroys human bonds and that shame—one of the key bonds—causes escalation of conflict and thus a new cycle of anger, insults, and aggression. The cycle entraps both sides in a conflict that can easily end in catastrophe. Shriver suggests that reconciliation may be hastened by an acknowledgment of interdependence and a willingness to apologize for previous transgressions. Scheff also suggests that forgiveness is crucial in terms of ending cycles of violence and retaliation. To reestablish a civil relationship between strangers.

If one crucial aspect of a peace process is to establish a new relationship between ancient enemies, it helps to begin by clarifying the record, compensating for past sins, and setting off with not a completely new slate but at least a slate that has been cleared of its worst grievances.[43]

So often closeted in an exclusively religious context, the words "forgiveness" and "repentance" are here creeping into a pragmatic, secular guise that is no less real for being at once religious and secular. Commonsense ethics tells us that the best human response to evil is not to do it. That axiom needs a corollary: the second best is to repent of it. And another: where there is repentance, forgiveness can follow. Together, these three are the best of preventive-action principles. Only for already perfect societies does Robert Frost's rule not apply: "To be social is to be forgiving."

THE VALUE OF HUMAN LIFE

It would seem motivationally impossible for anyone interested in violence prevention to sustain a commitment to it while believing that "humans are no damn good." The idea of human worth is so basic that it would go without mentioning, except for the fact that the escalation of the means of violence in our century has persuaded many that much human life *is* fundamentally expendable. There are religious dualisms that denigrate human life and material existence, and there are religious doctrines that legitimate killing. One can kill for deeply "spiritual" reasons, as when Hindus, Muslims, and Serbian Orthodox destroy each other in battles over temple, mosque, and church sites.

In the twentieth century, however, we have more typically killed for deeply political reasons, and on a larger scale than ever before in our history. The result is a profound philosophical crisis that simmers beneath many a rational attempt at conflict resolution: Who are we that we should value each other?

Here sneak back Stanton Burnett's "questions that were tossed out the back door by the Enlightenment."[44] It may not be a "self-evident truth" that all humans are "created equal," in value or in any other sense. A scholar with a long acquaintance with Rwanda,

William O'Neill, writes that neither liberal Enlightenment philosophy nor postmodernism provides a rationale for a fundamental "prejudice of respect" that all humans owe each other. From Auschwitz to Rwanda, the logic of mass killing begins with "divesting the imagined 'other' of moral standing"—with a neighbor refusing "to 'see' the neighbor's face upon which was inscribed the command: 'Thou shalt not kill.'"[45]

Historians of philosophy have suggested that the famous categorical imperative of Immanuel Kant contained the ghost of the pietist Protestantism in which the great Prussian philosopher was raised. Subsequent Western thinkers had difficulty sustaining the awed consciousness that Kant believed was endemic to all thoughtful humans. Furthermore, his primordial "imperative" had no inherent moral content, and even when a modern philosopher like John Rawls seeks to ground human respect for the other in a mythical "original position," the resulting ethic is procedural, not substantive.[46]

Do human beings have *ontological* dignity and worth? Do they have it on the basis of higher authority than their own, individually or collectively? Religious believers answer "yes," affirming that human worth is grounded in a Creation and a Creator. To end this paper so, however, is to court the liberal, secular criticism: "You mount an apologetic for religion." I would prefer to be credited with mounting an apology for the unnegotiable worth of the human being!

"How shall we account each other valuable?" remains a critical question for our time. Even agnostics have reason to search for an answer. In his first literary account of Auschwitz, Elie Wiesel offered a now-famous answer to the question when recounting the atrocious execution of a young boy. "Where is God now?" asked one despairing camp witness.

"And I heard a voice within me answer him: 'Where is He? Here He is—He is hanging here on this gallows.'"[47]

We will recognize the sacred in the face of every human, says William O'Neill; or we will be tempted to lose a perception of the authority behind the command, "Thou shalt not kill!" O'Neill draws fresh confirmation of this claim from a Rwandan theologian, Augustin Karekezi, who speaks of the agony of the Rwandan genocide as derived from a "culture of impunity" that permitted killing without regret:

> We now know the consequences of such a culture, not only for the moral standing of the nation but for the survival chances of any group within the nation. It is now clear that

what is known in Rwanda as "the revolution of 1959" ended up eating its own children, precisely because of the false premises on which it was based. Instead of being a social revolution, in the end it institutionalized an awful ethnic polarization. A pervasive lack of respect for human life led to a general decline in the quality of life in the whole country—and eventually to genocide.

Who could ever have imagined that Rwandese, after having refused their fellow countrymen all their human and civil rights, would use their bones to build fires?[48]

Members of the species did imagine it. Then they did it, at Auschwitz and elsewhere. In his 1982 book *The Fate of the Earth*, Jonathan Schell resorted finally to theology to justify his hope that we would not effect a true "end of history" through nuclear suicide. In some quarters he was staunchly criticized for turning theological. Nevertheless, if religion has nothing else to contribute to us but the stubborn assertion that we are creatures worth *loving*, it will not totally fail the human project. Whatever else it does for peace, it should stand for the hope that human life is worth the throttling of our collective capacities for murder, because we are loved by Another who loves us better than we love ourselves. If there are other powerful groundings for the same indispensable assertion, religion will gladly celebrate them and work with their adherents.

PROGRAM

CENTER FOR PREVENTIVE ACTION'S
THIRD ANNUAL CONFERENCE, DECEMBER 12, 1996

INTRODUCTION AND WELCOME

JOHN W. VESSEY, Center for Preventive Action
DAVID A. HAMBURG, Carnegie Commission on Preventing Deadly
    Conflict
RICHARD C. LEONE, Twentieth Century Fund

BREAKOUT SESSIONS I

A) *South Balkans*
    Chair: SEYMOUR TOPPING, Columbia University
    Paper: STEVEN L. BURG, Brandeis University

B) *Burundi / Great Lakes*
    Chair: LIONEL A. ROSENBLATT, Refugees International
    Paper: MICHAEL S. LUND, Creative Associates International

C) *Nigeria*
    Chair: VIVIAN LOWERY DERRYCK, Africa Leadership Forum/
    Academy for Educational Development
    Paper: PETER M. LEWIS, American University

KEYNOTE SPEAKER

GENERAL GEORGE A. JOULWAN, Supreme Allied Commander, Europe, North Atlantic Treaty Organization

BREAKOUT SESSIONS II

D) *Small Weapons Disarmament*
Chair: HARRY D. TRAIN II, Science Applications International Corporation
Paper: EDWARD J. LAURANCE, Monterey Institute of International Studies

E) *Religion and Preventive Action*
Chair: M. WILLIAM HOWARD JR., New York Theological Seminary
Paper: DONALD W. SHRIVER JR., Union Theological Seminary

F) *Economic Tools of Conflict Prevention*
Chair: RICHARD N. HAASS, The Brookings Institution
Paper: DAVID CORTRIGHT, Fourth Freedom Forum, GEORGE A. LOPEZ, Kroc Institute, University of Notre Dame

REPORTS FROM THE BREAKOUT GROUPS AND CONCLUDING REMARKS

Chair: SAMUEL W. LEWIS, Washington Institute for Near East Policy
JANE E. HOLL, Carnegie Commission on Preventing Deadly Conflict
BARNETT R. RUBIN, Center for Preventive Action

DIRECTORIES OF ORGANIZATIONS WORKING IN CONFLICT PREVENTION AND RESOLUTION

Handbook on Human Rights in Situations of Conflict
by Janelle M. Diller
ISBN: 0-929293-35-5
Order through sponsoring organization below:

> Minnesota Advocates for Human Rights
> 310 Fourth Avenue South, Suite 1000
> Minneapolis, MN 55415-1012
> tel: (612) 341-3302
> fax: (612) 341-2971
> mnadvocates@igc.apc.org
> http://www.umn.edu/humanrts/mnadvocates

International Conflict Resolution: A Guide to Organizations and Practitioners
ISBN: 1-878597-17-5
Order through sponsoring organization below:

> ACCESS, An International Affairs Information Service
> 1701 K Street, NW, 11th Floor
> Washington, D.C. 20006
> tel: (202) 223-7949
> fax: (202) 223-7947
> http://www.4access.org

International Guide to NGO Activities in Conflict Prevention and Resolution
The entire guide is available on the Internet, or contact the sponsoring organization below to order:

> Conflict Resolution Program
> The Carter Center
> One Copenhill
> 453 Freedom Parkway
> Atlanta, GA 30307
> tel: (404) 420-5151
> fax: (404) 420-5196
> http://www.emory.edu/CARTER_CENTER

Prevention and Management of Conflicts: An International Directory
Contact sponsoring organization below to order:

> Paul van Tongeren
> European Centre for Conflict Prevention
> Janskerknof 30
> 3512 BN Utrecht
> The Netherlands
> tel: +31 (30) 253-7528
> fax: +30 (30) 253-7529

APPENDIX C
SELECTED BIBLIOGRAPHY

This is only a sample of the available literature on the topics specified below.

CONFLICT PREVENTION

Adelman, Howard, and Astri Suhrke. "Early Warning and Conflict Management: Genocide in Rwanda." *Study II of the Evaluation of Emergency Assistance to Rwanda.* Bergen, Norway: Christian Michelson Institute, 1995.

Bauwens, Werner, and Luc Reychler, eds. *The Art of Conflict Prevention.* London: Brassey's, 1994.

Boutros-Ghali, Boutros. *An Agenda for Peace: Preventive Diplomacy, Peacemaking and Peace-Keeping.* New York: United Nations Doc. S/24111, June 17, 1992.

Brown, Sheryl J., and Kimber M. Schraub, eds. *Resolving Third World Conflict: Challenges for a New Era.* Washington, D.C.: United States Institute of Peace, 1992.

Cahill, Kevin M., ed. *Preventive Diplomacy: Stopping Wars before They Start.* New York: Basic Books, 1996.

Chayes, Abram, and Antonia Handler Chayes, eds. *Preventing Conflict in the Post-Communist World: Mobilizing International and Regional Organizations.* Washington, D.C.: The Brookings Institution, 1996.

Conflict Prevention: Strategies to Sustain Peace in the Post–Cold War World. Report of the Aspen Institute Conference, July 30–August 3, 1996. Aspen, CO: The Aspen Institute, 1997.

Crocker, Chester A., Fen Osler Hampson, and Pamela Aall, eds. *Managing Global Chaos: Sources of and Responses to International Conflict.* Washington: United States Institute of Peace, 1996.

DeMars, William. *Precarious Partnership: Government-NGO Collaboration for Conflict Prevention.* Notre Dame, IN: University of Notre Dame, 1995.

Diamond, Louise, and John McDonald. *Multi-Track Diplomacy: A Systems Approach to Peace.* West Hartford, CT: Kumarian Press, 1996.

Gelb, Leslie H. "Quelling the Teacup Wars: The New World's Constant Challenge." *Foreign Affairs* 73, no. 6 (November/December 1994), pp. 2–6.

Gurr, Ted Robert. *Minorities at Risk: A Global View of Ethnopolitical Conflicts.* Washington, D.C.: United States Institute of Peace, 1993.

Haass, Richard N. *The Reluctant Sheriff: The United States after the Cold War.* New York: Council on Foreign Relations, 1997.

Kuroda, Michiko, and Kumar Rupesinghe, eds. *Early Warning and Conflict Resolution.* New York: St. Martin's Press, 1992.

Lederach, John Paul. *Building Peace: Sustainable Reconciliation in Divided Societies.* Washington, D.C.: United States Institute of Peace, 1997.

Lund, Michael S. *Preventing Violent Conflicts: A Strategy for Preventive Diplomacy.* Washington, D.C.: United States Institute of Peace, 1996.

Lund, Michael S., et al. *Preventing and Mitigating Violent Conflicts: A Revised Guide for Practitioners.* Prepared for the Greater Horn of Africa Initiative, the U.S. Department of State, and U.S AID. Washington, D.C.: Creative Associates International, April 1997.

Mitchell, Christopher and Michael Banks. *Handbook of Conflict Resolution: The Analytical Problem-Solving Approach.* London: Pinter, 1996. Montville, Joseph V., ed. *Conflict and Peacemaking in Multiethnic Societies.* New York: Lexington Books, 1991.

Preventing Violent Conflict: A Study. Swedish Ministry of Foreign Affairs, 1997.

Rothberg, Robert I., ed. *Vigilance and Vengeance: NGOs Preventing Ethnic Conflict in Divided Societies.* Washington, D.C.: Brookings Institution, 1996.

Rupesinghe, Kumar, ed. *Conflict Transformation.* New York: St. Martin's Press, 1995.

Sisk, Timothy D. *Power Sharing and International Mediation in Ethnic Conflicts.* Washington, D.C.: United States Institute of Peace, 1996.

Stedman, Stephen John. "Alchemy for a New World Order—Overselling 'Preventive Diplomacy'." *Foreign Affairs* 74, no. 3 (May/June 1995), pp. 14–20.

Zartman, William I. *Collapsed States: The Disintegration and Restoration of Legitimate Authority.* Boulder, CO: Lynne Rienner, 1995.

Zartman, William I., and J. Lewis Rasmussen, eds. *Peacemaking in International Conflict: Methods and Techniques.* Washington, D.C.: United States Institute of Peace, 1997.

THE SOUTH BALKANS

Burg, Steven L. *War or Peace? Nationalism, Democracy and American Foreign Policy in Post-Communist Europe.* New York: New York University Press, 1996.

Burg, Steven L., and Michael L. Berbaum. "Community, Integration, and Stability in Multi-National Yugoslavia." *American Political Science Review* 83 (June 1989), pp. 535–54.

Duijzings, Ger, Dusan Janjic, and Shkelzen Maliqi, eds. *Kosovo-Kosova: Confrontation or Coexistence?* Nijmegen: Peace Research Center, University of Nijmegen, 1997.

Janjic, Dusan and Shkelzen Maliqi, eds. *Conflict or Dialogue?* Subotica: Open University, 1994.

Rubin, Barnett R., ed. *Toward Comprehensive Peace in Southeast Europe: Conflict Prevention in the South Balkans*. New York: Twentieth Century Fund Press, 1996. The executive summary may also be found at www.foreignrelations.org.

Rychlik, Jan. "National Consciousness and the Common State: A Historical-Ethnological Analysis." In Jiri Musil, ed. *The End of Czechoslovakia*. Budapest: Central European University Press, 1995; pp. 95–105.

Sekulic, Dusko, et al. "Who Were the Yugoslavs? Failed Sources of a Common Identity in the Former Yugoslavia." *American Sociological Review* 59 (February 1994), pp. 83–97.

BURUNDI

Chrétien, Jean Pierre. *Burundi: L'Histoire Retrouvée*. Paris: Éditions Karthala, 1993.

Guichaoua, André, ed. *Les Crises Politiques au Burundi et au Rwanda: 1993–1994*, 2e édition. Paris: Université des Sciences et Technologies de Lille, 1995.

Lemarchand, René. *Burundi: Ethnocide as Discourse and Practice*. Cambridge: Cambridge University Press, 1994.

"Les politiques de la haine: Rwanda, Burundi, 1994–1995." *Les Temps Modernes* no. 583 (Juillet/Août).

Ould Abdallah, Ahmedou. *La Diplomatie Pyromane: Burundi, Rwanda, Somalie, Bosnie . . .* Paris: Calmann-Lévy, 1996.

Prunier, Gérard. "Burundi: Descent into Chaos or a Manageable Crisis." *WRITENET Country Papers* (March 1995) at http://www.unhcr.ch/refworld/country/writenet/wribdi01.htm.

Prunier, Gérard. "Burundi: Update to Early August 1995." *WRITENET Country Papers* (August 1995) at http:// www.unhcr.ch/refworld/country/writenet/wribdi02.htm.

Prunier, Gérard. "Burundi: Update to Early February 1996." *WRITE-NET Country Papers* (February 1996) at http:// www.unhcr.ch/ref-world/country/writenet/wribdi03.htm.

Prunier, Gérard. "The Geopolitical Situation in the Great Lakes Area in Light of the Kivu Crisis." *WRITENET Country Papers* (February 1997) at http://www.unhcr.ch/refworld/country/writenet/wrilakes.htm.

NIGERIA

Annual Report on Human Rights in Nigeria, 1995. Lagos: Civil Liberties Organization, 1996.

Diamond, Larry. "Nigeria: The Uncivic Society and the Descent into Praetorianism." In Larry Diamond, Juan Linz, and Seymour Martin Lipset, eds., *Politics in Developing Countries: Comparing Experiences with Democracy*, 2d ed. Boulder, CO: Lynne Rienner, 1995; pp. 417–91.

Dudley, Billy. *An Introduction to Nigerian Government and Politics.* Bloomington: University of Indiana Press, 1982.

Forrest, Tom. *Politics and Economic Development in Nigeria*, 2d ed. Boulder, CO: Westview Press, 1995.

Joseph, Richard. *Democracy and Prebendal Politics in Nigeria.* Cambridge: Cambridge University Press, 1987.

Joseph, Richard. "Nigeria: Inside the Dismal Tunnel." *Current History* (May 1996), pp. 193–200.

Lewis, Peter M. "Endgame in Nigeria? The Politics of a Failed Democratic Transition." *African Affairs* 93 (July 1994), pp. 323–40.

Lewis, Peter M. "Nigeria: Domestic Crisis Challenges International Influence." *SAIS Review* (Summer/Fall 1995), pp. 17–38.

Suberu, Rotimi. "The Travails of Federalism in Nigeria." *Journal of Democracy* 4, no. 4 (October 1993), pp. 39–53.

Sanctions and Incentives

Baldwin, David. *Economic Statecraft*. Princeton: Princeton University Press, 1985.

Bergeijk, Peter van. *Economic Diplomacy, Trade and Commercial Policy: Positive and Negative Sanctions in a New World Order*. Aldershot, England: Edward Elgar, 1994.

Cortright, David, ed. *The Price of Peace: Inducement Strategies and International Conflict Prevention*. Landover, MD: Rowman and Littlefield, 1997.

Cortright, David, and George Lopez eds. *Economic Sanctions: Panacea or Peacebuilding in a Post–Cold War World?* Boulder, CO: Westview Press, 1995.

Crumm, Eileen. "The Value of Economic Incentives in International Politics." *Journal of Peace Research* 32, no. 3 (1995), pp. 313–30.

Damrosch, Lori Fisler, ed. *Enforcing Restraint: Collective Intervention in Internal Conflicts*. New York: Council on Foreign Relations, 1993.

Doxey, Margaret P. *International Sanctions in Contemporary Perspective*. New York: Macmillan Press, 1996.

George, Alexander L. *Forceful Persuasion: Coercive Diplomacy as an Alternative to War*. Washington, D.C.: United States Institute of Peace, 1991.

Hufbauer, Gary C., Jeffrey J. Schott, and Kimberly Ann Elliott. *Economic Sanctions Reconsidered: History and Current Policy*, 2d ed. Washington, D.C.: Institute for International Economics, 1990.

Long, William J. *Economic Incentives and Bilateral Cooperation*. Ann Arbor: University of Michigan Press, 1996.

Nincic, Miroslav, and Peter Wallensteen, eds. *Dilemmas of Economic Coercion: Sanctions and World Politics*. New York: Praeger, 1983.

Osgood, Charles E. *An Alternative to War or Surrender*. Urbana: University of Illinois Press, 1962.

Weiss, Thomas G., David Cortright, George A. Lopez, and Larry Minear, eds. *Political Gain and Civilian Pain: Humanitarian Impacts of Economic Sanctions.* Landover, MD: Rowman & Littlefield, 1997.

SMALL WEAPONS DISARMAMENT

Bonn International Center for Conversion. "Small Arms and Light Weapons: The Perpetuation of Conflicts." *Conversion Survey 1997.* Oxford: Oxford University Press, 1997; pp. 141–74.

Boutwell, Jeffrey, Michael T. Klare, and Laura Reed, eds. *Lethal Commerce: The Global Trade in Small Arms and Light Weapons.* Cambridge, MA: American Academy of Arts and Sciences, 1995.

Disarmament: A Periodic Review by the United Nations 14, no. 2 (1996).

Goose, Stephen D., and Frank Smyth. "Arming Genocide in Rwanda." *Foreign Affairs* 73, no. 5 (September/October 1994), pp. 86–96.

Latham, Andrew. "The Light Weapons Problem: Causes, Consequences and Policy Options." In Andrew Latham, ed., *Multilateral Approaches to Non-Proliferation: Proceedings of the 4th Canadian Non-Proliferation Workshop.* Toronto: York University, 1996; pp. 33–54.

Laurance, Edward J. *The New Field of Micro-Disarmament: Addressing the Proliferation and Buildup of Small Arms and Light Weapons.* Bonn: Bonn International Center for Conversion, Brief 7, September 1996.

Managing Arms in Peace Processes: Croatia and Bosnia-Herzegovina. Geneva: United Nations Institute for Disarmament Research (UNIDIR), 1996.

Rana, Swadesh. *Small Arms and Intra-State Conflicts.* Geneva: United Nations Institute for Disarmament Research, 1995.

Singh, Jasjit, ed. *Light Weapons and International Security.* Delhi: Indian Pugwash Society and British American Security Information Council, 1995.

RELIGION AND CONFLICT PREVENTION

Bailie, Gil. *Violence Unveiled: Humanity at the Crossroads.* New York: Crossroad, 1995.

Girard, René. *Violence and the Sacred*, tr. Patrick Gregory. Baltimore: Johns Hopkins University Press, 1977.

Henderson, Michael. *The Forgiveness Factor: Stories of Hope in a World of Conflict*. London: Grosvenor Books, 1996.

Johnston, Douglas, and Cynthia Sampson, eds. *Religion, the Missing Dimension of Statecraft*. New York: Oxford University Press, 1994.

Scheff, Thomas J. *Bloody Revenge—Emotions, Nationalism, and War*. Boulder, CO: Westview Press, 1994.

Shriver, Donald W., Jr. *An Ethic for Enemies: Forgiveness in Politics*. New York: Oxford University Press, 1995.

Tavuchis, Nicholas. *Mea Culpa: A Sociology of Apology and Reconciliation*. Stanford University Press, 1991.

Wink, Walter. *Engaging the Powers: Discernment and Resistance in a World of Domination*. Minneapolis: Fortress Press, 1992.

Witte, John, Jr., and Johan D. van der Vyver, eds. *Religious Human Rights in Global Perspective: Religious Perspectives*. The Hague: Martinus Nijhoff Publishers, 1996.

AUTHORS' BIOGRAPHIES

STEVEN L. BURG is a professor in the Department of Politics at Brandeis University, where he served as dean of the College of Arts and Sciences from 1990 to 1992 and is presently director of the Center for German and European Studies. His research focuses on Eastern Europe and former Yugoslavia. Professor Burg was a consultant to CPA's South Balkans Working Group and is a contributor to *Toward Comprehensive Peace in Southeast Europe: Conflict Prevention in the South Balkans* (Twentieth Century Fund Press) and the author of *War or Peace? Nationalism, Democracy, and American Foreign Policy in Post-Communist Europe* (New York University Press).

SUSANNA CAMPBELL is a research associate for the Center for Preventive Action. She received her B.A. in international relations from Tufts University.

DAVID CORTRIGHT is president of the Fourth Freedom Forum. He is also a visiting fellow at the Joan B. Kroc Institute for International Peace Studies at the University of Notre Dame and a visiting professor in the Peace Studies department at Goshen College. He was executive director of the peace organization SANE from 1977 to 1987.

FABIENNE HARA is a research associate for the Center for Preventive Action's project on the Great Lakes region of Africa. She received her M.A. and diplôme d'Etudes Approfondies in international relations from the Institut d' Etudes Politiques de Paris. Previously, she was the team coordinator for Doctors of the World's mission in Burundi.

EDWARD J. LAURANCE is professor of international policy studies at the Monterey Institute of International Studies (MIIS). He currently directs the Program for Arms Control, Disarmament, and Conversion at the Center for Nonproliferation Studies at MIIS. He has been a consultant to the U.N. Centre for Disarmament Affairs since 1992.

PETER M. LEWIS is assistant professor at American University's School of International Service. His research focuses on economic reform and political transition in Sub-Saharan Africa, with special emphasis on contemporary Nigerian issues. He directed CPA's project on Nigeria.

GEORGE A. LOPEZ is a faculty fellow at the Joan B. Kroc Institute for International Peace Studies and professor of government and international studies at the University of Notre Dame. His research focuses on the problems of state violence and coercion, especially human rights and economic sanctions.

MICHAEL S. LUND is a senior associate at the Center for Strategic and International Studies and at Creative Associates International. Previously, he was a senior scholar at the United States Institute of Peace, which published his book entitled *Preventing Violent Conflicts: A Strategy for Preventive Diplomacy*. He traveled to Burundi for CPA and is currently completing a study of preventive action in that country. He is a member of CPA's Advisory Board.

BARNETT R. RUBIN is the director of the Center for Preventive Action of the Council on Foreign Relations. He was associate professor of political science and director of the Center for the Study of Central Asia at Columbia University from 1990 to 1996. Previously, he was a peace fellow at the United States Institute of Peace and assistant professor of political science at Yale University.

DONALD W. SHRIVER, JR. was president of Union Theological Seminary from 1975 to 1991 and William E. Dodge Professor of Applied Christianity there, and is now *emeritus*. He is currently teaching in the Human Rights Program of Columbia University as an adjunct professor in the School of Law. He has previously held adjunct appointments in the Jewish Theological Seminary, the School of Business, and the School of Journalism at Columbia. He is a member of CPA's Advisory Board.

THE ADVISORY BOARD OF THE CENTER FOR PREVENTIVE ACTION

Chair:
JOHN W. VESSEY
former chairman of the Joint
Chiefs of Staff

Vice-Chairs:
FRANCES FITZGERALD
The New Yorker

SAMUEL W. LEWIS
Washington Institute for Near
East Policy

Members:
MORTON I. ABRAMOWITZ
Council on Foreign Relations

GRAHAM T. ALLISON
Harvard University

CRAIG B. ANDERSON
General Theological Seminary

JAMES E. BAKER

DENIS A. BOVIN
Bear, Stearns & Company

ANTONIA HANDLER CHAYES
Conflict Management Group

VIVIAN LOWERY DERRYCK
Africa Leadership Forum/
Academy for Educational
Development

ROBERT P. DEVECCHI
Council on Foreign Relations

LESLIE H. GELB (ex officio)
Council on Foreign Relations

LOUIS GERBER
Communications Workers of
America (CWA)

ANDREW J. GOODPASTER
Atlantic Council

ERNEST G. GREEN
Lehman Brothers

RICHARD N. HAASS
The Brookings Institution

SIDNEY HARMAN
Harman International Industries

JAMES W. HARPEL
Harpel Partners, L.P.

ARTHUR HERTZBERG
New York University

JANE E. HOLL
Carnegie Commission on
Preventing Deadly Conflict

SCOTT HORTON
Patterson, Belknap, Webb &
Tyler

M. WILLIAM HOWARD, JR.
New York Theological Seminary

HENRY KAUFMAN
Henry Kaufman & Company

RICHARD C. LEONE
Twentieth Century Fund

WENDY W. LUERS
Foundation for a Civil Society

MICHAEL S. LUND
Creative Associates International

ERNEST R. MAY
Harvard University

JAY MAZUR
Union of Needletrades,
Industrial and Textile Employees
(UNITE)

GAY J. MCDOUGALL
International Human Rights Law
Group

DONALD F. MCHENRY
Georgetown University

JOSEPH A. O'HARE, SJ
Fordham University

PEARL T. ROBINSON
Tufts University

LIONEL A. ROSENBLATT
Refugees International

KENNETH ROTH
Human Rights Watch

KURT L. SCHMOKE
Mayor, City of Baltimore

DONALD W. SHRIVER, JR.
Union Theological Seminary

HEDRICK L. SMITH
Johns Hopkins University

JOHN D. STEINBRUNER
The Brookings Institution

FRITZ STERN
Columbia University

JULIA V. TAFT
InterAction

SEYMOUR TOPPING
Columbia University

HARRY D. TRAIN II
Science Applications
International Corporation

BERNARD E. TRAINOR
Harvard University

ROBERT C. WAGGONER
Burelle's Information Services

MICHAELA WALSH
Women's Asset Management

H. ROY WILLIAMS
International Rescue Committee

R. JAMES WOOLSEY
Shea & Gardner

ARISTIDE R. ZOLBERG
New School for Social Research

NOTES

— 1 —

1. Please refer to the Preface of this volume for a more detailed description of the Center for Preventive Action's activities.

2. Please refer to Appendix A for the program of the conference, which was held on December 12, 1996.

3. For an analysis of this phenomenon in Southwest Asia, see Barnett R. Rubin, *The Search for Peace in Afghanistan: From Buffer State to Failed State* (New Haven: Yale University Press, 1995). On the proliferation of conflicts, see Leslie H. Gelb, "Quelling the Teacup Wars: The New World's Constant Challenge," *Foreign Affairs* 73, no. 6 (November/December 1994): 2–6. On deregulation of the international system, see Richard N. Haass, *The Reluctant Sheriff: The United States after the Cold War* (New York: Council on Foreign Relations, 1997).

4. No one did more to focus attention on prevention than former UN secretary-general Boutros Boutros-Ghali, who included it as one of the four basic elements of UN peace operations in his 1992 *Agenda for Peace: Preventive Diplomacy, Peacemaking and Peace-Keeping* (New York: United Nations Doc. A/47/277, S.2411, June 1992).

5. When Burundi's second Hutu president, Cyprien Ntaryamira, was killed in the April 1994 plane crash that killed Rwandan president Habyarimana in Kigali, Ahmedou Ould Abdallah, the UN secretary-general's special representative, coordinated a crisis response effort that effectively prevented a possible repetition of the 1993 massacres. As usual it is impossible to prove what might have happened otherwise, but the fact that there was no violence is quite striking.

6. The Security Working Group is a confidential meeting sponsored by the Great Lakes Policy Forum. Please refer to the Preface for a description.

7. See "Report of the Fact-finding Mission of the Secretary-General to Nigeria," Annex I of *Human Rights Questions: Human Rights Situations and Reports of Special Rapporteurs and Representatives* (New York: United Nations Doc. A/50/960, May 28, 1996).

8. Peter M. Lewis, "Nigeria: The Challenge of Preventive Action," in Barnett R. Rubin, ed., *Cases and Strategies for Preventive Action* (New York: Twentieth Century Fund Press, 1997), p. 109.

9. The other conditions were full compliance with the Dayton Accords and delivery of indicted war criminals to the International War Crimes Tribunal for the former Yugoslavia.

10. Stephen John Steadman, "Alchemy for a New World Order— Overselling 'Preventive Diplomacy,'" *Foreign Affairs* 74, no. 3 (May/June 1995): 14–20.

11. Michael S. Lund, *Preventing Violent Conflicts: A Strategy for Preventive Diplomacy* (Washington, D.C.: United States Institute of Peace, 1996).

12. Kalevi J. Holsti, *The State, War, and the State of War* (Cambridge: Cambridge University Press, 1996).

13. Gérard Prunier, "The Geopolitical Situation in the Great Lakes Area in Light of the Kivu Crisis" (http: //www.unhcr.ch /refworld/country /writenet /wrilakes.htm, February 1997).

14. Guides to this field have also proliferated. See Appendix B for a partial list.

15. See Donald W. Shriver, Jr., "Religion and Violence Prevention," in Rubin, *Cases and Strategies*. See also Cameron Hume, *Ending Mozambique's War: The Role of Mediation and Good Offices* (Washington, D.C.: United States Institute of Peace, 1994).

16. Alvaro de Soto and Graciana del Castillo, "Obstacles to Peacebuilding," *Foreign Policy*, no. 94 (Spring 1994): 69–83; James K. Boyce, *Economic Policy for Building Peace: The Lessons of El Salvador* (Boulder, Colo.: Lynne Rienner, 1996).

17. Among these efforts are the Great Lakes (formerly Burundi) Policy Forum in Washington, cosponsored by CPA, Search for Common Ground, and Refugees International, and the EuroForum on the Great Lakes in Brussels, cosponsored by CPA, the European Centre for Common Ground, and International Alert. Together with the Carter Center and Synergies Africa, CPA also sponsored an international and multisectoral consultation with Ambassador Mohamed Sahnoun, special envoy to the Great Lakes of the UN and OAU.

— 2 —

1. Note from volume editor: Kosovo is the province where the leaders of the overwhelmingly ethnic Albanian population (probably more than 90 percent of the total) claim the right to political independence, despite international recognition of Serbia's claim to it. Serbia's hold on the province was reinforced by the revocation of the province's autonomy in 1989 and a virtual military occupation since then. The Republic of Macedonia, one of socialist Yugoslavia's successor states, also contains a

sizable Albanian population (about 22 percent by official and international estimates, though Albanians claim 40 percent). Albanian parties in Macedonia have raised various nationalist demands, including political parity with ethnic Macedonians as a "constitutive nation" (rather than a national minority) in the republic, territorial autonomy for western Macedonia, where they constitute a majority, and a complete parallel system of education in the Albanian language. They recognize, however, that they are part of the state by participating in politics (including in the governing coalition), while Albanian parties in Kosovo boycott Serbian and Yugoslav institutions, denying that they are part of a common state.

Macedonia also includes other minorities, such as Turks, Roma, Vlach, and Serbs. Greece has contested the right of that republic to become independent under the name "Macedonia," which it claimed implied revanchist intentions toward the Greek province of the same name. Bulgaria has not recognized that Macedonians are ethnically or linguistically different from Bulgarians. In deference to Greek sensitivities, international organizations and some states refer to Macedonia as the "Former Yugoslav Republic of Macedonia," or FYROM.

2. For more comprehensive background material, see Chapter Three of the *Report of the Working Group on the South Balkans* (Steven L. Burg, "Stabilizing the South Balkans") in Barnett R. Rubin, ed., *Toward Comprehensive Peace in Southeast Europe: Conflict Prevention in the South Balkans* (New York: Twentieth Century Fund Press, 1996). The Executive Summary may also be found at http://www.foreignrelations.org.

3. For a brief discussion of this literature, see Timothy D. Sisk, *Power Sharing and International Mediation in Ethnic Conflicts* (Washington, D.C.: United States Institute of Peace, 1996).

4. Arend Lijphart, *Democracy in Plural Societies* (New Haven: Yale University Press, 1977), and "The Power-Sharing Approach," in Joseph V. Montville, ed., *Conflict and Peacemaking in Multiethnic Societies* (Lexington, Mass.: Lexington Books, 1990), pp. 491–509. Cf. the definitions contributed by Kenneth McRae, ed., in *Consociational Democracy: Political Accommodation in Segmented Societies* (Toronto: McClelland and Stewart, 1974).

5. Cf. "The Belgian Example of Cultural Coexistence in Comparative Perspective," in Arend Lijphart, ed., *Conflict and Coexistence in Belgium* (Berkeley: University of California, Institute of International Studies, 1981), pp. 1–12.

6. For a brief account of this process, see Richard Lewis, "The Example of Belgium," *Global Forum Series Occasional Paper* No. 96–01.2 (Durham, N.C.: Center for International Studies, Duke University, April 1996).

7. This argument is made at greater length in Steven L. Burg, *War or Peace? Nationalism, Democracy and American Foreign Policy in Post-Communist Europe* (New York: New York University Press, 1996).

8. See Steven L. Burg and Michael L. Berbaum, "Community, Integration, and Stability in Multi-National Yugoslavia," *American Political*

Science Review 83 (June 1989): 535–54; Dusko Sekulic et al., "Who Were the Yugoslavs? Failed Sources of a Common Identity in the Former Yugoslavia," *American Sociological Review* 59 (February 1994): 83–97; and Jan Rychlik, "National Consciousness and the Common State: A Historical-Ethnological Analysis," in Jiri Musil, ed., *The End of Czechoslovakia* (Budapest: Central European University Press, 1995), pp. 95–105.

9. Lewis, "The Example of Belgium," p. 15.

10. Arend Lijphart, *The Politics of Accommodation: Pluralism and Democracy in the Netherlands*, 2d ed. (Berkeley: University of California Press, 1975).

11. Refer to Chapter 3 of this volume, "Learning from Burundi's Failed Democratic Transition, 1993–96: Did International Initiatives Match the Problem?" p. 61.

12. This argument is made in greater detail in Steven L. Burg, "Bosnia-Herzegovina: A Case of Failed Transition" (paper prepared for Project on Democratization and Political Participation in Post-Communist Societies, Washington, D.C., October 1993).

13. Janie Leatherman, "Untying Macedonia's Gordian Knot" (Paper presented to the Center for Preventive Action's Working Group on the South Balkans, Council on Foreign Relations, New York, 1995).

14. Donald L. Horowitz, *Ethnic Groups in Conflict* (Berkeley: University of California Press, 1985), especially pp. 628–51 on electoral systems and conflict reduction, and Horowitz, *A Democratic South Africa?* (Berkeley: University of California Press, 1991), pp. 172ff.

15. For a history of such efforts and insight into the controversy surrounding them, see Bernard Grofman et al., *Minority Representation and the Quest for Voting Equality* (Cambridge: Cambridge University Press, 1992), and Lani Guinier, *The Tyranny of the Majority: Fundamental Fairness in Representative Democracy* (New York: Free Press, 1994).

16. For discussion of such a system, see James Coleman, "Democracy in Permanently Divided Systems," *American Behavioral Scientist* 35 (March–June 1992): 363–74.

17. The influx of weapons has been reported privately to the author by diplomatic sources and by well-informed individuals in Kosovo, and publicly in the *New York Times*, April 24, 1997.

18. This census and its results are reported in Victor Friedman, "Observing the Observers: Language, Ethnicity, and Power in the 1994 Macedonian Census and Beyond," in Rubin, ed. *Toward Comprehensive Peace*, pp. 81–105. For official results, see Statistical Office of the Republic of Macedonia, *The 1994 Census of the Population, Households, Dwellings, and Agricultural Holdings in the Republic of Macedonia* (Skopje: November 1996).

19. Owing to publishing constraints, diacritical marks have been omitted from this chapter.

20. Lewis, "Nigeria: The Challenge of Preventive Action," p. 109.

21. This very brief overview of Search for Common Ground in Macedonia (SCGM) activities is drawn from reports and other materials distributed by SCGM—e.g., letter from Kim Stalnaker, Program Coordinator, SCGM (October 4, 1996).

22. "Proposal of the Law on Higher Education," part I, article 9 (mimeographed).

23. Letter and supporting material from Kenneth D. Wollack, President, National Democratic Institute (September 27, 1996).

24. Statement of September 1, 1996, released by the Community of Sant' Egidio (mimeographed).

25. See, e.g., Dusan Janjic and Shkelzen Maliqi, eds., *Conflict or Dialogue?* (Subotica: Open University, 1994), and Ger Duijzings, Dusan Janjic, and Shkelzen Maliqi, eds., *Kosovo-Kosova: Confrontation or Coexistence?* (Nijmegen: Peace Research Center, University of Nijmegen, 1997).

26. David Phillips, "Practical Experience in Preventive Action" (Paper presented at the Center for Preventive Action's Third Annual Conference, held on December 12, 1996, at the Council on Foreign Relations, New York).

— 3 —

1. This paper is a preliminary result of an analysis of the international involvement in Burundi sponsored by the Center for Preventive Action of the Council on Foreign Relations. It is also a case within a larger research project of one author (Lund) to identify policy-relevant factors that explain why post-cold war national transition conflicts—such as disputes over ethnic group claims, secession efforts, and democratization—have in some cases led to violent conflict or repression (e.g., Serbia/Croatia/Bosnia, Moldova, Chechnya, Rwanda, Burundi), while, in other cases, violence has been prevented through more peaceful means (e.g., Macedonia, Hungary/Slovakia, Estonia, Tatarstan, Congo/Brazzaville, South Africa). The authors are indebted to the United States Institute of Peace, the Winston Foundation, Stiftung Wissenschaft und Politik, the Carnegie Corporation of New York, the Norwegian Institute for International Relations, and the Carnegie Commission for Preventing Deadly Conflict for partial support of this project.

2. This section distills certain variables prevalent in recent research on so-called "ethnic" conflicts, on early warning indicators of genocide and other national conflicts, and on cases of peaceful settlement of disputes. Several of these were preliminarily tested vis-à-vis successful and unsuccessful cases of post–cold war preventive initiatives in Chapter 3 of Michael S. Lund, *Preventing Violent Conflicts: A Strategy for Preventive Diplomacy* (Washington, D.C.: United States Institute of Peace, 1996). This is work in progress, so conclusions are not definitive. But based as

they are on a wider literature as well as on preliminary assessments of several cases, the factors are not merely speculative.

3. See, e.g., Hugh Miall in "Peaceful Settlement of Post-1945 Conflicts: A Comparative Study," in Kumar Rupesinghe and Michiko Kuroda, eds., *Early Warning and Conflict Resolution* (New York: St. Martin's Press, 1992), p. 77; Hugh Miall, *The Peacemakers: Peaceful Settlement of Disputes since 1945* (New York: St. Martin's Press, 1992), p. 30.

4. See Donald L. Horowitz, *Ethnic Groups in Conflict* (Berkeley: University of California Press, 1985).

5. Thomas S. Szayna, *Ethnic Conflict in Central Europe and the Balkans: A Framework and U.S. Policy Options* (Santa Monica, Calif.: Rand, 1994). Cf. David Carment, "The Ethnic Dimension in World Politics: Theory, Politics, and Early Warning," *Third World Quarterly* 15, no. 4 (1994): 563; and "The International Dimensions of Ethnic Conflict: Concepts, Indicators, and Theory," *Journal of Peace Research* 30, no. 2 (1993): 137–50.

6. But when these massacres occurred, Burundi leaders also took steps to calm down the resulting anxieties. Thus, an opposite effect of regionalization can be "cross-conflict learning"—when horrible analogous conflicts occur nearby, and domestic leaders are repelled from violent escalation because they want to avoid the horrors they observe in these situations. Such turmoil may temper the inclination of state leaders to push disagreements too far, for if domestic constituencies rise up in uncontrollable anger that destabilizes their own states, the conflicts might spiral outside the control of the leaders.

7. Timothy D. Sisk, *Living Together? International Intervention and Power-Sharing in Ethnic Conflicts* (Washington, D.C.: United States Institute of Peace, 1996), p. vii.

8. Carment, "The Ethnic Dimension," pp. 6–9; Miall, *The Peacemakers*, p. 83.

9. Gérard Prunier, "Burundi: Descent into Chaos or Manageable Crisis?" (March 1995), http://www.unhcr.ch/refworld/ country/writenet/ wribdi01. htm.

10. Adam Przeworski, "Material Bases of Consent: Economics and Politics in a Hegemonic System," *Political Power and Social Theory* I (1980): 21–67.

11. Patrick D. Gaffney, "Burundi on the Brink: The Long Somber Shadow of Ethnic Instability," revised draft of paper for UNU/WIDER project on The Political Economy of Humanitarian Emergencies, Helsinki, October 4–6, 1996.

12. Ibid.

13. Prunier, "Burundi: Descent into Chaos," section 4.1

14. Ibid.

15. Ibid.

16. These observations derive primarily from interviews conducted in Bujumbura by Lund and Hara during their trip to Burundi, May 18–June 2, 1996.

17. "Report of the Secretary-General on the Situation in Burundi," S/1996/116, February 15, 1996, paragraphs 44–45.

18. The quotation is from "Letter of the Secretary-General to the Security Council on the Situation in Burundi," S/1995/1068, December 29, 1995, but similar phrases were used by many, including the Center for Preventive Action and its partners in the initial statement of the goals of the Burundi Policy Forum.

19. Michael Ignatieff, "Alone with the Secretary General," *The New Yorker*, August 14, 1995, pp. 33–39

20. There was a controversy over the publication of the report, as the UN Secretariat at first kept it confidential. It named individuals responsible for the killing of President Ndadaye and might have incited them to pressure or overthrow Buyoya. Eventually the report was released, and Buyoya dismissed several officers.

21. In a fax to the Center for Preventive Action dated August 25, 1995, Ould Abdallah wrote, "Situation in Burundi is presently dominated by the problem of Burundese and Rwandese refugees now in Zaire, a serious question long overshadowed by the litany of worst case scenario for Burundi."

22. *Cairo Declaration on the Great Lakes Region,* Cairo, November 29, 1995; *Tunis Declaration on the Great Lakes Region,* Tunis, March 18, 1996.

23. "Letter of the Secretary-General to the Security Council on the Situation in Burundi," S/1995/1068, December 29, 1995.

24. "Report of the Secretary-General on the Situation in Burundi," February 15, 1996.

25. "Report to the Security Council on the Situation in Burundi," S/1996/660, August 15, 1996.

26. Innocent Mukozi, quoted in Stefan Lovgren, "Burundi on Edge over an 'Invasion,'" *Christian Science Monitor*, July 8, 1996.

27. Gérard Prunier claims that this was one of the goals that led Gen. Paul Kagame of Rwanda to launch the uprising in Kivu. See "The Geopolitical Situation in the Great Lakes Area in Light of the Kivu Crisis" (February 1997), http://www. unhcr.ch/refworld /country/writenet /wrilakes.htm.

28. Speech at Council on Foreign Relations, June 25, 1997. Quoted with permission.

29. For instance, after Nyangoma left the government Ould Abdallah arranged a fellowship in the United States for him. When a Swedish institute invited Nyangoma to participate in a dialogue, however, Ould Abdallah claims that he decided to remain in the region and found his organization, the CNDD. The authors have no independent information on Nyangoma's decision-making process.

30. Prunier, "Burundi: Update to Early February 1996" (February 1996), http://www.unhcr.ch/refworld/country/writenet/wribdi03.htm. From the legal point of view, some, including the legal office of the U.S.

Department of State, argued that the gradual killings by both sides fulfilled the Genocide Treaty's definition of killings with the intention of destroying a group "in whole or in part." The discourse about genocide in Burundi, however, continually made reference to Rwanda, a well-organized, intense effort by a government and its supporters to kill all the members of one group. The average daily rate of killing in Rwanda was equal to or higher than that of Jews by the Nazis during 1941–45.

31. Ibid.

32. But the polemic that humanitarian efforts have been insufficient to resolve the Burundi crisis misses the point that aid to the victims of violent conflicts has never been widely seen as intended to treat its causes.

33. For an early effort to identify and evaluate the range of policy tools available for conflict prevention and mitigation, see Michael S. Lund et al., *Preventing and Mitigating Conflicts: A Guide for Practitioners*, prepared for U.S. AID and the U.S. Department of State, Greater Horn of Africa Initiative (Washington, D.C.: Creative Associates International, Inc., 1996).

4

1. These events are discussed the reports by Human Rights Watch/Africa, *Nigeria: Democracy Derailed* (Washington, D.C., August 1993) and *Nigeria: The Dawn of a New Dark Age* (Washington, D.C., October 1994). See also Peter M. Lewis, "Endgame in Nigeria? The Politics of a Failed Democratic Transition," *African Affairs* 93 (July 1994): 323–40.

2. See Richard Joseph, "Nigeria: Inside the Dismal Tunnel," *Current History* (May 1996): 193–200.

3. These issues are reviewed by Rotimi Suberu in "The Travails of Federalism in Nigeria," *Journal of Democracy* 4, no. 4 (October 1993): 39–53.

4. Larry Diamond reviews this history in "Nigeria: The Uncivic Society and the Descent into Praetorianism," in Larry Diamond, Juan Linz, and Seymour Martin Lipset, eds., *Politics in Developing Countries: Comparing Experiences with Democracy*, 2d ed. (Boulder, Colo.: Lynne Rienner, 1995), pp. 417–91.

5. The evolution of the Nigerian economy is recounted by Tom Forrest in *Politics and Economic Development in Nigeria*, 2d ed. (Boulder, Colo.: Westview Press, 1995).

6. See James S. Coleman, *Nigeria: Background to Nationalism* (Berkeley: University of California Press, 1958).

7. Billy Dudley covers this period in *An Introduction to Nigerian Government and Politics* (Bloomington: University of Indiana Press, 1982).

8. The characteristic electoral pattern in Nigeria since 1979 has been a sequence of elections beginning with local governments, state assemblies, and governorships, followed by National Assembly polls (including the House of Representatives and the Senate) and culminating with the

presidential vote. During the Second Republic, elections were held at weekly intervals, but the spacing has been more protracted in recent years.

9. See Richard A. Joseph, *Democracy and Prebendal Politics in Nigeria: The Rise and Fall of the Second Republic* (Cambridge: Cambridge University Press, 1987).

10. Adebayo Olukoshi and Tajudeen Abdulraheem, "Nigeria: Crisis Management under the Buhari Regime," *Review of African Political Economy*, no. 34 (December 1985): 95–101.

11. Thomas M. Callaghy discusses the genesis of the adjustment program in "Lost between State and Market: The Politics of Economic Adjustment in Ghana, Zambia, and Nigeria," in Joan Nelson, ed., *Economic Crisis and Policy Choice* (Princeton: Princeton University Press, 1990), pp. 257–319.

12. Lewis, "Endgame in Nigeria?"

13. Ibid.

14. External responses to Nigeria are covered in Peter M. Lewis, "Nigeria: Domestic Crisis Challenges International Influence," *SAIS Review* (Summer/Fall 1995): 17–38.

15. Utibe Ukim, "The New Offensive," *Newswatch*, September 12, 1994, pp. 8–13. See also the report by Human Rights Watch/Africa, *Nigeria: The Dawn of a New Dark Age*.

16. Howard French, "In Nigeria, A Strongman Tightens the Vise," *New York Times*, March 31, 1995.

17. The sentence for Yar'Adua was changed to life imprisonment, while Obasanjo received fifteen years.

18. These events are covered in the report by the Civil Liberties Organization, *Annual Report on Human Rights in Nigeria, 1995* (Lagos, 1996).

19. See Attahiru Jega, "Professional Associations and Structural Adjustment," in Adebayo Olukoshi, ed., *The Politics of Structural Adjustment in Nigeria* (London: James Currey, 1993), pp. 97–111.

20. Abacha's handling of the politicians is described by Mike Akpan in "The Joker," *Newswatch*, February 20, 1995, pp. 13–18.

21. Paul Adams, "Reign of the Generals," *Africa Report*, November/December 1994, pp. 27–29.

22. In 1994, a pamphlet appeared in Nigeria supposedly detailing a "Yoruba Agenda" to destabilize the country and capture political dominance. The document, of unknown origin, is attributed to the "Yoruba Solidarity Forum" and, in the classic manner of conspiracy literature, purports to reveal confidential documents substantiating Yoruba intrigues. The pamphlet has circulated widely among northern elites and has been cited by prominent northerners as evidence of a cabal among southwestern elements. This is one conspicuous manifestation of the deep mistrust and antipathy among regional groups. See the Yoruba Solidarity Forum, *The Master-Plan: The Agenda that Conquered IBB* (n. p., 1994).

23. The violent conflict among Itsekiri, Urhobo, and Ijaw groups in the area of the Niger Delta was reported in *The Week* (Lagos), April 7, 1997, pp.

20–21. On the battles between Ife and Modakeke communities in western Nigeria, see *The Week*, September 8, 1997, pp. 21–23.

24. The term "road to Kinshasa" was used by Shell Oil analysts in a projection of alternative scenarios for political and economic change in Nigeria, although they have moderated their terminology to label this scenario as one of "strife." See the Shell Petroleum Development Corporation, *Nigeria Scenarios 1996–2010* (Lagos, 1996), pp. 10, 19.

25. As this volume went to press, reports of General Abacha's failing health raised doubts about his ability to stand for election in 1998. On September 8, 1997, according to Agence France-Presse, a leading Nigerian news magazine reported that Abacha was suffering from advanced cirrhosis of the liver. If these accounts prove credible, then the possibility of self-succession by the military leader is largely eliminated.

26. Several of these factors are discussed by Michael S. Lund in *Preventing Violent Conflicts: A Strategy for Preventive Diplomacy* (Washington, D.C.: United States Institute of Peace, 1996).

27. This "toolbox" of engagement is elaborated by Lund in *Preventing Violent Conflicts*, pp. 203–5. The threat and application of military force is also available as a policy instrument, although such considerations have not been relevant to policy debates on Nigeria. See also the chapter by Lund et al. in this volume.

28. Petroleum accounts for more than 95 percent of Nigeria's export income. Taking 1994 as a convenient benchmark, nearly 90 percent of Nigeria's petroleum exports (in dollar value) went to North America and Western Europe, with negligible amounts purchased by Japan. Most of these exports were purchased by eight countries: In order of importance, they were the United States (46 percent of total value), France (12 percent), Spain (8 percent), the Netherlands (6 percent), Canada (3 percent), Italy (2.1 percent), Germany (0.6 percent), and the United Kingdom (0.6 percent). (These percentages have been rounded.) The figures are provided by the Central Bank of Nigeria in its *Annual Report and Statement of Accounts, 1994* (Lagos, 1995), p. 129. At the end of the 1980s, the principal sources of imports into Nigeria were, in order, the United Kingdom, West Germany, France, Japan, the United States, and the Netherlands; these figures are found in the Federal Republic of Nigeria, *Digest of Statistics* (Lagos: Federal Office of Statistics, December 1989), pp. 102–5.

29. The prospects and liabilities of sanctions are assessed in the report by the U.S. General Accounting Office, *International Trade: Issues Regarding Imposition of an Embargo against Nigeria*, GAO/GGD-95-24, November 10, 1994.

30. John Harbeson, Donald Rothchild, and Naomi Chazan, eds., *Civil Society and the State in Africa* (Boulder, Colo.: Lynne Rienner, 1995).

31. Samuel P. Huntington elaborates the problem of civilian-military relations in *The Third Wave: Democratization in the Late Twentieth Century* (Norman: University of Oklahoma Press, 1991).

— **5** —

1. See David Cortright and George A. Lopez, eds., *Economic Sanctions: Panacea or Peacebuilding in a Post-Cold War World?* (Boulder, Colo.: Westview Press, 1995); and David Cortright, ed., *The Price of Peace: Inducement Strategies and International Conflict Prevention* (Lanham, Md.: Rowman and Littlefield, 1997).

2. Alexander L. George, David K. Hall, and William R. Simons, *The Limits of Coercive Diplomacy: Laos-Cuba-Vietnam* (Boston: Little, Brown and Company, 1971), p. 25; David Baldwin, "The Power of Positive Sanctions," *World Politics* 24, no. 1 (October 1971): 25.

3. Alexander L. George and Richard Smoke, *Deterrence in American Foreign Policy: Theory and Practice* (New York: Columbia University Press, 1974), p. 608; Alexander L. George, *Forceful Persuasion: Coercive Diplomacy as an Alternative to War* (Washington, D.C.: United States Institute of Peace, 1991), p. 11.

4. Martin Patchen, *Resolving Disputes between Nations: Coercion or Conciliation?* (Durham, N.C.: Duke University Press, 1988), p. 271; Russell Leng, "Influence Techniques among Nations," in Philip E. Tetlock et al., eds., *Behavior, Society, and International Conflict* (Oxford: Oxford University Press, 1993), p. 115.

5. Arnold Wolfers, "Power and Influence: The Means of Foreign Policy," in Arnold Wolfers, ed., *Discord and Collaboration: Essays on International Politics* (Baltimore: Johns Hopkins Press, 1962), pp. 107–8.

6. Patchen, *Resolving Disputes*, p. 269.

7. See, for example, Jim Hoagland, "The Sanctions Bromide," *The Washington Post*, November 12, 1993.

8. Margaret P. Doxey, *International Sanctions in Contemporary Perspective* (New York: St. Martin's Press, 1987), p. 92.

9. Gary C. Hufbauer, Jeffrey J. Schott, and Kimberly Ann Elliott, *Economic Sanctions Reconsidered: History and Current Policy*, 2d ed. (Washington, D.C.: Institute for International Economics, 1990).

10. Alan Dowty, "Sanctioning Iraq: The Limits of the New World Order," *The Washington Quarterly* (Summer 1994): 192.

11. Hufbauer et al., *Economic Sanctions Reconsidered*, p. 94.

12. See Barry M. Blechman and Stephen S. Kaplan, *Force without War: U.S. Armed Forces as a Political Instrument* (Washington, D.C.: Brookings Institution, 1978). Blechman and Kaplan studied the use of military force to achieve political objectives and found long-term success rates for "compellence" of only 18 percent and for inducement of 22 percent. See the discussion of these findings and a comparison with success rates using economically coercive instruments in David Baldwin, *Economic Statecraft* (Princeton: Princeton University Press, 1985), p. 318–19.

13. Hufbauer et al., *Economic Sanctions Reconsidered*, p. 101.

14. United Nations Security Council Sanctions Committee, *Report of the Copenhagen Round Table on United Nations Sanctions in the Case of Former Yugoslavia, held at Copenhagen on 24 and 25 June 1996*. Annex prepared by the Security Council Sanctions Committee, established pursuant to Resolution 724 (1991) concerning Yugoslavia, S/1996/776, September 24, 1996.

15. See the comments of Edward N. Luttwak in "Toward Post-Heroic Warfare," *Foreign Affairs* 74, no. 3 (May/June 1995): 117–18.

16. Hufbauer et al., *Economic Sanctions Reconsidered*, pp. 63ff.

17. Johan Galtung, "On the Effects of International Sanctions," in Miroslav Nincic and Peter Wallensteen, eds., *Dilemmas of Economic Coercion: Sanctions and World Politics* (New York: Praeger, 1983), pp. 26–27.

18. Baldwin, *Economic Statecraft*, p. 63.

19. Ivan Eland, "Economic Sanctions as Tools of Foreign Policy," in Cortright and Lopez, *Economic Sanctions*, pp. 32–33.

20. U.S. General Accounting Office, *International Trade: Issues regarding Imposition of an Oil Embargo against Nigeria* (Report prepared for the chairman, Subcommittee on Africa, Committee on Foreign Affairs, U.S. Congress, House, 103d Cong., 2d sess., November 1994), GAO/GGD-95-24, p. 12.

21. See Jennifer Davis, "Sanctions and Apartheid: The Economic Challenge to Discrimination," in Cortright and Lopez, *Economic Sanctions*, pp. 173–86.

22. American Friends Service Committee, *Dollars or Bombs: The Search for Justice through International Sanctions* (Philadelphia, 1993), p. 9.

23. Lori Fisler Damrosch, "The Civilian Impact of Economic Sanctions," in Lori Fisler Damrosch, ed., *Enforcing Restraint: Collective Intervention in Internal Conflicts* (New York: Council on Foreign Relations, 1993), p. 302.

24. Robert Axelrod, *The Evolution of Cooperation* (New York: Basic Books, 1984).

25. George and Smoke, *Deterrence*, pp. 608–9.

26. Paul W. Schroeder, "The New World Order: A Historical Perspective," *The Washington Quarterly* (Spring 1994): 35.

27. Lloyd Jensen, "Negotiating Strategic Arms Control, 1969–1979," *Journal of Conflict Resolution* 28 (1984): 535–59.

28. William Gamson and Andre Modigliani, *Untangling the Cold War* (Boston: Little, Brown and Company, 1971).

29. "An Assault on Nuclear Arms," *U.S. News and World Report*, October 7, 1991, pp. 24–28; "Nuclear Weapons: Going, Going," *The Economist*, October 12, 1991, p. 54.

30. Charles E. Osgood, *An Alternative to War or Surrender* (Urbana: University of Illinois Press, 1962). See Alexander George's analysis in Alexander L. George, Philip J. Farley, and Alexander Dallin, eds., *U.S.-Soviet Security Cooperation: Achievements, Failures, Lessons* (New York: Oxford University Press, 1988), pp. 705–7.

31. Wolfers, "Power and Influence," pp. 107–8.

32. See Joan M. Nelson and Stephanie J. Eglinton, *Global Goals, Contentious Means: Issues of Multiple Aid Conditionality* (Washington, D.C.: Overseas Development Council, 1993).

33. Virginia I. Foran and Leonard S. Spector, "The Application of Incentives to Nuclear Proliferation," in Cortright, *The Price of Peace*.

34. William J. Long, *Economic Incentives and Bilateral Cooperation* (Ann Arbor: University of Michigan Press, 1996).

35. Roger Fisher, *International Conflict for Beginners* (New York: Harper and Row, 1969), pp. 119–24.

36. Axelrod, *Evolution of Cooperation*, p. 185.

37. William J. Long, "Trade and Technology Incentives and Bilateral Cooperation," *International Studies Quarterly* 40, no. 1 (March 1996).

38. Etel Solingen, "The New Multilateralism and Nonproliferation: Bringing in Domestic Politics," *Global Governance* 1, no. 2 (May–August 1995): 214, 218.

39. Denis Goulet, *Incentives for Development: The Key to Equity* (New York: Horizons Press, 1989), p. 11.

40. Baldwin, "Power of Positive Sanctions," p. 23.

41. Hans Morgenthau, "A Political Theory of Foreign Aid," *American Political Science Review* 56 (June 1962): 308.

42. Goulet, *Incentives for Development*, pp. 145, 159–61.

43. Toumas Forsberg, "The Efficacy of Rewarding Conflict Strategies: Positive Sanctions as Face Savers, Payments, and Signals" (Paper prepared for the annual meeting of the International Studies Association, San Diego, April 16–20, 1996), p. 10.

44. Remarks of Kimberly Ann Elliott, Conference on Economic Sanctions and International Relations, University of Notre Dame, Notre Dame, Indiana, April 1993.

45. Long, *Economic Incentives*, esp. chapter 2.

46. Eileen Crumm, "The Value of Economic Incentives in International Politics," *Journal of Peace Research* 32, no. 3 (1995): 326.

47. See William H. Kaempfer and Anton D. Lowenberg, "The Problems and Promise of Sanctions," in Cortright and Lopez, *Economic Sanctions*, pp. 61–72.

48. See Richard Rosecrance, *The Rise of the Trading State* (New York: Basic Books, 1987).

49. Peter van Bergeijk, *Economic Diplomacy, Trade and Commercial Policy: Positive and Negative Sanctions in a New World Order* (Aldershot, England: Edward Elgar, 1994), p. 12.

50. Jeffrey E. Garten, "Congress Wages War on Free Trade," *The New York Times*, May 28, 1997.

51. Baldwin, "Power of Positive Sanctions," p. 32.

52. Ibid.

53. Fisher, *International Conflict*, p. 28.

54. Ibid., p. 35.

55. Long, *Economic Incentives*, chapter 2.
56. Fisher, *International Conflict*, p. 106.

1. Quoted in Colum Lynch, "African Trade in Arms Soars in Ethnic Wars," *Boston Globe*, November 12, 1996.
2. James Rupert, "Zaire Reportedly Selling Arms to Angolan Ex-Rebels," *Washington Post*, March 21, 1997.
3. Alison DesForges, quoted in Stephen Buckley, "Gunmen in Camps Loom Large: Dealing with Hutus Called Unavoidable," *Washington Post*, November 15, 1996.
4. There is a significant literature developing around the problems associated with the proliferation of small arms and light weapons. Key works include: the entire series of case studies produced as part of the Geneva-based United Nations Institute for Disarmament Research, Disarmament and Conflict Resolution Project (case studies have been completed on Somalia, Rhodesia/Zimbabwe, Bosnia and Croatia, Southern Africa, Cambodia, Angola/Namibia and Liberia); the entire issue of *Disarmament: A Periodic Review by the United Nations* 19, no. 2 (1996); Jeffrey Boutwell, Michael T. Klare, and Laura Reed, eds., *Lethal Commerce: The Global Trade in Small Arms and Light Weapons* (Cambridge, Mass.: American Academy of Arts and Sciences, 1995); Andrew Latham, "The Light Weapons Problem: Causes, Consequences and Policy Options," in Andrew Latham, ed., *Multilateral Approaches to Non-Proliferation: Proceedings of the 4th Canadian Non-Proliferation Workshop* (Toronto: York University, 1996), pp. 33–54; Edward J. Laurance, *The New Field of Micro-Disarmament: Addressing the Proliferation and Buildup of Small Arms and Light Weapons* (Bonn: Bonn International Center for Conversion, Brief 7, September 1996); Christopher Louise, *The Social Impacts of Light Weapons Availability and Proliferation*, Discussion Paper No. 59 (Geneva: UNRISD, 1995); Swadesh Rana, *Small Arms and Intra-State Conflicts*, (Geneva: United Nations Institute for Disarmament Research, 1995); Jasjit Singh, ed., *Light Weapons and International Security* (Delhi: Indian Pugwash Society and British American Security Information Council, 1995).
5. The UN Register is a voluntary reporting system designed to increase the transparency of arms exports and imports in order to defuse destabilizing arms buildups. The Wassenaar Arrangement is a supplier cartel-like approach, in which a select group of supplier states is attempting to limit exports of conventional weapons by mutual agreement. It is designed to succeed its cold war predecessor, COCOM (Coordinating Committee), a cartel designed to restrict exports of strategic technology to Warsaw Pact countries and the People's Republic of China during the cold war.

6. I am indebted to Michael Klare's pioneering work in developing this typology of acquisition modes. See Michael J. Klare, "Light Weapons Diffusion and Global Violence in the Post-Cold War Era," in Singh, *Light Weapons*, pp. 1–40.

7. For an example of a case where a buildup of light weapons was instrumental in the outbreak of conflict, see Stephen D. Goose and Frank Smyth, "Arming Genocide in Rwanda," *Foreign Affairs* 73, no. 5 (September /October 1994): 86–96.

8. The author is the consultant to the United Nations Panel of Experts on Small Arms.

9. Boutros Boutros-Ghali, *Supplement to an Agenda for Peace: Position Paper of the Secretary-General on the Occasion of the Fiftieth Anniversary of the United Nations*, A/50/60, S/1995/1, January 3, 1995.

10. *General Assembly Resolution A/ROES/50/70 B* (1995).

11. I am indebted to Jill Sinclair of the Canadian Department of Foreign Affairs and International Trade for reminding me that disarmament actions differ in type and effectiveness according to the phase of conflict. For two basic and complementary treatments on how conflict prevention tools vary by phase of conflict, see Michael S. Lund, *Preventing Violent Conflicts: A Strategy for Preventive Diplomacy* (Washington, D.C.: United States Institute of Peace, 1996); and Kalypso Nicolaidis, "International Preventive Action: Developing a Strategic Framework," in Robert I. Rothberg, ed., *Vigilance and Vengeance: NGOs Preventing Ethnic Conflict in Divided Societies* (Washington, D.C.: Brookings Institution, 1996), pp. 23–72.

12. Lund, *Preventing Violent Conflicts*, pp. 109–13.

13. Ibid., p. 113.

14. Ibid., pp. 148–51, Table 4.1.

15. Ibid., p. 141.

16. Ibid., p. 145.

17. For a summary of the literature on "ripeness," see ibid., p. 133.

18. "Remember Rwanda?" *Washington Post*, July 24, 1995; Peter De Ionno, "PWOs 'Chocolate Box Sailor' Implicated in Rwanda Arms Deal," *Sunday Times* (London), April 4, 1995; William Branigin, "Arms Flows to Rwandans Raise Alarms," *Washington Post*, July 19, 1995; Chris McGreal, "Zaire Helps Rearm Hutu Killers," *The Guardian*, May 30, 1995; "Les français réarmeraient l'ancienne armée rwandaise," *Libération*, May 29, 1995; United Nations Security Council, *Resolution 997*, S/1995/997.

19. United Nations Security Council, *Report of the International Commission of Inquiry (Rwanda)*, S/1996/195, March 14, 1996.

20. "Arms to Rwanda," *The Times* (London), November 19, 1996.

21. Lund, *Preventing Violent Conflicts*, p. 92.

22. Alison DesForges, "Making Noise Effectively: Lessons from the Rwandan Catastrophe," in Rothberg, *Vigilance and Vengeance*, pp. 213–32.

23. Government of South Africa, "Firearms in South Africa: An Escalating Problem" (Presentation made to the United Nations Workshop on Small Arms, Pretoria, September 24, 1996).

24. Juanita Darling, "Gun-Swap Project Overwhelmed by Response in War-Weary Land," *Los Angeles Times*, October 5, 1996.

25. These examples are based on interviews with ECCM and UNPROFOR personnel who served in the former Yugoslavia, and on *Managing Arms in Peace Processes: Croatia and Bosnia-Herzegovina* (Geneva: United Nations Institute for Disarmament Research [UNIDIR], 1996).

26. Prvoslav Davinic, "Press Briefing by Director of Centre for Disarmament Affairs," United Nations, April 3, 1996.

27. Jean Houngtounbe, "Former Foes in Mali's Tuareg War Seal Peace by Burning Weapons," Agence France-Presse, March 28, 1996.

28. "Mali President Burns Weapons to Seal Peace," Reuters, March 27, 1996.

29. Davinic, "Press Briefing."

30. The FMLN had held back a significant number of weapons in caches; their discovery almost led to a breakdown of the process. But as in the case of Srebrenica, its compliance was deemed "good enough." By that time the political process had evolved to where the FMLN had really decided that its fighting days were over.

31. Tom Hundley, "GIs in Bosnia Face New Tensions," *Chicago Tribune*, November 24, 1996.

32. Interview with former IFOR officers, November 1996.

33. Information for this section is based on notes from and interviews with Neil O'Connor, from the Program on Arms Control, Disarmament, and Conversion at the Monterey Institute of International Studies. He spent a week in Haiti in the fall of 1995 researching the weapons collection program. Additional interviews were conducted with U.S. Army officers who had participated in the disarmament activities described.

34. "UN Offers to Buy Weapons from Croatian Serbs," *OMRI Daily Digest* 3, no. 192 (October 1996).

35. "Croatia: Gun Buyback," *Washington Times*, February 3, 1997.

36. Frank Millar, "Debate on Arms Needs Injection of Reality," *Irish Times*, November 18, 1996.

37. The World Bank has established a small office with a mandate to address the demobilization process and is active in developing weapons collection and turn-in programs.

38. Birgit Brauer, "Simmering Ethnic Unrest in China Gains Attention," *San Jose Mercury News*, February 27, 1997.

39. Stephen John Steadman, "Alchemy for a New World Order— Overselling 'Preventive Diplomacy,'" *Foreign Affairs*, 74, no. 3 (May/June 1995): 20.

40. Nicolaidis, "International Preventive Action," p. 29.

41. Lund, *Preventing Violent Conflicts*, p. 153.

42. "Museveni Seeks Help for Rebels in Southern Sudan," *Financial Times*, January 27, 1997.

43. United Nations Disarmament Commission, *Guidelines for International Arms Transfers in the Context of General Assembly Resolution 46/36H of December 6, 1991*, A/CN.10/1996/CRP.3, May 3, 1996.

1. David Little and William Vendley, "Implications for the Foreign Policy Community," in Douglas Johnston and Cynthia Sampson, eds., *Religion: The Missing Dimension of Statecraft* (New York: Oxford University Press, 1994), p. 295.

2. Robert L. Rothstein, "After the Peace: The Political Economy of Reconciliation" (The Inaugural Rebecca Meyerhoff Memorial Lecture for the Harry S. Truman Research Institute for the Advancement of Peace, Hebrew University of Jerusalem, May 1996), p. 4.

3. Cf. Hannah Arendt, *On Violence* (New York: Harcourt, Brace, and World, 1969), pp. 52–56. *Legitimacy* is the distinctive ingredient of real political power, she contends, not violence. Violence can destroy legitimacy but it cannot create it. "Violence appears when power is in jeopardy, but left to its own course it ends in power's disappearance" (p. 56).

4. Paul Tillich, *Systematic Theology*, vol. 1 (Chicago: University of Chicago Press, 1951), pp. 14–17.

5. Cf. I Kings 22:13–28 and II Samuel 11–12, where Hebrew prophets defy kings to great popular effect.

6. Harold H. Saunders, "Prenegotiation and Circum-negotiation: Arenas of the Peace Process," in Chester A. Crocker et al., eds., *Managing Global Chaos: Sources of and Responses to International Conflict* (Washington: United States Institute of Peace, 1996), p. 426.

7. See John W. Dower's study of the American and Japanese resort to racism, *War without Mercy: Race and Power in the Pacific War* (New York: Pantheon Books, 1986).

8. As quoted in Michael Henderson, *The Forgiveness Factor: Stories of Hope in a World of Conflict* (Salem, Ore.: Grosvenor Books, 1996), p. 76.

9. As quoted by Henry Wooster, "Faith at the Ramparts: The Philippine Catholic Church and the 1986 Revolution," in Johnston and Sampson, *Religion: The Missing Dimension*, p. 167.

10. Ron Kraybill, "Transition from Rhodesia to Zimbabwe: The Role of Religious Actors," in ibid., p. 243. He goes on to remark that the Quakers

in that conflict demonstrated not only "trust in God" but also trust in human beings—on all sides.

11. Robert M. Cover, "The Supreme Court, 1982 Term, Forward: *Nomos* Narrative," 97 *Harvard Law Review* 33 (1983).

12. Harvey Cox, "World Religions and Conflict Resolution," in Johnston and Sampson, *Religion: The Missing Dimension*, p. 279.

13. Charles Villa-Vicencio, "Identity, Culture, and Belonging: Religious and Cultural Rights," in John Witte, Jr. and Johan D. van der Vyver, eds., *Religious Human Rights in Global Perspective: Religious Perspectives* (The Hague: Martinus Nijhoff Publishers, 1996), pp. 531–36. This concluding chapter of this volume (pp. 517–37) is a careful answer, drawing from many major religions, to the accusation (reversing the axiom of Learned Hand) that "the spirit of religion is the spirit that is too sure it is right."

14. Samuel P. Huntington, "Religion and the Third Wave," *National Interest*, Summer 1991, p. 31, as quoted in Wooster, "Faith at the Ramparts," p. 165.

15. Abdullah A. An-na'im, "Islamic Foundations of Religious Human Rights," in Witte and van der Vyver, *Religious Human Rights*, p. 345.

16. One state legislator said to me twenty-five years ago, "If I could count on having fifty people come to hear what I had to say once a week for an hour, I could develop an organization to win most elections. The clergy have more potential political power than most of them admit."

17. Huntington, "Religion and the Third Wave," pp. 29–42, as quoted in Wooster, "Faith at the Ramparts."

18. Cf. David Steele, "At the Front Lines of the Revolution: East Germany's Churches Give Sanctuary and Succor to the Purveyors of Change," in Johnston and Sampson, *Religion: The Missing Dimension*, pp. 127–28 and the entirety of the chapter, pp. 119–52.

19. Timerman has been quoted as saying that he owes his life to the human rights policies of President Jimmy Carter, whose support for that policy had some roots in Carter's religion. Religion also played a part in the human rights policies of his UN ambassador (and ordained minister) Andrew Young. Saving politically threatened life is a very basic form of "resolving" conflict, even though this occasional service of religion to dissidents is not always tagged as a form of conflict resolution. Without his base in a major local synagogue, Marshall Meyer would probably have himself become a victim of the Argentine junta. In the Taiwan case, Stated Clerk C. M. Kao was jailed for four years for his protection of a political dissident—and his release was due mostly to the pressure of international Presbyterian and ecumenical bodies on the government of Taiwan.

20. Mary L. Gautier, "Was the Church Sheltering Democrats? The Effect of Church Attendance on Support for Democratic Values in Postcommunist Societies" (Paper presented at the Annual Meeting of the Society for the Scientific Study of Religion, November 1996). Citations here are from pp. 1, 7, and 17–18 and are used by permission. Gautier

makes no reference to the role of the churches in Germany during the Nazi era, when there was little parallel to the sort of freedoms that the DDR Communists apparently felt they had to grant the churches, the peace movement, and the environmental movement.

21. "One can identify, for example, the roles of instigator, communicator, persuader, organizer, precipitator, legitimizer, convenor, moderator, manager, funder, teacher, idea formulator—all played by different combinations of actors." Saunders, "Prenegotiation and Circumnegotiation," p. 425. With the possible exception of "manager," every one of these roles was played, at one time or another, in the East German, Rhodesian, and other cases referred to here, by religiously motivated actors.

22. For a more extensive analysis of the Quaker role, cf. Kraybill, "Transition from Rhodesia to Zimbabwe," pp. 233–44, on which this summary of the Rhodesian-Zimbabwe history is based.

23. Gene Sharp, *The Politics of Nonviolent Action* (Boston: Porter Sargent, 1973); Walter Wink, *Engaging the Powers: Discernment and Resistance in a World of Domination* (Minneapolis: Fortress Press, 1992), pp. 244–51.

24. Wink, *Engaging the Powers*, p. 250.

25. David Little makes useful distinctions between four different religious stances, historical and contemporary, toward the question of violence: (1) violent intolerance—the use of violence to promote religious conformity; (2) civic intolerance—the promotion of religious conformity through government; (3) nonviolent tolerance—"a spirit that is as militant [in advocacy of social change] as it is nonviolent [in tactics]"; and (4) civic tolerance—the promotion of societywide religious tolerance, with the possible use of legal violence to *enforce* that tolerance. Martin Luther King, Jr., accepted both (3) and (4), as does Desmond Tutu. Little, "Religious Militancy," in Crocker, *Managing Global Chaos*, pp. 79–91.

26. According to Human Rights Watch, no outsider knows the name or fate of this famous student. China's ability to inhibit worldwide knowledge of the mass peasant deaths in the late 1950s is a contrary case in point.

27. Wink, *Engaging the Powers*, pp. 251–52.

28. Ibid., p. 255. B. H. Liddell-Hart, military historian, reports on the frustration of Nazi generals in World War II at their "complete inability to cope with nonviolence as practiced in Denmark, Holland, Norway, and, to a lesser extent, in France and Belgium. . . . The generals found friendly noncompliance more frustrating than any other form of resistance, and had no effective means to counter it." ("Lessons from Resistance Movements—Guerilla and Nonviolent," in Adam Roberts, ed., *The Strategy of Civilian Defence: Non-Violent Resistance to Aggression*, (London: Faber, 1967), pp. 205–7.

29. Cf. *Minutes of the General Assembly of the Presbyterian Church, USA, 1983* (Atlanta, 1984).

30. Kraybill, "Rhodesia to Zimbabwe," p. 213, quoting Ian Linden, *The Catholic Church and the Struggle for Zimbabwe* (London: Longman, 1980), p. 196. Linden calls this commission "the first formal commitment to social justice made by the hierarchy" in Rhodesia.

31. Ibid., pp. 236–37.

32. Cynthia Sampson, "To Make Real the Bond between Us All: Quaker Conciliation during the Nigerian Civil War," in *Religion: The Missing Dimension*, p. 108.

33. Rothstein, "After the Peace," p. 31.

34. Saunders, "Prenegotiation and Circum-negotiation," pp. 420, 427–28.

35. Burg prefers the term "consociation" to "segregation," but the barbed-wire image is pertinent to this strategy: constituencies that remain cordoned off from each other while their representative leaders negotiate and share power. "Integration" implies pluralist civil society in which previously hostile groups meet each other over time at institutionalized social interstices.

36. Thomas Friedman, "It's Time to Separate," *New York Times*, January 29, 1995.

37. Rothstein, "After the Peace," p. 20.

38. Duncan J. Morrow, "Seeking Political Peace amidst Memories of War in Northern Ireland" (Address at conference "After the Peace: The Political Economy of Reconciliation," held at Colgate University, February 7, 1997). Morrow is a lecturer in politics at the University of Ulster.

39. Anthony Lewis, "No Messianic Dreams," *New York Times*, September 19, 1996.

40. See Marc Sommers, "The Mending of Hearts: Conflict Resolution and Reconciliation Activities among Rwandan Refugee Religious Groups in Ngara District, Tanzania" (Unpublished paper prepared for the African Studies Center of Boston University). The paper is based on interviews conducted in the camp over a period of three weeks in October 1996 with members of the three largest religious groups there—Catholic, Anglican, and Pentecostal—as well as with Muslims and members of other smaller bodies.

41. Ibid., p. 12.

42. The normative Jewish and Christian traditions take up the subject in connection with the story of Cain and Abel (Genesis 4:1-16). Recent thinking about violence by Christian theologians has acquired particular impetus from the writings of Rene Girard. Cf. his *Violence and the Sacred*, tr. Patrick Gregory (Baltimore: Johns Hopkins University Press, 1977), and Gil Bailie's *Violence Unveiled: Humanity at the Crossroads* (New York: Crossroad, 1995).

43. Rothstein, "After the Peace," pp. 31–32; cf. Thomas J. Scheff, *Bloody Revenge: Emotions, Nationalism, and War* (Boulder, Colo.: Westview Press, 1994), pp. 3–6; and Donald W. Shriver, Jr., *An Ethic for Enemies:*

Forgiveness in Politics (New York: Oxford University Press, 1995). See also Nicholas Tavuchis, *Mea Culpa: A Sociology of Apology and Reconciliation* (Stanford, Calif.: Stanford University Press, 1991).

44. Little and Vendley, "Implications for the Foreign Policy Community," in Johnston and Sampson, *Religion: The Missing Dimension,* p. 295.

45. William O'Neill, "Death's Other Kingdom: Human Rights and the Politics of Genocide in Rwanda" (Paper presented at the Annual Meeting of the Society of Christian Ethics, January 10, 1997), p. 3.

46. John Rawls, *A Theory of Justice* (Cambridge: Harvard University Press, 1970).

47. Elie Wiesel, *Night* (New York: Discus Books, 1969), p. 76.

48. Augustin Karekezi, "In Memory of the Victims of the Genocide in Rwanda," p. 6, quoted in O'Neill, "Death's Other Kingdom," p. 24.

— INDEX —